Lecture Notes in Computer Science   13294

More information about this series at https://link.springer.com/bookseries/558

Simon Collart-Dutilleul · Anne E. Haxthausen ·
Thierry Lecomte (Eds.)

Reliability, Safety, and Security of Railway Systems

Modelling, Analysis, Verification, and Certification

4th International Conference, RSSRail 2022
Paris, France, June 1–2, 2022
Proceedings

Springer

Editors
Simon Collart-Dutilleul
Université Gustave Eiffel
Villeneuve d'Ascq, France

Anne E. Haxthausen [iD]
Technical University of Denmark
Lyngby, Denmark

Thierry Lecomte [iD]
ClearSy
Aix en Provence, France

ISSN 0302-9743   ISSN 1611-3349   (electronic)
Lecture Notes in Computer Science
ISBN 978-3-031-05813-4   ISBN 978-3-031-05814-1   (eBook)
https://doi.org/10.1007/978-3-031-05814-1

This Springer imprint is published by the registered company Springer Nature Switzerland AG
The registered company address is: Gewerbestrasse 11, 6330 Cham, Switzerland

Preface

This volume contains papers presented at the fifth international conference on Reliability, Safety and Security of Railway Systems: Modelling, Analysis, Verification and Certification (RSSRail 2022) We are pleased to propose a mainly physical meeting during June 1–2, 2022, organized by University Gustave Eiffel in the UIC (The Worldwide Railway Organization) building in Paris. The conference is back in Paris after its first loop: The series of conferences started in Paris in 2016 and continued in 2017 in Pistoia. In 2019, the conference took place in Lille and the 2021, edition was a special issue of the journal Formal Aspects of Computing. In 2022 we were back to where we started, after a long period of pandemic, filled with expectations for a fruitful physical event fostering networking activities and an informal but fundamental sharing of knowledge.

Developing the complex railway systems of the future faces a number of challenges:

– To improve and demonstrate railway system safety, security and reliability
– To reduce production costs, time to market, and running costs
– To increase system capacity and reduce carbon emissions

In the context of current digital transformations, we require integrated environments and methods that support different abstraction levels and different views, including:

– System architecture
– Safety analysis
– Security analysis
– Verification tools and methods

The RSSRail 2022 conference brought together researchers and engineers interested in building critical railway application and systems, as a working conference in which research advances are discussed and evaluated by both researchers and engineers, focusing on their potential to be industrially deployed, keeping in mind the current digital transformation. Bringing together researchers, developers and stakeholders, working on reliability, safety and security of railway systems, to leads to contribute to a range of key objectives. A key goal is the development of advanced methods and tools that will ensure that rail system meet the requirements imposed both by standards and in building the arguments for compliance. The conference covered topics related to all aspects of reliability, safety and security engineering for railway systems and networks including:

– Safety in development process and safety management
– Integrated approaches to safety and security
– System safety analysis
– Formal modelling and verification techniques
– System reliability
– Validation according to the standards

- Safety and security argumentation
- Fault and intrusion modelling and analysis
- Evaluation of system capacity, energy consumption, cost and their interplay
- Tool and model integration, tool-chains
- Domain specific language and modelling frameworks
- Model reuse for reliability, safety, and security
- Modelling for maintenance strategy engineering

The fifth occurrence of RSSRail attracted 31 submissions from 16 countries. 16 papers were selected after a rigorous review process in which every paper received at least three reviews from committee members or from subreviewers of committee members.

Two prominent researchers working on railway engineering, Frédéric Henon from UIC (France) and Juliette Marais from University Gustave Eiffel (France). Kindly agreed to deliver keynote talks. The corresponding abstracts of these keynotes are included in the current volume.

We would like to thank all the committee members and the additional reviewers for all their efforts. We are indebted to the Gustave Eiffel University for their involvement in the planning and organization of this event, particularly for administrative tasks which the evolving pandemic context made even more complex. We would like to mention the precious advice from Tom Anderson, Joan Atkinson and Alexander Romanovsky. Thanks to the UIC, for kindly providing us preferential access to their conference hall. We are very grateful to Ronan Nugent from Springer for supporting the publication of these proceedings in the LNCS series. But most of all, our thanks go to all the contributors and those who attended the conference for making this conference a success and great new start after the interruption due to the pandemic.

Simon Collart-Dutilleul
Thierry Leconte
Anne Haxthausen

Organization

Conference Chairs

Anne E. Haxthausen   Technical University of Denmark, Denmark
Simon Collart-Dutilleul   University Gustave Eiffel, France
Thierry Lecomte   Clearsy, France

Local Organization Chairs

Simon Collart-Dutilleul   University Gustave Eiffel, France
Philippe Bon   University Gustave Eiffel, France
Nathalie Boticchio   University Gustave Eiffel, France

Web Designers

Sébastien Martinez   University Gustave Eiffel, France
Dalay Israel de Almeida Pereira   University Gustave Eiffel, France

Steering Committee

Anne Haxthausen   Technical University of Denmark, Denmark
Alessandro Fantechi   University of Florence, Italy
Alexander Romanovski   The Formal Route Ltd., UK
Mario Gleirscher   University of Bremen, Germany
Simon Collart-Dutilleul   University Gustave Eiffel, France
  (President)
Thierry Lecomte   Clearsy, France

Program Committee

Abderrahim Ait Wakrime   University Mohammed V, FSR, Morocco
Alessandro Fantechi   University of Florence, Italy
Alexander Romanovski   The Formal Route Ltd., UK
Alexei Iliasov   The Formal Route Ltd., UK
Barbara Gallina   Mälardalen University, Sweden
Bas Luttik   Eindhoven University of Technology, Netherlands
Carlo Becheri   Alstom, Italy
Christophe Ponsard   Cetic, Belgium

Elena Troubitsyna	KTH Royal Institute of Technology, Sweden
Etienne Prun	Clearsy, France
Francesco Flammini	Linnaeus University, Sweden
Frank Golatowski	Univ. of Rostock, Germany
Hironobu Kuruma	Hitachi, Japan
Jan Peleska	Verified Systems Int., Germany
Jens Braband	Siemens, Germany
Kenji Taguchi	CAV Technologies, Japan
Klaus Reichl	Thales, Austria
Laurent Voisin	Systerel, France
Mariëlle Stoelinga	Univ. of Twente, Netherlands
Mario Gleirscher	University of Bremen, Germany
Maurice ter Beek	ISTI, CNR, Pisa, Italy
Michael Leuschel	University of Düsseldorf, Germany
Nadia Chouchani	IRT Railenium, France
Philippe Bon	University Gustave Eiffel, France
Sana Debbech	IRT Railenium, France
Stefano Tonetta	FBK-irst, Italy

Additional Reviewers

Michael Nast	University of Rostock, Germany
Benjamin Rother	University of Rostock, Germany
Marco Papini	University of Florence, Italy
Mark Bouwman	Eindhoven University of Technology, Netherlands
Daisuke Shimbara	Hitachi, Japan
Stefano Marrone	University of Naples Federico II, Italy
Usman Sanwal	Mälardalen University, Sweden
Bob Janssen	Siemens, Netherlands

Sponsors

Clearsy

University Gustave Eiffel

DTU

IRT Railenium

EPSF

The Formal Route Ltd.

Abstracts of Keynotes

New Methods for Safety Demonstration in the Frame of Railway System

Frédéric Henon

International Union of Railways, Paris, France
henon@uic.org

Abstract. The main research priorities for the future of rail are 1. new techs, 2. mass transit systems, 3. digital transformation, 4. safety as a whole. These imply long-term disruptive technologies, where new challenges regarding safety demonstrations will arise. These challenges must be tackled today, as it is highly expected that intermediate but actual and near future digital/innovative solutions, come into the railway system, delivering opportunities of safety tools or loops.

The 4th Industrial Revolution

The new and innovative systems, especially the ones that are using artificial intelligence and/or complex digital systems, thanks to the 4th industrial revolution, will increasingly need intensive collaborations between the proposers of new solutions, and the supervisory authorities who are responsible for authorizing the placing on the market, that is the very end objective to achieve.

The fourth industrial revolution will have an impact on three different areas:

– global or integrated mobility systems,
– long-term disruptive railway technologies,
– methods regarding safety demonstrations.

Future is Today

Some of today's short-term solutions for railways (somehow, some necessary pre-4th revolution achievements), are driven by long term research activities, such as these on automated systems, autonomous trains, hyperloop, etc. For instance, the 5G specifications for rail, geolocalization systems, video computing, etc., are on the path of targeted integrated systems.

The different techniques involved, such as AI, solve problems, but remain rather opaque about how they actually solve them. Interoperability is therefore an essential question. That is why authorization to place AI on the market, particularly for safety cases, will be granted only if the human-machine system as a whole is considered, and thus if the role of human experts remains central.

Thus, the new paradigm for railway engineers and safety engineers is not future, but already actual and real.

One the other hand, end-users are expecting these intermediate digital and innovative solutions, to be brought quickly as new "safety loops" or "safety barriers", in the railway system, that will deserve the global performance of the system.

These new opportunities, for the whole business, are making this safety challenge, for operators but also for the regulatory bodies worldwide, to be tackled today.

New Relationships are Necessary

"Authorization" processes for these future systems will be modified considerably, as the regulating bodies in the railway system will have to evolve with these new technologies. These new issues have already been identified and are related particularly to the risk assessment methods and the definition of the safety requirements.

The future scope of use-cases involves a range of unquantifiable different situations (different lines, operational situations, etc.). The answer may be a combination of several elements of proof for the new systems, to likely make that these guarantees will become sufficient:

- A formal demonstration of the software involved in the safety functions,
- Tests on the operational network or in rail test centers,
- Digital simulations in conjunction with physical tests to guarantee that the implemented tests are representative,
- Live monitoring & control,
- etc.

Science on Safety

The field of safety science is uncertain and controversial. There is no consensus on how to answer the question "what is the purpose of the science of safety"?

There is not even a single paradigm on the science of safety, that makes it indisputable scientific discipline.

A profound crisis of professional identity affects the scientific community as a group of researchers and safety professionals.

This is the time where the safety must be considered as safety as a service (SaaS), and considered in the globality and the completeness of the system.

Satellite-Based Train Localization for Safety Critical Applications. The Challenges of Performance Demo and Certification

Juliette Marais

Université Gustave Eiffel, France
juliette.marais@univ-eiffel.fr

Abstract. GNSS (Global Navigation Satellite System) is recognized as a game changer for ERTMS. The use of this equipment, handled in the pocket of millions of people every day, for safe railway localization necessarily puts several challenges before us! What is nominal performance and what is the real performance encountered in a railway environment? The presentation will highlight the remaining challenges and highlight ongoing and future to reach performance demonstration and certification.

Presentation

Almost everybody has today a GNSS (Global Navigation Satellite System) receiver in his pocket. But how many of us know how it works? GNSS are satellite-based localisation systems. They are composed of satellites, in orbit at 20 000 km from earth and controlled from the ground, that continuously broadcast navigation signals. The receiver is the doing the rest of the job: it computes the time of propagation of available signals and extract the satellite-to-receiver distance, called pseudo range. A trilateration principle, meaning the reception of at least 4 signals, result in a 3D position, in an absolute coordinate system. This cost-effective chip offers absolute continuous position, all over the globe, without any frontier, with quite good accuracy (meters).

After first explorative research projects, GNSS has finally be recognized as a game changer for ERTMS. Through the adoption of the own-initiative procedure 2019/2191 (INI) in July 2021, the European Parliament highlights the need to take advantage of the potential cost savings that GNSS offers in railway signalling. Indeed, GNSS may be used to increase the capacity of the railway network by allowing the development of future train operations such as moving block or virtual coupling.

Did you already try to close your eyes and let you guided by your GNSS receiver? Would you try? In an urban environment, you may have already experienced some large errors, or unavailability. This is caused by the surrounding environment and a result of the GNSS principle! As long as we measure the time of propagation, GNSS performance is sensitive to the different path the signal will follow to reach the receiver.

In land transport environment, so in a railway environment, GNSS performance is suffering from masking effects, multipath or reflected signals and interferences. These effects can be seen as random or almost, as they depend on the very close surrounding of the antenna.

For non-safety critical applications (cargo tracking, digital freight…), where requirements can be relaxed, COTS receivers already travel with trains and wagons over Europe. For safety-critical applications such as signalling, performance have to be enhanced and ensured, before being demonstrated and certified.

During the talk, these issues will be highlighted: how can we mitigate local effects? How to protect against unacceptable performance, causing failures? Some answers are developed or investigated in Eu R&D projects: development of detection techniques; mapping of GNSS reception quality along railway lines; error modelling; integrity monitoring concepts (integrity being the measure of trust placed in the position provided), multi-sensor fusion solutions…

GNSS-based solutions should ensure fail-safe train location and location integrity. For example, this allows a reduction in trackside location equipment such as the replacement of physical balises (beacons) with virtual ones, or to compute a continuous and accurate train position. However, the use of GNSS requires current railway regulations and operations to be adapted.

To complexify the process, GNSS satellites are moving around the earth and what happens at 10h will not happen or happen differently at 15h because of the satellite configuration.

The demonstration and certification of GNSS-based solutions will need new solutions and tools in order to consider parameters among which: propagation conditions, time, geometry (of both satellites and surrounding environment), analysis of rare events consequences. Can experimentation help for this performance quantification? How can we reach zero-on-site testing and what are the test bed to be developed? These are some of the topics that will be addressed.

Contents

ATO

Safe and Secured Telecom for Railway

Safe Interlocking

Compositional Verification of Railway Interlockings: Comparison of Two Methods

Alessandro Fantechi[1], Gloria Gori[1(✉)], Anne E. Haxthausen[2], and Christophe Limbrée[3]

[1] University of Florence, Firenze, Italy
gloria.gori@unifi.it
[2] DTU Compute, Technical University of Denmark, Lyngby, Denmark
[3] Belgian Railway Infrastructure Manager, Brussels, Belgium

Abstract. Formal verification of safety of interlocking systems and of their configuration on a specific track layout is conceptually an easy task for model checking. Systems that control large railway networks, however, are challenging due to state space explosion problems. A possible way out is to adopt a compositional approach that allows safety of a large system to be deduced from the formal verification of parts in which the system has been properly decomposed. Two different approaches have been proposed in this regard, differing for the decomposition assumptions and for the adopted compositional verification techniques. In this paper we compare the two approaches, discussing the differences, but also showing how the different concepts behind them are essentially equivalent, hence producing comparable benefits.

Keywords: Compositional verification · Model checking railway · Railway interlocking systems

1 Introduction

Railway signalling is one of the domains in which formal methods have been applied in industry with multiple success stories since decades. In particular, *interlocking systems*, that control the train movements inside a railway network, called for a direct application of model checking, since required safety properties can be conveniently expressed in temporal logic. These systems need to be configured with *application data* that are closely related to the network layout in terms of tracks, points, signals, etc. Formal verification aims to verify both the generic algorithms for safe allocation of routes to trains, and the specific configuration for the network at hand, given by the application data. However, due to the high number of variables involved, automatic verification of sufficiently large networks typically incurs in combinatorial state space explosion [9].

State space explosion in model checking has been addressed by several techniques, e.g., adopting abstraction techniques, that preserve the validity of model

© Springer Nature Switzerland AG 2022
S. Collart-Dutilleul et al. (Eds.): RSSRail 2022, LNCS 13294, pp. 3–19, 2022.
https://doi.org/10.1007/978-3-031-05814-1_1

checking results: the abstraction technique to be chosen typically depends on the nature of the system. Indeed, interlocking systems typically exhibit a high degree of *locality*: if we consider a typical safety property desired for an interlocking system, e.g., that the same track element shall not be reserved by more than one train at a time, it is likely that this property is not influenced by a train moving on a distant, or parallel, track element. Locality of a safety property can be exploited for verification purposes, so limiting the state space on which to verify it, by abstracting away the said "movement of distant trains". This principle has been exploited in [26] to define domain-oriented optimisation of the variable ordering in a BDD-based verification. Locality has been used also for *model slicing*, as suggested in [9,13,14], where only the portion of the model that has influence on the property to be verified (*cone of influence*) is considered: this allows for a more efficient verification of the single property, at the price of repeating the slicing and the verification for every property, and of separately checking that this abstraction preserves property satisfaction.

Locality also enables the adoption of a *compositional* approach that separately verifies portions of a network layout that are shown to be rather independent by the said locality principle. The residual dependency between the portions needs however to be properly addressed.

In [8,10,18,19] a compositional verification approach based on dividing the network layout into two (or more) portions has been proposed. Extra track sections and signals are added at the border between two portions in order to abstract in one portion the behaviour of the other one.

A different approach [15–17] has addressed the same issue by resorting to the criteria for functional decomposition of interlocking systems as defined by Belgian railways; these criteria address the control of large networks by dividing the layout into subnetworks, each possibly controlled by separate interlocking systems. The cited study has considered the very same criteria as efficient as well as a basis for a compositional verification approach.

We were therefore interested in comparing the two compositional approaches. Indeed, they appear at a first glance quite different both for the definition of possible decomposition procedure and for the formal verification machinery adopted. The comparison presented in this paper shows in the end, instead, a high degree of similarity, that strengthens the confidence on the actual applicability of compositionality to attack formal verification of interlocking systems of large networks.

The paper is structured as follows: Sect. 2 introduces some necessary terminology for interlocking systems. With reference to the two different approaches, Sect. 3 describes "normal" formal verification of interlocking systems, while compositional reasoning is introduced in Sect. 4. Section 5 compares the two compositional approaches and discusses the differences. Section 6 introduces a case study, that has been useful to compare the methods, and which shows the advantages of the compositional methods. A related work section (Sect. 7) and a concluding section (Sect. 8) follow.

2 Background

In this section we briefly introduce the main notions of interlocking systems: we restrict to assumptions consistent with the European ETCS Level 2 resignalling program, for which we refer to [24,25] for a more detailed introduction, and to Belgian signalling principles. Different terminology and assumptions are often used as well, as can be found in most of the literature on interlocking systems cited in this paper. We also take a simplified view, that is sufficient for our discussion, although ignoring some details of real systems.

A railway network consists of a number of track and track-side elements of different types, of which we limit to consider *linear sections, points, and signals*. Figure 1 shows an example railway network layout, introducing the graphic representation of these elements:

- A *linear section*, identified with a magenta box in Fig. 1, is a track section with up to two neighbours: one in the *up* end, and one in the *down* end. For simplicity, in the following examples and figures, the *up* (*down*) direction is assumed to be the left-to-right (right-to-left) direction.
- A *point*, identified with a red box in Fig. 1, can have up to three neighbours: one at the *stem*, one at the *plus* end, and one at the *minus* end. The *stem* and *plus* ends form the straight (main) path, and the *stem* and *minus* ends form the branching (siding) path. A point can be switched between two positions: PLUS and MINUS, selecting the main or siding paths, respectively.
- Linear sections and points are collectively called *(train detection) sections*, as they are provided with train detection equipment used by the interlocking system to detect the presence of trains.
- Along each linear section, up to two *signals* (one for each direction) can be installed. Two signals, one for the up direction and one for the down direction, are indicated in Fig. 1 using two green boxes. A signal can only be seen in one direction and has two aspects (OPEN or CLOSED). In ETCS Level 2, signals are actually virtual and their aspect is communicated to the onboard computer via a radio network.
- A *route*, identified with a blue arrow in Fig. 1, is a path from a *source* signal to a *destination* signal in the given railway network.
- By *setting* a route we denote the process of allocating the resources – i.e., sections, points, and signals – for the route, and then *locking* it exclusively for only one train when the resources are allocated. When the train has left all the sections of the allocated route, the route is free again, to be allocated to another train.

Further examples of network layouts are deferred to Sect. 5.

Typical safety properties required of an interlocking system can be reduced to the following generic safety conditions:

1. **No collisions:** Two trains must never occupy the same track section at the same time.

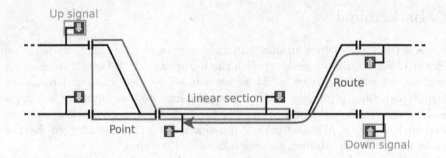

Fig. 1. Railway network: track and track-side elements. (Color figure online)

2. **No derailments:** A point must not be switched, while being occupied by a train.

All required safety properties are expressed as *generic* conditions leading to *specific* conditions for each specific case of a network. The *No collisions* property is enforced by a mutually exclusive allocation of a route to a train asking for it. Notice that considering such typical safety properties, a route defines the maximal subset of elements whose status affects the safety property, that is, no element outside a route, or, at most, two conflicting routes, can affect a safety property for that route(s).

In this paper we focus on No collisions and No derailments safety properties. Other properties, e.g., liveness, can be proven using both methods.

3   Formal Verification by Model Checking

Interlocking systems called for a direct application of model checking, since required safety properties can be conveniently expressed in temporal logic. The verification process based on model checking can be represented as in Fig. 2, where dashed boxes represent artefacts related to a specific network topology: typically, from the network layout a *control table* (aka *interlocking table* or *application data*) is derived, that contains information about routes, their sections, points and signals, their conditions for safe allocation, and their conflicts with other routes. From this data, a behavioural model in the form of a transition system is derived, according to realistic assumptions and principles of train movements, that also follow specific national regulations.

The two derivation steps of a model from the network layout can be automated, but the generation of the control table may ask for a manual intervention of signalling engineers to take into account specific physical constraints or other peculiarities [11].

The network layout guides the instantiation of generic safety properties as well. As usual, the model checker verifies whether the properties are satisfied by the model, returning a diagnostic counterexample in the case they are not.

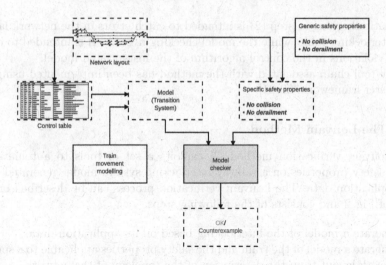

Fig. 2. Monolithic verification process.

In this paper we consider two verification approaches that implement, with a few differences, the process of Fig. 2.

3.1 The RobustRailS Method

The RobustRailS verification method [22–25] is based on a combination of formal methods and a domain-specific language (DSL) to express network diagrams and interlocking tables. A tool is provided by the RobustRailS environment to transform the DSL description into the transition system model and the required safety properties given as Linear Temporal Logic (LTL) formulae.

The RobustRailS tools can be used to verify the design of an interlocking system in the following steps:

1. A DSL specification of the configuration data (a network layout and its corresponding interlocking table) is constructed in the following order:
   (a) first the network layout,
   (b) and then the interlocking table (this is either done manually or generated automatically from the network layout).
2. The static checker [12] verifies whether the configuration data is statically well-formed according to the static semantics [24] of the DSL.
3. The generators instantiate a generic behavioural model and generic safety properties with the well-formed configuration data to generate the model input of the model checker and the safety properties.
4. The generated model instance is then checked against the generated properties by the bounded model checker, performing a k-induction proof.

The static checking in step (2) is intended to catch errors in the network layout and interlocking table, while the model checking in step (4) is intended to catch safety violations in the control algorithm of the instantiated model.

The tool chain associated with the method has been implemented using the RT-Tester framework [20, 21].

3.2   The Louvain Method

The Louvain verification method [3] exploits a set of tools to automatically verify safety properties on a railway interlocking system model generated from the application data. The Louvain verification process can be described on the basis of Fig. 2 and consists of the following steps:

1. Generate a model of the interlocking based on its application data.
2. Generate a model of the train and the safety properties applicable to a specific network layout from the description of the topology of the network.
3. Combine the models of the interlocking with two instances of the train in a SMV model and verify the properties with nuXmv.

4   Compositional Verification

Figure 3 represents a generic compositional verification method, in which a complex network layout is divided into two or more subnetworks/components, and the previous process is applied to each of them, including control table generation, model generation, safety properties instantiation and model checking. A formal proof allows to extend the model checking results obtained on the subnetworks to the whole network: typically, if all the subnetworks satisfy the related safety properties, then the full network satisfies its own ones.

Within both the RobustRailS and the Louvain methods a compositional approach that instantiates the process of Fig. 3 has been developed.

4.1   The RobustRailS Compositional Method

In [8, 10, 18, 19] a method for performing compositional verification in connection with RobustRailS has been developed. It provides a general definition of allowed network cuts that divide a network into multiple subnetworks. Using such a network cut the compositional verification is done in the following steps:

1. Cut the network N into n subnetworks $N_1, \ldots, N_n$, applying allowed network cuts.
2. For $i = 1, \ldots, n$, use the RobustRailS tools verification steps described above to create a model m_i and properties ϕ_i and verify that m_i satisfies ϕ_i.

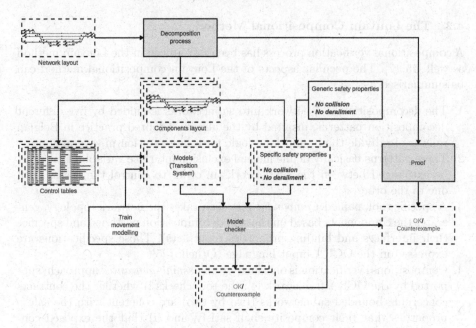

Fig. 3. Compositional verification process.

The identification of the points where to cut a network is manual[1], while a tool has been developed to generate the two subnetwork descriptions from the whole network and the identified cut points. Note that an interlocking system controlling a subnetwork (e.g. a station) is connected to the rest of the railway network by means of incoming/outcoming tracks, which are not under the control of the interlocking. The RobustRailS method assumes that a subnetwork includes at each of its connections with the outside a *border* section and a pair of signals: an *exit signal* which is not controlled by the interlocking, since the authority to exit the subnetwork area is not a responsibility of the interlocking, and an *entry signal* under the control of the interlocking. In the RobustRailS compositional method, a cut needs to add border track segment and signals in order to maintain the previously mentioned assumptions for the subnetworks as well (as shown in Fig. 4a, 4b). Under these assumptions, it is demonstrated that proving (by model checking) safety of both subnetworks implies the safety of the full network [10]. The "Proof" box in Fig. 3 is therefore in this case an a priori proof.

---

[1] The automatization of cut placements for RobustRailS tool is currently an undergoing activity.

4.2   The Louvain Compositional Method

A compositional verification process has been introduced in the Louvain method as well [15,17]. The peculiar aspects of the Louvain compositional method can be summarised as:

1. The decomposition of a network into subnetworks is guided by five different decomposition patterns, inspired by the already adopted practice in Belgian railways to divide the interlocking logic for a large station in several zones;
2. These patterns basically define mutual exclusion interface variables that must be exchanged between the subnetworks in order to control the access from one to the other;
3. A specific tool, named *Component retriever*, takes the network topology, generates the components based on the said decomposition patterns, and specifies their interfaces and binding properties (contracts). Those specifications are expressed in the OCRA input language (Othello) [5];
4. Compositional verification is obtained by an *assume-guarantee* approach, supported by the OCRA framework [4]: the tool checks i) whether the contracts concerning bounded subnetworks (two by two) are coherent with the safety properties that their composite shall satisfy, and ii) that the exposed contracts of each subnetwork are satisfied by their implementation (model in SMV), according to the contracts-refinement proof system for component-based systems proposed in [6].
5. In a third verification step, safety properties are verified on the SMV model representing each subnetwork with the NuXmv model checker (Sect. 3.2).

The "Proof" box in Fig. 3 in this case refers to the contract verification by OCRA, while the component verification activities are run employing nuXmv, taking advantage of k-liveness and ic3 algorithms [2,7] in order to verify LTL properties on the components.

5   Comparison of the Two Methods

To discuss the details of each compositional method we refer to a simple example station shown in Fig. 4.

Both methods decompose the station into two components (A and B, respectively left and right) with a similar cut. The two models differ in the way the interactions between the components are managed. On one hand, RobustRailS adds linear sections and signals to abstract the other part of the network. On the other hand, Louvain retrieves and uses mutual exclusion variables (called BSP variables) already defined in the interlockings in order to define binding properties between subnetworks.

Let us consider the simple network of Fig. 4a, where the drawing represents the network layout in terms of tracks, points and signals. Two tracks converge from the left on a single track (up direction), and symmetrically from the right (down direction).

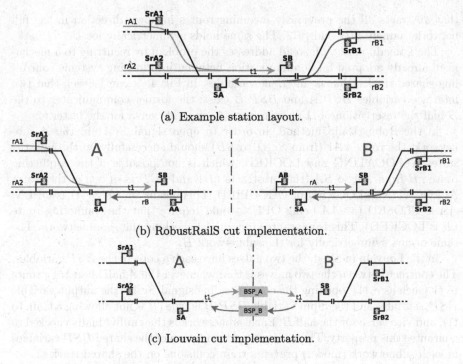

(a) Example station layout.

(b) RobustRailS cut implementation.

(c) Louvain cut implementation.

Fig. 4. Cut methods.

The coloured arrows represent the routes that make possible to reach the central track $t1$ from the left and the right. Obviously, routes $rA1$ and $rA2$ are in conflict with routes $rB1$ and $rB2$ to gain access to the central track. The No-collision property reads as "No two trains can enter track $t1$ together" and $t1$ is actually a shared resource with mutually exclusive access by the trains. The interlocking system guarantees the property by granting only one of the conflicting routes to be allocated to a train, and communicating this to the trains by means of signals at the beginning of the routes ($SrA1, SrA2, SrB1, SrB2$ for $rA1, rA2, rB1, rB2$ respectively).

When applying a decomposition that cuts the network into two symmetrical halves A and B, the two halves are managed as if they were controlled by two different interlocking systems. Hence, mutual exclusion on $t1$ is distributed among the two halves.

The definition of cut[2] given by the RobustRailS method includes $t1$ in both subnetworks and adds the signals AA and AB to A and B subnetworks, respectively (Fig. 4b); focusing on A, the extra signal adds a route rB from AA to SA,

---

[2] Note that the operated cut is the one defined in [19], which slightly differs from the *single cut* defined in [10], since the $t1$ section is present in both subnetworks. The compositionality proof of [10] covers this case as well.

that abstracts all the previously incoming routes in down direction in the full network, namely $rB1$ and $rB2$. The same holds symmetrically for B.

The Louvain method instead addresses the problem by recurring to a mechanism already adopted for communication between interlocking systems controlling shared tracks, that is, interface variables. In Fig. 4c it can be seen that two interface variables BSP_A and BSP_B exist: the former communicates to the B half the reservation of $t1$ as seen from A, and vice versa for the latter.

In the RobustRailS method, in order to open signal $SrA1$ in the A subnetwork, the route $rA1$ (from $SrA1$ to SB) should successfully go through the states ALLOCATING and LOCKED, which is not possible if the conflicting route rB from AA to SA (that abstracts $rB1$ and $rB2$) is in one of the states ALLOCATING, LOCKED or OCCUPIED. This means that if $SrA1$ is OPEN, AA is CLOSED (as AA being OPEN would require that the conflicting route rB is LOCKED). This is guaranteed by model checking the A subnetwork. The same occurs symmetrically for the subnetwork B.

In the Louvain method, the two halves have each a copy of the BSP variables. The contract between the two halves is that whenever the A half allocates a route to $t1$ (such as $rA1$), opening the corresponding signal $SrA1$, the output variable BSP_A is false and the input variable BSP_B is true (B is not allowing a train to $t1$), and vice versa for the half B. Each subnetwork is then individually checked to guarantee this property. The proper implementation of the shared BSP variables in each subnetwork (model) prevents train collisions on the shared track $t1$.

We can therefore observe that in the RobustRailS method, the added signals AA and AB play the role of the variables BSP_A and BSP_B of the Louvain method, respectively.

We can conclude therefore that the two methods are equivalent for the considered cut[3]. Similar arguments can be used to show that this holds also for the other four decomposition patterns considered by the Louvain method. We claim that different decomposition patterns, addressed by the RobustRailS method, that have not been considered by the Louvain one, could be expressed by means of interface variables and contracts according to the latter by properly mimicking the added RobustRailS signals with interface mutual exclusion variables.

The two verification methods are different in the sense that while the Louvain one builds on the adoption of established compositional model checking techniques and tools, applied to the specific problem, the RobustRailS approach has been tailored in its very definition to the specific problem, hence it is a domain dependent solution: this is apparent in the fact that in the former contracts are established for each interface between two components, while in the latter the interface models are built by adding extra railway elements.

6   Case Study: La Louvière-Sud

We develop further our comparison by applying the two methods on a common case study, with the main aim to confirm the advantages of compositionality in

---

[3] The formal equivalence of the two presented methods is out of scope of this paper.

both frameworks. Our case study concerns a real railway network: a portion of La Louvière-Sud in Belgium, which was already decomposed into three subnetworks, namely LVR1, LVR7 and LVR9 represented in Fig. 5[4].

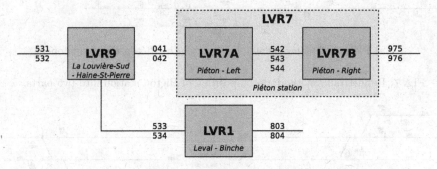

Fig. 5. La Louvière-Sud: topology of the verified components.

LVR1 and LVR9 are small and have a limited number of routes (18), so it is expected that for both methods they can be verified without recurring to decomposition. On the other hand, LVR7, the Piéton station represented in Fig. 6, has three main line platforms, a marshalling yard with two tracks, and contains many routes. So we will investigate how a decomposition of LVR7 can help the verification.

In the following subsection we describe how LVR7 can be decomposed using the two methods.

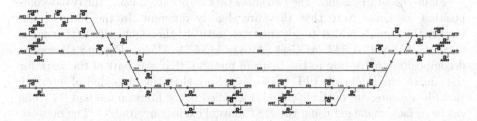

Fig. 6. Piéton station scheme represented according to the RobustRailS conventions: sections (plain label), points (red label) and signals (bold label). In particular the scheme includes the pair of signals at the borders. (Color figure online)

---

[4] The models are available at https://github.com/gorigloria/compositionalverification models.

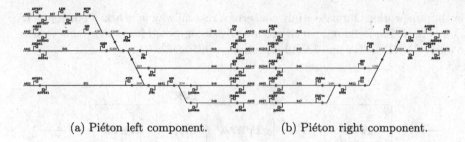

(a) Piéton left component.   (b) Piéton right component.

Fig. 7. RobustRailS method: decomposition of Piéton station into two parts.

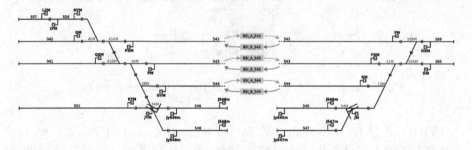

Fig. 8. Louvain method: decomposition of Piéton station into two parts.

6.1 Decomposition of LVR7 - Piéton station

Figure 6 shows the Piéton station scheme represented according to the Robust-RailS conventions.

Figure 7 and Fig. 8 show the two subnetworks, obtained using the two decomposition methods. Note that they are slightly different. In the RobustRailS model, the signals added to abstract respectively the right (the left) component are AIX542, AI543, AIY544 (AI542, AIX543, AI544). Figure 8 shows the decomposition according to the Louvain method, that was part of the work for the Christophe Limbrée's PhD thesis [17]. Note that only one kind of interface variable appears, out of the five kinds identified in the Louvain method [17]. The cut is, in fact, managed using the BSI mutual exclusion variables. The network modelled with the Louvain method relies on extensions of track-side equipment previously described in Sect. 2: in particular, the network has points with more than one branch and it uses *sectioning points*, i.e., points with an associated signal (see points 36M and 14M in Fig. 8). These extensions have been modelled with the RobustRailS methods as follows:

– Points with more than one branch have been splitted into multiple points;
– Sectioning points have been modelled as follows: 1) sectioning points have been treated as simple points; 2) an additional linear section has been placed adjacent to each sectioning point; 3) two signals, one for each direction, have been added to the additional linear section.

Another difference between the two methods is on the definition of routes. In the RobustRailS framework, every route starts at a signal and ends at the following one. This implies that no intermediate signal in the same travel direction is crossed in any given route. In the Louvain model, a route starts at a signal and ends on the destination track segment without crossing intermediate signals.

In the following subsections we report the experimentation results. The experiments were executed on a server with the following system specifications: Intel(R) Xeon(R) CPU E5-1650 @ 3.6 GHz, 125 GB RAM, and running Linux 4.4.0-47.x86_64 kernel. The execution time was limited to 1 day in order to fit with typically industrially acceptable times.

6.2 Verification Results Using the RobustRailS Method

We have applied the RobustRailS method on LVR7 and its decomposed subnetworks as well as on LVR1 and LVR9. The RobustRailS control table generator allows for two options, one of which enforces the so-called *flank protection*, in which points and signals not belonging to the route are properly set in order to avoid hostile train movements into the route at an incident point. Table 1 reports the results when flank protection is chosen for all the modelled components. It can be seen that all networks were verifiable and that the time for verifying both LVR7A and LVR7B is around three times faster than that for LVR7, while the max needed memory usage (2083 MB) is around a third.

Table 1. Verification of the models for LVR1, LVR9, and LVR7 and LVR7's decomposed networks LVR7A and LVR7B using the RobustRailS tools.

ID	Name	Routes	Time (s)	Memory (MB)
LVR7	Piéton	48	2387	5467
LVR7A	Piéton - Left	30	670	2083
LVR7B	Piéton - Right	18	108	846
LVR1	Leval - Binche	18	38	413
LVR9	La Louvière-Sud - Haine-St-Pierre	18	33	415

6.3 Verification Results Using the Louvain Method

Table 2 contains the verification metrics obtained by the OCRA/nuXmv tools for all the networks, with the same server used for RobustRailS experiments. The models of LVR1, LVR9, LVR7A and LVR7B were, as expected, verifiable, but the verification of the monolithic model of Piéton (LVR7) had to be stopped after one day, which is the maximal time considered to be feasible. The sum of the verification times of the models of the two decomposed networks is 23.210 s ∼ 6.5 h, which shows that the decomposition not only made the verification feasible, but also fast (compared to more than one day). We highlight the small amount of memory occupied by the verification tasks.

Table 2. Verification of the models for LVR1, LVR9 and LVR7 and LVR7's decomposed networks LVR7A and LVR7B using the Louvain method.

ID	Name	Routes	Time (s)			Memory (MB)
			OCRA	nuXmv	Total	
LVR7	Piéton	48	Not feasible			–
LVR7A	Piéton - Left	30	15673	1997	17670	152
LVR7B	Piéton - Right	18	4791	749	5540	125
LVR1	Leval - Binche	18	287	245	532	48
LVR9	La Louvière-Sud - Haine-St-Pierre	18	3407	59	3466	81

6.4   Discussion

The shown performance figures are not meant to support an efficiency comparison between the two methods: indeed the actual verification performance depends on many factors that differ in the two methods. However, the figures on models LVR7, LVR7A and LVR7B clearly show the advantages given by compositional verification in both methods. Moreover, one interesting thing can be observed if we compare the verification times for all the networks: while the ones by the Louvain tools is generally 15–50 times longer than those by the RobustRailS tools, the time for the LVR9 component is of the order of 100 times longer. This can be explained by the fact that LVR9 is a simple junction that has few routes and a low internal complexity, but that connects with different components through several interfaces: the Louvain method requires to separately check the component w.r.t. all contracts related to the interfaces; the RobustRailS method takes the proof of compliance between components as granted once for all – when the added border sections and signals comply with the standard format (compliance assured by the static analysis engine included in RT-Tester).

Another main difference between the two methods is on the decomposition technique. On one hand, cuts are manually applied to a network for the Robust-RailS method. On the other hand, Louvain method exploits automatic decomposition starting from the existing description of the network layout, which in turn is automatically generated from their application data. The automatic decomposition performed by Louvain method requires a couple of minutes, hence it can be neglected. The manual decomposition performed by RobustRailS method requires more time, but it is limited and feasible as the number of rules for cuts is low. Furthermore, for RobustRailS method, the implementation of automatic cuts is currently in progress.

7   Related Work

We have already reported in the introduction how *locality* exhibited by interlocking systems has been exploited in different approaches aimed to optimise verification by model checking of large station layouts [1,9,13,14,26]. Still, in those approaches the verification process considers the full interlocking system defined over the full station layout.

The two approaches discussed in this paper are, at the best of our knowledge, the only ones that address verification of interlocking of large networks by decomposing the layout in smaller components and formally deduce safety of the whole from the safety verification of the parts.

Regarding a comparison of different formal verification methods of interlocking systems, not addressing compositionality, we can cite [11].

8   Conclusions

We have compared two different compositional approaches to address state space explosion in formal verification of railway interlocking systems: the RobustRailS compositional method and the Louvain compositional method. We made a comparison of methodological elements at a conceptual level rather than comparing concrete performance metrics of the two methods as they use different verification tools. The comparison revealed that different concepts behind the two methods are essentially equivalent when it comes to the division of the network of an interlocking system into two networks and the creation of interlocking models for these and their interfaces. However, the two methods are different in the sense that while the Louvain one builds on the adoption of established compositional model checking techniques and tools, applied to the specific problem, the RobustRailS approach has been tailored in its very definition to the specific problem, hence it is a domain dependent solution: this is apparent in the fact that in the former contracts are established for each interface between two components, while in the latter the interfaces are built by adding extra railway elements. A major difference between the two verification methods is also the amount of generated proof obligations: in both approaches, one must perform component verification (prove safety of the interlocking models for the two decomposed networks), however, for the Louvain compositional method there are additional verification obligations: the verification of the contracts, i.e. the verification that each component satisfies all contracts related to its interfaces. For the RobustRailS compositional method the soundness of the component verification has been proved a priori (once-and-for-all). A case study demonstrated that both methods had great benefits in terms of addressing state space explosion.

A further comparison of the RobustRailS method with the Louvain one could be done by extending the reasoning shown in this paper to the other four kinds of interface variable adopted in [17]. This extension is straightforward, due to the similarity of the different cases, but the detailed study is left to future work.

As a final remark, we observe that verification of interlocking systems in the end boils down to mutual exclusion verification. Operating a cut in the network typically distributes the mutual exclusion mechanisms over two or even more components, whether such decomposition is physical, to exploit the advantages of distributed computing, or logical, to remain in the low ends of the exponential state space explosion in verification. To this respect, the presented reasonings may reveal useful in other domains where some notion of distributed mutual exclusion may help verification of large systems.

Acknowledgement. The authors wish to thank Jan Peleska and Linh H. Vu with whom Anne Haxthausen developed the RobustRailS verification method and tools, and Hugo D. Macedo, who collaborated in the initial work of Anne Haxthausen and Alessandro Fantechi on the RobustRailS compositional approach.

References

1. Bonacchi, A., Fantechi, A., Bacherini, S., Tempestini, M.: Validation process for railway interlocking systems. Sci. Comput. Program. **128**, 2–21 (2016)
2. Bradley, A.R.: SAT-based model checking without unrolling. In: Jhala, R., Schmidt, D. (eds.) VMCAI 2011. LNCS, vol. 6538, pp. 70–87. Springer, Heidelberg (2011). https://doi.org/10.1007/978-3-642-18275-4_7
3. Busard, S., Cappart, Q., Limbrée, C., Pecheur, C., Schaus, P.: Verification of railway interlocking systems. In: Proceedings of the ESSS 2015, Oslo, Norway, 22 June 2015. EPTCS, vol. 184, pp. 19–31. Open Publishing Association (2015)
4. Cimatti, A., Dorigatti, M., Tonetta, S.: OCRA: a tool for checking the refinement of temporal contracts. In: 28th IEEE/ACM International Conference on Automated Software Engineering, Silicon Valley, CA, USA, 11–15 November 2013, pp. 702–705. IEEE (2013)
5. Cimatti, A., Tonetta, S.: A property-based proof system for contract-based design. In: 38th Euromicro Conference on Software Engineering and Advanced Applications, pp. 21–28. IEEE (2012)
6. Cimatti, A., Tonetta, S.: Contracts-refinement proof system for component-based embedded systems. Sci. Comput. Program. **97**, 333–348 (2015)
7. Claessen, K., Sörensson, N.: A liveness checking algorithm that counts. In: Formal Methods in Computer-Aided Design, FMCAD 2012, Cambridge, UK, 22–25 October 2012, pp. 52–59. IEEE (2012)
8. Fantechi, A., Haxthausen, A.E., Macedo, H.D.: Compositional verification of interlocking systems for large stations. In: Cimatti, A., Sirjani, M. (eds.) SEFM 2017. LNCS, vol. 10469, pp. 236–252. Springer, Cham (2017). https://doi.org/10.1007/978-3-319-66197-1_15
9. Ferrari, A., Magnani, G., Grasso, D., Fantechi, A.: Model checking interlocking control tables. In: Schnieder, E., Tarnai, G. (eds.) FORMS/FORMAT 2010, pp. 107–115. Springer, Heidelberg (2010). https://doi.org/10.1007/978-3-642-14261-1_11
10. Haxthausen, A.E., Fantechi, A.: Compositional verification of railway interlocking systems. Submitted for publication (2021)
11. Haxthausen, A.E., Nguyen, H.N., Roggenbach, M.: Comparing formal verification approaches of interlocking systems. In: Lecomte, T., Pinger, R., Romanovsky, A. (eds.) RSSRail 2016. LNCS, vol. 9707, pp. 160–177. Springer, Cham (2016). https://doi.org/10.1007/978-3-319-33951-1_12
12. Haxthausen, A.E., Østergaard, P.H.: On the use of static checking in the verification of interlocking systems. In: Margaria, T., Steffen, B. (eds.) ISoLA 2016. LNCS, vol. 9953, pp. 266–278. Springer, Cham (2016). https://doi.org/10.1007/978-3-319-47169-3_19

13. James, P., Möller, F., Nguyen, H.N., Roggenbach, M., Schneider, S., Treharne, H.: Decomposing scheme plans to manage verification complexity. In: FORMS/FORMAT 2014, pp. 210–220. Institute for Traffic Safety and Automation Engineering, Technische Univ. Braunschweig (2014)

14. James, P., et al.: Verification of solid state interlocking programs. In: Counsell, S., Núñez, M. (eds.) SEFM 2013. LNCS, vol. 8368, pp. 253–268. Springer, Cham (2014). https://doi.org/10.1007/978-3-319-05032-4_19

15. Limbrée, C., Cappart, Q., Pecheur, C., Tonetta, S.: Verification of railway interlocking - compositional approach with OCRA. In: Lecomte, T., Pinger, R., Romanovsky, A. (eds.) RSSRail 2016. LNCS, vol. 9707, pp. 134–149. Springer, Cham (2016). https://doi.org/10.1007/978-3-319-33951-1_10

16. Limbrée, C., Pecheur, C.: A framework for the formal verification of networks of railway interlockings - application to the belgian railway. Electron. Commun. Eur. Assoc. Softw. Sci. Technol. **76** (2018)

17. Limbrée, C.: Formal verification of railway interlocking systems. Ph.D. thesis, UCL Louvain (2019)

18. Macedo, H.D., Fantechi, A., Haxthausen, A.E.: Compositional verification of multi-station interlocking systems. In: Margaria, T., Steffen, B. (eds.) ISoLA 2016. LNCS, vol. 9953, pp. 279–293. Springer, Cham (2016). https://doi.org/10.1007/978-3-319-47169-3_20

19. Macedo, H.D., Fantechi, A., Haxthausen, A.E.: Compositional model checking of interlocking systems for lines with multiple stations. In: Barrett, C., Davies, M., Kahsai, T. (eds.) NFM 2017. LNCS, vol. 10227, pp. 146–162. Springer, Cham (2017). https://doi.org/10.1007/978-3-319-57288-8_11

20. Peleska, J.: Industrial-strength model-based testing - state of the art and current challenges. In: 8th Workshop on Model-Based Testing, Rome, Italy, vol. 111, pp. 3–28. Open Publishing Association (2013)

21. Verified Systems International GmbH: RT-Tester Model-Based Test Case and Test Data Generator - RTT-MBT - User Manual (2013). http://www.verified.de

22. Vu, L.H., Haxthausen, A.E., Peleska, J.: A Domain-Specific Language for Railway Interlocking Systems. In: FORMS/FORMAT 2014. pp. 200–209. Institute for Traffic Safety and Automation Engineering, Technische Universität Braunschweig (2014)

23. Vu, L.H., Haxthausen, A.E., Peleska, J.: A domain-specific language for generic interlocking models and their properties. In: Fantechi, A., Lecomte, T., Romanovsky, A. (eds.) RSSRail 2017. LNCS, vol. 10598, pp. 99–115. Springer, Cham (2017). https://doi.org/10.1007/978-3-319-68499-4_7

24. Vu, L.H.: Formal development and verification of railway control systems - in the context of ERTMS/ETCS level 2. Ph.D. thesis, Technical University of Denmark, DTU Compute (2015)

25. Vu, L.H., Haxthausen, A.E., Peleska, J.: Formal modelling and verification of interlocking systems featuring sequential release. Sci. Comput. Program. **133**, Part 2, 91–115 (2017)

26. Winter, K.: Optimising ordering strategies for symbolic model checking of railway interlockings. In: Margaria, T., Steffen, B. (eds.) ISoLA 2012. LNCS, vol. 7610, pp. 246–260. Springer, Heidelberg (2012). https://doi.org/10.1007/978-3-642-34032-1_24

Safety Invariant Verification that Meets Engineers' Expectations

Alexei Iliasov[1], Linas Laibinis[2]([✉]), Dominic Taylor[3], Ilya Lopatkin[1],
and Alexander Romanovsky[1,4]

[1] The Formal Route Ltd., London, UK
[2] Institute of Computer Science, Vilnius University, Vilnius, Lithuania
linas.laibinis@mif.vu.lt
[3] Systra Scott Lister, London, UK
[4] Newcastle University, Newcastle upon Tyne, UK

Abstract. This industrial experience report discusses the problems we have been facing while using our formal verification technology, called SafeCap, in a substantial number of live signalling projects in UK mainline rail, and the solutions we are now developing to counter these problems. Symbolic execution and safety invariant verification are well-understood subjects and yet their application to real life high assurance systems requires going a few steps beyond the conventional practice. In engineering practice it is not sufficient to simply know that a safety property fails: one needs to know why and hence where and what exactly fails. It is also crucial to positively demonstrate that no safety failure is omitted from consideration. In this industrial report we show how to derive a list of all potential errors by transforming a safety invariant predicate using information from the constructed state transition system. The identified possible errors are verified by an automated symbolic prover, while a report generator presents findings in an engineer-friendly format to guide subsequent rework steps. The scalability and the efficiency of the proposed mechanism (which is now fully integrated in the SafeCap technology) have been demonstrated in several live signalling projects.

1 Introduction

There is a growing number of railway signalling companies that use verification techniques based on formal proofs for demonstrating and assuring system safety. The automated technologies, including AtelierB [1,2], Ovado/Rodin [3], Prover [4] and Spark Ada [5], formally verify that a system satisfies a collection of identified safety properties. These tools report violations found during verification to the signalling engineers, who use that information to guide the rework process.

One of the earliest forms of computer-based interlocking was the Solid State Interlocking (SSI) [6], developed in the UK in the 1980s through an agreement between British Rail and two signalling supply companies, Westinghouse and GEC General Signal. SSI is the predominant technology used for computer-based interlockings on UK mainline railways. It also has applications overseas, including in India, Australia, New Zealand, France and Belgium.

© Springer Nature Switzerland AG 2022
S. Collart-Dutilleul et al. (Eds.): RSSRail 2022, LNCS 13294, pp. 20–31, 2022.
https://doi.org/10.1007/978-3-031-05814-1_2

In the last two years we have been applying a modern verification technology called SafeCap as part of a number of industrial signalling projects to verify the safety of SSI designs. Safety verification of 30 mainline interlockings, developed by different suppliers and design offices, has been successfully conducted for our industrial partners [7].

SafeCap was originally developed as an open toolkit for modelling railway capacity and verifying railway network safety in a number of public projects led by Newcastle University [8]. In the last 5 years the tool has been fully redesigned to deliver scalable and fully-automated verification of industrial interlockings [7,9]. The resulting toolset has been proven in commercial applications through the verification of signalling projects that use SSI, and successor technologies. The two distinguishing features of SSI SafeCap are a fully automated verification process and complete hiding of formalisation details. As a result, engineers receive diagnostics reports describing the found safety problems in terms familiar to them, i.e., by explicitly referring to the applicable railway layouts (schemas) and SSI data.

Our approach to proving safety of signalling data is based on expressing signalling principles as a collection of predicates constituting *safety invariants*, translating the source data (the schema and SSI data) into a formal model – a *state transition system*, and then generating and discharging proof obligations (i.e. verification conjectures) to establish that every system transition maintains the predefined safety invariants. At the basic level, the output is a list of names of violated signalling safety principles. This is clearly inadequate and hence we provide further detail about the identified violations in two ways:

- a particular transition leading to a failed proof obligation is used to define the source code location of a potential error;
- the state of an undischarged proof obligation is used to report the probable cause of proof failure and thus indicate the actual cause of an error in the source data.

The second way is a heuristic and is not guaranteed to succeed in producing a useful commentary. In particular, it cannot, in general, identify all errors in the sense of an error as understood by engineers, i.e., as a specific mistake in the source data. Such a rift between the tool output and engineers' expectations could not be bridged without changing the underlying approach to verification of a safety invariant.

Our initial industrial projects have highlighted deficiencies of the conventional safety invariant verification procedure, most critically, that a single verification pass cannot produce the list of all possible errors due to masking of unreported errors by reported ones. In particular, safety invariant verification relies on the conditions of an invariant to be fulfilled in an initial system state; with any other violation detected, this is no longer the case and verification becomes potentially unsound.

The setting can be made sound again by "patching" a safety invariant to exclude a detected violation (by explicitly provisioning for an exception to the set of safety rules), but in practice such an approach is untenable due to unwieldy safety predicates arising from an applied patching routine. It also makes verification a sequential process or, alternatively, requires a new safety critical proof scheduling component.

It is our belief that a more promising approach is an automatic safety invariant verification procedure that constructs proof obligations in a different way. The procedure is designed in such a manner that every constructed proof obligation aligns exactly with one potential engineering error in the source data. Thus, with the same technique, we give a formal definition of an engineering error and a method to produce all their instances for a given system.[1]

2   Reporting Safety Invariant Violations

2.1   Establishing System Correctness

The central question in the verification of signalling correctness is what constitutes a safe signalling design. Certain basic principles are universally accepted, for instance, the absence of train collisions and derailment. However, it is almost hopeless to verify the absence of such hazards in the strictest possible sense, not least because there are many real-world limitations [7]. Moreover, interlockings, by themselves, provide only one level of protection against driver errors through the provision of overlaps and control of signal aspects. This is an area where there is significant variation in practice across different geographic regions and times. Interlockings also do little to protect against equipment failures, but are themselves designed to be resilient to such failures.

For these reasons, correctness is established not against the basic principles but rather against the lower level signalling principles (that are expected to adequately address foundational safety principles) and designed to enforce railway operation with an acceptable level of risk and failures. Such principles are carefully designed by domain experts, documented in standards [10–12], can vary between regions, and do change over time. At the time of writing this paper, the SSI SafeCap is capable to verify about 60 formalised signalling safety principles.

2.2   The Running Example

In the following we shall use a simple, but real-life, case of a signalling safety principle to illustrate our approach. The principle states that

For every set route, it holds that all sub routes of the route that are within the interlocking control area are locked.

---

[1] It is a somewhat circular argument: we do cover all engineering errors but only because we get to define what they mean formally; we are guided by our prior practical experience to choose the right level of granularity for the definition of an engineering error to match engineers' expectations.

In other words, when setting a route, all the sub routes of the route path must be commanded locked or detected locked. In the mathematical notation we employ, which is a combination of first order logic and set theory (based upon the B-Method mathematical notation [13]), the rule can be formally expressed as the following safety invariant:

$$route\_subrouteset[\text{route\_s} \setminus \text{route\_s'p}] \cap SubRoute.ixl \subseteq \text{subroute\_l} \,, \qquad (1)$$

where *route_subrouteset* is a constant defined by a *signalling plan document* (a formalised data set describing a geographical interlocking area), stating which sub routes comprise the path of a route; *SubRoute.ixl* is a signalling plan constant defining the current interlocking sub routes; route_s and route_s'p are the current and previous states of a model variable recording the route locking status (i.e., $r \in$ route_s implies that route r is currently locked). Finally, $f[s]$ denotes the relational image of f (that must be a set of a pairs) over given set s.

2.3 Symbolic Verification of Signalling Safety Principles

For the purposes of verification, each signalling principle is rendered as an *inductive safety invariant* – a system property that must hold when a system boots up and must be maintained (or, equivalently, reestablished) after any possible update to a new system state. Verification is then understood as the problem of checking that any safety invariant is respected by every state update. Technically this is done be generating conjectures of the form *"if an invariant holds in a previous state and a state update happens, is it true that the invariant holds for the new state?"*. Formally, such a conjecture (also called a *proof obligation* (PO)) is represented as a logical sequent consisting of a number of hypotheses (H) and a goal (G), denoted as $H \vdash G$.

In general, a schematic proof obligation for the preservation of a safety invariant (for a state transition $j \in J$) takes the following form:

$$M(c) \wedge A(c, v) \wedge I(c, v) \wedge P_j(c, v) \wedge Q_j(c, v, v') \Rightarrow I(c, v'), \qquad (2)$$

where $M(c)$ and $A(c, v)$ are constants and constraints from the formalised signalling plan, defined over constants c and model state (variables) v, a state transition is characterised by a pre-condition predicate $P_j(c, v)$ and a post-condition $Q_j(c, v, v')$ relating a next state v' to the current state v and constants c, J represents the set of all such state transitions, and $I(c, v)$ stands for the invariant property to be preserved.

The number of such proof conjectures is $m * n$, where m is the number of safety invariant predicates (67 defined so far) and n is the number of possible state updates (for the industrial projects we have carried out, this value varies between 4000 and 140000 with the mean value of 17641). This is a small number when contrasted against the number of potentially reachable states[2]. As

---

[2] Somewhere in the region of 2^{2000}, where 2000 is the typical number of Boolean model variables in an electronic interlocking; there are also a couple of hundreds of bit vectors and integers.

the number of safety invariant predicates is fixed for all projects, the complexity measured in the number of conjectures grows linearly with the interlocking complexity.

When a prover fails to discharge (i.e., to complete automated proof of) a proof obligation derived from a safety invariant, we presume that a safety invariant is violated[3]. Clearly this alone is not sufficient since a typical interlocking data has thousands lines of code. However, a failed proof obligation itself can be traced, via the associated state transition, to the data source code and, more precisely, to one or more control flow threads of the verified data. This gives us an initial error localisation in terms of the available signalling data.

Such a localisation alone is still not enough since many errors result in hundreds of failed proof obligations with often distinct control flow traces. Therefore, ascertaining the actual cause of each failed proof obligation is extremely laborious; in cases of hundreds or thousands of failed proof obligations it becomes simply impracticable.

Previously, we have processed every failed proof obligation at the report generation stage in order to identify its likely cause. This processing is more involved than simply looking at an *open goal*, i.e., a current proving conjecture that the prover failed to discharge. First, there can be a number of open goals (in fact, there can be hundreds of open goals arising from prover attempts to simplify the goal hypotheses by splitting internal disjunctions). Second, an open goal could be stated in terms that are of no relationship (i.e., having no common free identifiers) to the original transition and safety invariant predicate (e.g., due a translation into a logical expression suitable for subsequent treatment with an SMT solver).

One technique that we have employed to overcome this shortcoming was automatic backtracking of a failed subgoal to find a state most amenable to reporting. The backtracking acts on an open goal and reverts the attempted proof steps in a search of a goal predicate matching one of the predefined expression templates. Such a technique brings no guarantee of arriving at a satisfactory result, however, in our applications it was reasonably successful.

Knowing the identified causes of failed proof obligations allowed us to collate identical errors and produce usable reports. The compression factor here was quite significant: there could be between 10 to 50 failed proof obligations for every reported violation.

2.4   The Running Example, Continued

The formal definition of our running example safety principle, as given in (1), is a typical set-theoretic statement of a safety predicate; however, any arising failed goals are difficult to backtrack and analyse. Expression *route_subrouteset* [route_s \ route_s'p] relates all the routes being set to all of their sub routes,

---

[3] Here we 'presume', since we cannot know for sure because the logic we rely on is undecidable. Thus a failed conjecture could mean a false positive – a risk we are prepared to accept.

therefore, when a proof of (1) fails, all we can hope to know is that one or more of the routes being set is not locking of one or more sub routes. However, we can rewrite this property into an equivalent (predicate) one:

$$\forall r \in Route$$
$$r \in \mathsf{route\_s} \setminus \mathsf{route\_s'p}$$
$$\Rightarrow$$
$$\forall \mathsf{sr} \in SubRoute$$
$$\mathsf{sr} \in route\_subrouteset[\{r\}] \cap SubRoute.ixl$$
$$\Rightarrow$$
$$\mathsf{sr} \in \mathsf{subroute\_l}$$

In the rewritten proof obligation, expression route_s \ route_s'p becomes replaced by a constant set of routes involved in a deterministic state transition. This allows the prover to eliminate the outer quantifier and introduce a free identifier with constraint $r = R_1 \lor r = R_2 \lor \dots$. The proof then proceeds by analysing cases of this disjunction. This, in turn, allows the prover to infer that $route\_subrouteset[\{r\}]$ is a constant set, and to continue in the same manner for the inner quantifier. The advantage of the predicate form above is the ability, in most cases, to identify a specific combination of route r and sub route sr that give rise to a violation for a considered proof obligation.

3   Positive Demonstration of the Absence of Violations

Decoding the proof state to infer an error has proven to be insufficient for finding all its causes and all the circumstances of its occurrence. It is possible for a failed proof obligation to reveal one error and, at the same time, mask the presence of another. Logically, nothing wrong happens here: analysis of a violated safety invariant, involving the backtracking process, reveals one likely cause of the violation.

Yet reporting all such causes associated with specific source data errors is one of the principal requirements for an automated safety verification process. Hence, to continue the running example, if some route were missing the locking of two (or more) sub routes on its path, a failed proof obligation would be able to point to only one of them.

The simplest solution would be to fix all the identified problems and re-run the verification process, which would reveal previously masked errors. Unfortunately, this is not a practical scenario for the following reasons: 1) changes to the signalling data can take months and conducting multiple re-verification cycles might be impossible due to delivery constraints; 2) generic signalling principles can, at times and subject to risk assessment, be deliberately violated to meet site-specific operational needs; 3) we cannot rule out the presence of false positives, partly due to the complexity and constant evolution of real-life signalling data, and partly due to automated theorem proving being undecidable. A false positive can turn from being a benign issue to a critical one when it masks another error.

To rule out the masking of one error by another, we approach safety invariant verification from a slightly different perspective. Instead of a verification process as such, we focus initially on the enumeration of all potential non-trivial errors. This is achieved by altering the method of proof obligation generation, aiming to obtain a dedicated proof obligation for each non-trivial potential error. In the following sections we define the meaning of *a non-trivial potential error* via a process that constructs bespoke proof obligations for each state transition.

3.1 Synthesising a Focused Safety Invariant

Most of the attributes of SSI objects have two states (e.g., a route is set or unset, a sub route is locked or free, and so on). In line with the set theory underpinning our formalisation, such attributes are modelled as set membership tests for an object stored in the model variable corresponding to the attribute. For instance, the fact that some sub route $UAA\text{-}AB$ is locked is expressed as $UAA\text{-}AB \in$ subroute_l; the same sub route being free is, conversely, $UAA\text{-}AB \notin$ subroute_l.

In our formalisation, a state transition is represented as a pair of predicates $Pre(c,v)$ and $Post(c,v,v')$. In a general case, that is all we can say. However, in the case of a state transition derived from the signalling data, the restrictions of the SSI language allow us to make stronger assumptions. First, since SSI is a fully deterministic language, transition postconditions are limited to conjunction of equalities of the form $v' = v \cup E_1 \setminus E_2$, where E_1 and E_2 are constant sets of the values to be added or removed. Second, the predicate language of SSI is also quite limited and, as a result, its translation yields a precondition that is conjunction of just few forms of clauses:

- membership clause $v \in S$, $v \notin S$ or $v \subseteq S$;
- equality clause $f(v) = c$, $v = c$, $v \neq c$, ...;
- disjunctive clauses;
- quantifiers, implications and other forms arising from the SSI axiomatisation.

By looking at a postcondition, it is possible to deduce, via simple pattern matching, sets of objects that are being added or removed from the corresponding set variables (i.e., constant sets E_1 and E_2). That is, from the predicate of a postcondition, we can unfailingly infer, e.g., which sub routes are locked or freed and so on. Another way to look at this is representing a resulting before-after predicate $S(c,v,v')$ as a deterministic assignment of a form $v := v \cup A \setminus B$, where A and B are constant sets.

We shall *describe* various model variables of interest as indexed set Z_i. For instance, Z_0 could describe the model variable subroute_l, Z_1 – track_o, and so on. The description of a variable is different from the variable itself – it characterises variable values (states) in relation to the precondition and the postcondition of a given state transition.

In particular, the postcondition part of the variable description contains the added and removed value sets of Z_i, referred as Z_i^+ and Z_i^-. There is a simple relationship between Z_i and its variable counterpart v_i:

$$v_i = \overline{v}_i \cup Z_i^+ \setminus Z_i^-. \tag{3}$$

Identifier $\overline{v}_i$ stands for the value of v_i in a state a transition occurs. For the moment, we only know that it must satisfy the safety invariant. In our running example, for postcondition subroute_l' = subroute_l' $\cup \{UAA\text{-}AB\} \setminus \{UAA\text{-}BA\}$, we have $Z_i^+ = \{UAA\text{-}AB\}$ and $Z_i^- = \{UAA\text{-}BA\}$.

Next, let us consider a transition precondition. The situation is less certain here as we can rely only on the first two precondition clause forms presented above (i.e., membership and equality) to deduce the precondition part of the current state variable description. Since we have to leave some clauses out, our knowledge of the previous state is generally incomplete.

Let us examine in more detail the first (membership) clause case. For every model variable, one can once again build two sets: values tested to be in a model variable and values tested to be not in it. These sets define Z_i as consisting of two components: for added, $\overline{Z}_i^+$, and removed, $\overline{Z}_i^-$, values. This allows us to relate these two sets to the previous (with respect to a considered transition) state of a model variable v_i:

$$\overline{v}_i = x_i \cup \overline{Z}_i^+ \setminus \overline{Z}_i^-, \tag{4}$$

where x_i is some previous (unknown) variable v_i state. Putting (3) and (4) together, we have the following:

$$v_i = x_i \cup (\overline{Z}_i^+ \cup Z_i^+ \setminus Z_i^-) \setminus (\overline{Z}_i^- \cup Z_i^- \setminus Z_i^+).$$

Intuitively, $\overline{Z}_i^+ \cup Z_i^+ \setminus Z_i^-$ is a set of objects that are known to be added (locked or set), while $\overline{Z}_i^- \cup Z_i^- \setminus Z_i^+$ is the known set of removed (unlocked, freed) objects.

3.2 Computing Potential Errors

Using model variable descriptions inferred for a state transition, we can transform a safety invariant predicate into a program computing the set of proof obligations. These new kinds of proof obligations are generally more numerous but also individually simpler. This is due to the fact that most invariant statements are written in a predicate form with quantifiers to facilitate reporting (via introduction of bound variables that may provide the error context) and such quantifiers can be eliminated, in the majority of cases, using the information contained in the description of model variables. The end result is a proof obligation with fewer or no quantifiers, with the previously bound variables instantiated to their constant values.

Each such derived proof obligation is a test for the presence of exactly one *engineering error*. A unique name generated for a proof obligation is the name of a corresponding potential error. Conversely, a proof obligation is the definition of a potential engineering error. All the proof obligations that can be derived for a given SSI source code and a safety invariant define the set of all potential engineering errors in a given interlocking.

It is quite possible to get an absolutely overwhelming number of proof obligations (e.g., hundreds of millions). The balance at play here is the granularity of errors. At one extreme we can declare a violation of a safety invariant to be exactly one error. Another extreme is to deduce every unique combination of schema entities that may give rise to this error and regard such a combination as an error. The practical solution is to control the degree of error granularity for each individual safety invariant predicate and, where necessary, prohibit more complex transformations involving deeply nested quantifiers.

We require the technique to be sound – it is fine to list errors that cannot possibly arise (and, we hope, will be filtered out by the prover), however it is not acceptable to omit errors that can potentially arise. The soundness proof is the subject for a future publication.

To refer to an identified error, we need to give it a name. As a starting point, the name of an error is taken as a combination of a safety invariant predicate (referenced by its label) and a (uniquely named) state transition. For instance, `inv1/transition5`. This level of error granularity identifies both principle violated and source code location.

When we drill down into what can go wrong for a specific transition with respect to a given invariant, we might discover that the original coarse-grained error name is refined (split) into a number of more specific errors: `inv1/transition5/a/b/.../goal`. Here `a` and `b` are some schema objects. Another addition here is a goal predicate – for `inv1/transition5/a/b/...` to uniquely refer to an identified error, such an error needs to be associated with its distinct proof obligation. To summarise, an error name is a combination of

- invariant,
- transition,
- identifying schema entities, and
- verification goal.

The identifying schema entities are automatically added to a proof obligation name (remember that a proof obligation is a concrete definition of an error) when a derived program computes its proof obligations.

Let us consider again the example invariant of sub route locking on route setting:

$$\forall r \in Route$$
$$r \in route\_s \setminus route\_s'p$$
$$\Rightarrow \dots$$

Predicate $r \in route\_s \setminus route\_s'p$ filters out the routes not commanded in the current state transition. Let some Z_p describe model variable $route\_s$, then Z_p^+ and Z_p^- correspond to the sets of routes being set and unset respectively. We can now reformulate the invariant, for the particular state transition and without any loss of precision, as

$$\forall p \in Z_p^+ \setminus Z_p^- \quad \Rightarrow \quad \ldots$$

Crucially, set $Z_p^+ \setminus Z_p^-$ is known (i.e., can be calculated exactly) from the description of route_s, which allows us to soundly replace the external quantification with iteration. We shall employ a distinct syntax to define *programs* that compute focused proof obligations. For instance, the fragment above can be translated into the following imperative notation:

$$\textbf{WITH } p \textbf{ FROM } Z_p^+ \setminus Z_p^- \quad \textbf{GOAL } (\forall \mathsf{sr} \in SubRoute \ldots).$$

Here p is iterated over a set of values (derived from a given transition) and, for each value of p, the program constructs a dedicated proof obligation, as defined by the GOAL clause. The derived error names then would take form of, for instance, inv1/<transition name>/R123/<goal>.

The improvement over the base case is that any found violation can be readily attributed to some route p_i even without analysing the proof state.

We can continue in the same manner, now focusing on the inner universal quantifier. This would deliver an extra level of refinement (granularity) reflected in an error name at the price of producing one proof obligation for each sub route of a route.

$$\textbf{WITH } p \textbf{ FROM } Z_p^+ \setminus Z_p^-$$
$$\textbf{WITH } sr \textbf{ FROM } route\_subrouteset[\{r\}] \cap SubRoute.ixl$$
$$\textbf{GOAL } sr \in \mathsf{subroute\_l}\ .$$

The key point here is that set $route\_subrouteset[\{r\}] \cap SubRoute.ixl$ is known at this point (as the p value was already computed) so we can once again replace quantification with an iteration over a new, smaller goal.

We apply this constructed program to achieve two goals: to compute the list of all possible errors, and to compute proof obligations for all such errors. By iterating over all the combinations of state transitions and invariant predicates, we obtain the overall list of errors and their proof obligations.

There is one further potential refinement of the described procedure: we can use the variable description to deduce the cases where there is a definite error even before attempting a proof. This saves us from relying on the prover to fail to prove such cases or can be used to cross check the prover itself.

4   Discussion and Conclusions

The process outlined in the paper extends the employed safety invariant technique to produce error names and proof obligations at a finer level of granularity. Previously, a failed proof obligation could indicate one or more errors, while with the new approach a failed proof obligation is exactly one error.

On one extreme, the proposed process can filter out all proof obligations for a given invariant. On another, it can inflate their number by orders of magnitude. On the balance, the conducted experiments and initial application of the new approach in the life signalling projects show a significant but manageable (about ten fold) increase of the number of proof obligations. These proof obligations are individually much simpler and hence the overall proof time increase is generally between 2 and 5 times more than before the transformation is applied. It is an acceptable price to pay for increased assurance in the verification process.

We do not expect to see a bigger number of false positives arising from the transformation procedure itself. Indeed, the resultant proof obligations are simply instances of original proof obligations with some proof steps already applied to them at the stage of proof obligation generation. Experimental results so far confirm this hypothesis. It is difficult to give a non-empirical argument as to how provability is affected since symbolic proof in real life is resource limited (in time and memory domains) and mathematical equivalence between original and new proof obligations would not automatically entail equivalent (up to the transformation relation) set of false positives.

The proof of soundness of the applied transformation would require showing that every possible transformation applied to a safety principle predicate is a case of a valid proof step. We intend to formalise the described predicate transformation and the extraction of constant sets from symbolic transitions in the Why3 framework (benefiting from the existing work on an embedding of B mathematical notation in Why3) and carry out the formal proof of soundness.

The proposed improved verification process builds upon an already industrially successful application of formal methods in the railway domain. Using SafeCap, we routinely verify interlocking with hundreds of routes where the control logic is defined using several thousand variables (Boolean, integer and categorical). We have seen cases of 24 deep nestings of conditional operators and blocks of codes with nearly 200 conditional statements.

The verification process is completely automatic: due to the sheer scale of a system under verification it is impracticable to require manual intervention at any stage of the process. Needless to say that such systems cannot be verified to any level of assurance via simulation, testing or state space exploration (model checking) techniques.

In our experiments with the new approach the number of proof obligations is much higher: a typical interlocking verification results in between 20K and 100K proof obligations (derived from about 60 safety invariant predicates). This is after application of all the known reduction techniques to a constructed symbolic state transition system. The proof takes longer, however, it is still comfortably under 2–4 min for most complex projects, whilst for the majority of the projects it takes less than 10 s.

We expect this effort to contribute to substantial improvement of the Safe-Cap diagnostics reports, ensuring that the tool is fit for purpose and to eventual safety certification of our automated verification process as an alternative to manual checking. Moreover, the one-to-one mapping between "engineering" errors (deficiencies in the source data) and failed proof obligations permits a fairly straightforward implementation of a tracking of historic improvements in data.

References

1. Clearsy: AtelierB: The industrial tool to efficiently deploy the B method. https://www.atelierb.eu/en/
2. Butler, M., et al.: The first twenty-five years of industrial use of the B-method. In: ter Beek, M.H., Ničković, D. (eds.) FMICS 2020. LNCS, vol. 12327, pp. 189–209. Springer, Cham (2020). https://doi.org/10.1007/978-3-030-58298-2_8
3. Fredj, M., Leger, S., Feliachi, A., Ordioni, J.: OVADO - enhancing data validation for safety-critical railway systems. In: Fantechi, A., Lecomte, T., Romanovsky, A.B. (eds.) RSSRail 2017. LNCS, vol. 10598, pp. 87–98. Springer, Cham (2017). https://doi.org/10.1007/978-3-319-68499-4_6
4. Borälv, A.: Interlocking design automation using prover trident. In: Havelund, K., Peleska, J., Roscoe, B., de Vink, E. (eds.) FM 2018. LNCS, vol. 10951, pp. 653–656. Springer, Cham (2018). https://doi.org/10.1007/978-3-319-95582-7_39
5. Brosgol, B.M., Dross, C., Moy, Y.: Tutorial: a practical introduction to formal development and verification of high-assurance software with SPARK. In: 2019 IEEE Cybersecurity Development, SecDev 2019, Tysons Corner, VA, USA, 23–25 September 2019, pp. 1–2. IEEE (2019). https://doi.org/10.1109/SecDev.2019.00012
6. Stratton, D.H: Solid State Interlocking, 1st edn. IRSE Booklet, 28. Institution of Railway Signal Engineers (IRSE), p. 20 (1988)
7. Iliasov, A., Taylor, D., Laibinis, L., Romanovsky, A.B.: Formal verification of railway interlocking and its safety case. In: Proceedings of Safety-Critical Systems Symposium (SSS 2022), Bristol, UK, 8–10 February 2022. Safety-Critical Systems Club, UK (2022)
8. Iliasov, A., Lopatkin, I., Romanovsky, A.: The SafeCap platform for modelling railway safety and capacity. In: Bitsch, F., Guiochet, J., Kaâniche, M. (eds.) SAFE-COMP 2013. LNCS, vol. 8153, pp. 130–137. Springer, Heidelberg (2013). https://doi.org/10.1007/978-3-642-40793-2_12
9. Iliasov, A., Taylor, D., Laibinis, L., Romanovsky, A.: Practical verification of railway signalling programs. IEEE Trans. Dependable Secure Comput. 13 (2022, preprints). https://doi.org/10.1109/TDSC.2022.3141555
10. Commission Implementing Regulation (EU) No 402/2013 of 30 April 2013 on the common safety method for risk evaluation and assessment and repealing: Regulation (EC) No 352/2009, Official Journal of the European Union. https://www.orr.gov.uk/media/10711
11. Office of Rail and Road: Common Safety Method for Risk Evaluation and Assessment, Guidance on the application of Commission Regulation (EU) 402/2013, September 2018. https://eur-lex.europa.eu/legal-content/EN/TXT/?uri=CELEX%3A32013R0402
12. Interlocking Principles (Former Railway Group Standard GK/RT0060): Network Rail Company Standard NR/L2/SIG/30009/GKRT0060, Issue 2, 07 March 2015
13. Abrial, J.R.: The B-Book. Cambridge University Press, Cambridge (1996)

Innovation in Traffic Management

Formalization and Processing of Data Requirements for the Development of Next Generation Railway Traffic Management Systems

Airy Magnien[1]([✉])[iD], Gabriele Cecchetti[2][iD], Anna Lina Ruscelli[2][iD],
Paul Hyde[3][iD], Jin Liu[3][iD], and Stefan Wegele[4]

[1] SNCF and UIC, Paris, France
airy.magnien@sncf.fr
[2] Scuola Superiore Sant'Anna, Pisa, Italy
{g.cecchetti,a.ruscelli}@santannapisa.it
[3] School of Engineering, Newcastle University, Newcastle upon Tyne, UK
{paul.hyde,jin.liu}@newcastle.ac.uk
[4] Siemens, Munich, Germany
stefan.wegele@siemens.com

Abstract. Railway Traffic Management Systems (TMSs) handle data from multiple railway subsystems, including Rail Business Services (such as interlocking, RBC, maintenance service, etc.) and external services (such as passenger information systems, weather forecast, etc.). In turn, the data from these subsystems are described in several models or ontologies contributed by various organizations or projects which are in a *process* of converging or federation. The challenge of the Shift2Rail OPTIMA project, which is implementing a communication platform for virtual testing of new applications for railway TMS, is to allow the exchange of data between different services or users and to support new traffic management applications, enabling access to a large number of disparate data sources. In this paper, the core activities of the OPTIMA project related to the formulation and standardization of a common data model are described. A new Common Data Model is developed based on standardized data structures to enable the seamless exchange of large amounts of data between different and heterogeneous sources and consumers of data, that contributes to the building of next generation of a more effective and efficient railway TMS suitable to offer precise and real-time traffic information to railway operators and other end users.

Keywords: Railway Traffic Management System · Common Data Model · Model transformation · Context-free grammar

Supported by H2020 Shift2Rail OPTIMA project G.A. 881777.

S. Collart-Dutilleul et al. (Eds.): RSSRail 2022, LNCS 13294, pp. 35–45, 2022.
https://doi.org/10.1007/978-3-031-05814-1_3

1   Introduction

Railway Traffic Management Systems (TMSs) are used in Operation Control Centers to monitor and manage Railway Business Services like traffic management, maintenance and energy systems, and external services like the Passenger Information Systems. However, since current legacy TMSs are lacking in standardized communication interfaces with internal and external services and in interoperable data structures, the interoperability with different TMSs and the upgrade of these systems is difficult. Next generation TMSs aim to overcome these limitations and take advantage of the capability to access multiple disparate data sources in order to better optimize operational solutions, as well as increase the integration between system.

The European Commission promotes the design and implementation of innovative solutions suitable to outline an European railway transport mode more competitive, sustainable, interoperable, and efficient through the Shift2Rail (S2R) Joint Undertaking, set under the H2020 program that aims to specify and design railways systems based on standardised frameworks and a Common Data Model (CDM).

2   OPTIMA Project

One of the challenges of TD2.9 of Innovation Programme 2 in S2R Multi-Annual Action Plan [1,2] is to develop a Technological Demonstrator providing seamless data exchange to support future TMSs which enables the integration of status information from different services. The H2020 S2R OPTIMA (cOmmunication Platform for TraffIc ManAgement demonstrator) project [8], started in December of 2019, is strictly linked to TD2.9 as it aims to implement and validate a demonstrator of a communication platform for the testing and validation of novel industry solutions for next generation TMSs. The components of the communication platform developed by OPTIMA are conceived to ensure seamless access to persistent data from heterogeneous data sources with automated data exchange process, real time availability and configurable quality of service (QoS) levels for services [3,7]. The Integration Layer (IL) is the core component providing the functionalities of a middleware between the sources and consumers of data, and Traffic Control and Management Applications, hosted in the Applications Framework that provides a uniform deployment environment in which to deploy various TMS services into virtual machines or containers with a plug-and-play approach. The seamless exchange of data is ensured by the use of standardized and interoperable data structures and processes based on the definition of a CDM. Finally, in the Operations Center, newly designed Operator Workstations (OWs) enable operators to access the available data in IL via associated TMS applications. The OPTIMA demonstrator will be validated by connecting external prototypes from the S2R complementary projects X2RAIL-4 [10] and FINE-2 [4].

3   Railway System Modelling: State of Play

3.1   Shared Models

LinX4Rail [6], an ongoing Shift2Rail project, aims at the federation, and, ultimately, convergence of railway system models into a "Common Data Model". LinX4Rail developments rest on models that are provided by various entities for different purposes.

An example would be "signal", an term that is already present in four models. EULYNX and RSM decided to couple two classes, the EULYNX class taking care of signalling design aspects, while the RSM class takes care of its localisation on the network. IFC Rail provides additional information about signal structure and components, while X2RAIL-4 focuses on signal state and related data exchange.

Under such conditions, overlaps and mismatches are unavoidable. Model convergence requires, inter alia:

- harmonized semantics (Work Package 2), using ontologies;
- linking of models generally published in UML (Work Package 3);
- formalizing a shared railway system architecture and dealing with its governance (Work Package 5).

The current so-called "candidate models", expected to become parts of the model federation, are listed in the Table 1.

Table 1. Candidate models for federation.

Model	Purpose	Owner	Used technologies
RSM	Multi-purpose rail system model	UIC	UML
EULYNX DataPrep	Signalling assets (material or immaterial)	EULYNX	UML
IFC Rail	Railway infrastructure assets (all subsystems, mostly material)	buildingSMART Intl	EXPRESS, UML, OWL
TRANSMODEL	Multi-modal passenger traffic management and related assets	CEN	UML
X2RAIL-4	Data exchange model for operational purposes, incl. ATO	X2RAIL-4 consortium	JSON schema, Protobuf

All the models above are shared between project participants at least. With the exception of X2RAIL-4, all have been published by their owners at different stages of completion, using various licenses.

3.2   Platform-Specific Model: X2Rail-4

Amongst the models listed above, the X2RAIL-4 model has a special status due to its distinct purpose and the formats adopted (JSON and Protobuf). The X2Rail4-model was developed during several Shift2Rail projects dedicated to TMSs starting in 2015 and reached its current version in the X2Rail-4 project, therefore the model name. The TMS as a central controlling instance requires data from almost all railway domains, including the infrastructure, interlocking, energy system, timetables, etc. To allow evolutionary extension of TMS with new functionalities, a common data architecture (data model) and common communication architecture (Application Programming Interface - API for data access) were specified. This communication platform is used as a common backbone for several demonstrators developed by the complementary projects including Automatic Train Operation (ATO), Decision Support System, Connected Driver Advisory System, etc. [10]. The data model developed in X2Rail-4 is specially adapted for usage in this X2Rail-4-communication platform (called Integration Layer). It supports two serialisation formats, namely a human-readable format (JSON) and a binary format (Protobuf), which can be used interchangeably via API.

4   OPTIMA: From Requirements to Model

The initial intent of OPTIMA project was to rely on the "Common Data Model" prepared by Linx4Rail as the basis for deriving a platform-specific model, to be used by the IL. However, calendar constraints made such derivation difficult. Moreover, software applicable to the tasks had already been developed, using models prepared under other closed or running Shift2Rail projects. A pragmatic decision was made, which is to use the X2RAIL-4 model:

– the link between OPTIMA and the LinX4Rail CDM is preserved, even though indirectly (via X2Rail-4);
– the existing developments are preserved, but
– X2Rail-4 model evolution requires close cooperation between owner and user (here, OPTIMA) without creating undue dependencies.

While a cooperation agreement set the scene for that cooperation to happen, technical challenges remained.

4.1   Challenges of Model Evolution

The X2Rail-4 model is the basis for application developments using the IL. Such applications have been developed (implying backward compatibility of model changes) or are under development (implying openness to changes) in different projects, OPTIMA being one of them. The challenge is therefore to become able to extend an evolving model with requirements that are themselves evolving, avoiding cross-dependencies to the largest extent possible.

4.2   Previous Works

Model-to-Model transformation was extensively explored [5], requirements-to-model, much less so. The authors acknowledge that published solutions have potentially been overlooked. The most commonly investigated model-to-model transformation path is from natural text requirements to UML. The absence of any well-established, shared terminologies or ontologies in the railway field that are precisely defined, well-documented, and widely used, is a significant issue in terms of establishing data models.

5   Formalizing Data Requirements

In general, data requirements[1] are formulated in human-readable documents, and OPTIMA is no exception. Usage of requirement management tools is still uncommon, in international railway projects, although some project partners may be familiar with such tools. In this regard, the railway world does not seem to belong to the 17.8% of survey respondents having "strong knowledge" of using requirements management tools, but definitely to the 69% using a "systematic methodology" for collecting requirements [9].

Natural Language Processing can be excluded from the solutions, lacking comprehensive, published, and widely used domain ontologies[2]. As a matter of fact, Ontorail.org is the place where the ontology extractions from Linx4Rail candidate models are assembled, but the linkage of the extracted ontologies has just started.

Experience with some modelling endeavours in international projects (such as IFC Rail) showed that the set up of UML models would include two phases:

- domain requirement expression by domain experts, usually organized as collections of tables (with columns "objects", "description", "illustration"...);
- UML formalization by tandems, or teams, grouping domain experts and UML modelling experts.

Domain representation is time-consuming mainly because of the temptation of being complete and the resolution of overlaps, to ensure consistency and non-redundancy of the complete set of requirements.

UML formalization is time-consuming because it requires participants to understand some of the expertise or concerns of the other side (domain vs. modelling), which is no small effort, and because modelling choices have to be made. Additionally some domain knowledge is based on accepted practice and historical conventions, therefore certain domain concepts are sometimes expressed in requirements with contextual assumptions as to the meaning of terms.

---

[1] In our context, "data requirements" is the term commonly used for "information requirements", as metadata, context, etc. also need to be established.

[2] ifcOWL is one such initiative, but extension of ifcOWL to the scope of IFC Rail is pending. See https://technical.buildingsmart.org/standards/ifc/ifc-formats/ifcowl/.

Our goal was to find a *deterministic* solution to a *simplified* problem:

- requirements should be expressed in a formal, prescribed way, also dealing with semantic uncertainties;
- requirements should extend an existing model, not alter it;
- all transformations are done by code, using requirements and transformation options persisted in text files.

5.1   Minimal Requirements... for Requirements

Domain experts would spontaneously describe material or immaterial assets as "systems" composed of "objects" having "features" or "properties", a description that naturally evokes object-oriented modelling. Such views however collide with another valid world representation that would consider data exchange, resulting in bundling "data" into nested "data sets", i.e. coherent pieces of knowledge for a purpose.

In our case, we would only expect the domain expert to identify single objects and single object features, which is our "atomic" level. Formalizing the drilldown process, from general requirements to atomic ones, exceeds the scope of OPTIMA; it is however part of the parallel Linx4Rail[3] project.

Features are defined and described in the context of the object they characterize, which is restrictive: ontology properties for instance are classes, and LinkML allows to define "slots" (equivalent to our "features") to be defined separately from classes and shared by several classes[4].

This restriction is certainly old-fashioned, but simplifies the expression of requirements, at the cost of possible repetitions. Object features may be understood as attributes (or fields in a document), or references to other objects (or documents).

Fig. 1. Requirements sheet (excerpt)

Using spreadsheets for input is common practice, and unlikely to deter domain experts. An excerpt of the used spreadsheet is shown in Fig. 1. Each requirement is self-contained, and is expressed in a single row. While the actual requirements viewing and editing environment is MS Excel, the work does not require more than CSV capabilities. System views are outside the scope of the formalisation approach adopted, however, it does not preclude them:

---

[3] https://projects.shift2rail.org/s2r_ipx_n.aspx?p=LINX4RAIL.
[4] Link Modeling Language, see https://github.com/linkml/linkml.

- users may use multiple sheets and files to sort requirements, but the processor will ignore this sorting;
- by design, model extension will not break the input model structure and will respect the system (or documentation) breakdown that was initially intended.

5.2 Supporting Grammar

Some consideration was given to the data structure used to capture the requirements, particularly the grammar used, for instance, increasing the number of columns to accommodate finely tuned requirements would lead to "sparse matrices", the kind that is not easily edited, let alone reviewed. For example, an enumerated feature has a list of values, while a numeric feature has a unit, so two filled columns should be able to express both cases, instead of four columns with two irrelevant ones.

A pragmatic solution consisted of setting up a short context-free grammar, formalized in EBNF[5]. The purpose of the grammar is twofold with regard to current and potential future work:

- now: specification for the ad-hoc CSV parser;
- later: open the possibility of using an off-the-shelf parser, the grammar being one of its inputs.

The somewhat simplified grammar is shown below (many units are missing...). W3C conventions are used.

```
start        ::= requirement ( '#CR#LF' requirement )*
requirement ::= object_declaration | enum_declaration |
    feature_declaration
object_declaration ::= object_name ';;;' ( '*' superclass )?
    ';;;;'
enum_declaration ::= enum_name ';;;' 'enum' ';' enum_values
    ';;;'
feature_declaration ::= object_name ';' feature_description
superclass ::= object_name
object_name ::= identifier
identifier ::= [A-Za-z] [A-Za-z0-9_]*
feature_description ::= feature_name ';' info ';'
    feature_details ';' authority ';' time_dependency
feature_name ::= identifier
info ::= text
text ::= character*
character ::= [A-Za-z0-9,] | space
space        ::= [#x9#xA#xD#x20]
type   ::= numeric_type | nonnumeric_type
feature_details ::= 'optional'? ('sorted '? 'list of ' )? (
    numeric_type ';' unit | ( nonnumeric_type |
    object_reference ) ';' | 'enum' ';' enum_values |
    enum_reference ';')
```

---

[5] Extended Backus-Naur Form.

```
numeric_type  ::=  'int'  |  'float'
nonnumeric_type  ::=  'str'  |  'boolean'
unit        ::=  'counter'  |  'dimensionless'  |  'kg'  |  'm'  |  's'  |
   'Celsius'
enum_name  ::=  identifier
enum_values  ::=  enum_value ( ',' enum_value )*
enum_value  ::=  identifier
enum_reference  ::=  '*' ( module_name '.' )? enum_name
object_reference  ::=  '*' ( module_name '.' )? (type |
   object_name)
module_name  ::=  identifier
authority  ::=  priority ';' source ';' isdefinedby
priority  ::=  digit | 'skip' text?
source     ::=  text
isdefinedby  ::=  text
digit      ::=  [0-9]
time_dependency  ::=  'Static'  |  'Quasi_static'  |  'Dynamic'
```

Requirements may also express abstract datatypes (such as text or numeric), associations (using '*' as a prefix), and multiplicities (using "list of"). Exact multiplicities (lower and higher bound) and concrete datatypes (e.g. those defined in JSON) are left for later stage processing. Therefore, domain experts should not expend effort on such details, while semantics often remain unattended.

5.3 Semantics

A realistic design goal for UML class diagram-based models is to embed semantics in the model itself. This has been consistently achieved, for instance by EULYNX DataPrep, RSM, or TRANSMODEL, by extensive use of UML notes pertaining to diagrams, classes, attributes, or associations. Notes are, as far as possible, brought to the surface of the class diagrams, and in any case remain accessible when the diagrams are published in XML or other text formats.

To enable these high standards to be achieved, there should be a strong focus on the robustness, accuracy, completeness, and specificity, of the requirements formalisation by the domain experts from the beginning of the process.

Each data requirement (object, feature, enumeration...) is identified by a name (object name, feature name...) or a short phrase that should be expressive, unambiguous, and familiar to experts, as much as possible, unique across the whole set of requirements. These names will be used as identifiers after transformation (e.g. camel-casing).

Names alone are not sufficient to define the semantics of requirements, given the many-to-many relationship between names (labels) and the concepts they denote. An "info" key was introduced at an early stage in the JSON schema of the X2RAIL-4 model: an "info" column was provided accordingly in the input sheets, which is relevant to each single requirement and is intended for the specific definition and full explanation of the feature. Expected values are one sentence or two, without conditionals. Since one sentence is helpful, but not a reference, we recommend to point to a public, freely accessible resource. In the RDFS framework, the annotation property rdfs:isDefinedBy is dedicated to such purposes. However, isDefinedBy may point to any resource. In our context, we need the resource to be public and published, preferrably in the shape of a URI. Moreover, annotation properties are ignored by reasoners. Consequently, a "hasPublicDefinition" key was introduced, in line with object property ontorail:hasPublicDefinition.

5.4   Authorities

The authority *defining* the terms of the requirement have been separated from the authority that *expresses* the requirement. Two columns remain associated with the requiring authority:

- a priority level, the meaning of which is somewhat ambiguous: priority of requirement in view of model extension, or priority with respect to data exchange, e.g. in case of channel saturation. In the context of OPTIMA, the second meaning applies;
- a source, that ensures traceability of the requirement and, indirectly, identifies the authority expressing the requirement.

6   Transformation and Integration

Formalized requirements are intended to extend the source model (here: X2RAIL-4), leaving the existing parts unchanged. We expect extensions to be ignored by those applications that do not require them. However, the extended model must in any case conform the original JSON schema. Processing requirements takes four steps:

informal requirements → formal requirements → pre-processing → processing → post-processing.

6.1   Pre-processing

The pre-processing step of model transformation is partly automated. The automated part consists of:

- check the completeness of each single requirement, especially with respect to units or dangling references;
- suggest structures and properties matching objects and features formulated in the requirements;
- check whether features are static or dynamic, in view of expressing the time-dependency of feature values in JSON;
- express multiplicities using the JSON schema conventions.

The manual part of pre-processing then consists of:

- dealing with the warnings and errors provided by the pre-processing execution log,
- assigning requirements to existing JSON modules, and
- indicate the matching JSON structs and enums, when possible.

6.2   Processing and Post-processing

Both the processing and post-processing steps are fully automated, the output of the processing is the set of extended JSON modules, and post-processing checks JSON schema conformity. The salient features of the processing are:

- offering the choice to instantiate object features 1) as attributes, or 2) as references to a reified attribute, 3) possibly reversing the dependency direction (observer pattern);
- replacing subclassing (not supported by JSON) by having the subclass referring to the superclass, rather than inheriting its attributes;
- using the observer pattern to express "dynamic" attributes (having time-dependent values). In this case, the preferred solution is to pair the Foo class with a FooState class, which holds the dynamic attributes, a single timestamp, and a reference to Foo.

7   Conclusions and Further Works

Shift2Rail OPTIMA project deals with the design and validation of a demonstrator of a communication platform to test new TM applications. Requirement elicitation and transformation of the requirements into a data model is a part of the OPTIMA project. The requirement formalization and transformation toolset was developed in response to the complexity of the data model required for TMSs and the project timescales (as well as reducing the time for future work). There has already been interest from other projects and interested parties in both the formalization and toolsets (demonstrating the relevance of this work), which are intended to be shared under some sort of open source license

Since requirements were processed in a particular context (setting up a train management system) by knowledgeable experts, some formalization aspects were omitted, such as or process mining, or allocation of requirements to project phases. Such aspects would generally deserve more attention.

By further experimenting with model extension and combination, either using the proposed, semi-automated methodology or more creative, whiteboard-based methods, we are confident that OPTIMA will achieve its particular goal, i.e. running a TMS demonstrator. The somewhat unexpected bonus is however a contribution to building the CDM, which is one of the main goals pursued by the European Commission and could be of utility to the railway industry.

References

1. SJG Board: Shift2rail joint undertaking multi-annual action plan (2015). https://shift2rail.org/wp-content/uploads/2013/07/S2R-JU-GB_Decision-N-15-2015-MAAP.pdf
2. SJG Board: Shift2rail joint undertaking multi-annual action plan (2019). https://shift2rail.org/wp-content/uploads/2020/09/MAAP-Part-A-and-B.pdf. https://doi.org/10.2881/314331

3. Cecchetti, G., et al.: Communication platform concept for virtual testing of novel applications for railway traffic management systems. In: Proceedings of 24th Euro Working Group on Transportation Meeting (EWGT 2021) - Transportation Research Procedia (2022)
4. FINE-2: Furthering Improvements in Integrated Mobility Management (I2M), Noise and Vibration, and Energy in Shift2Rail, December 2019. https://projects. shift2rail.org/s2r_ipcc_n.aspx?p=fine-2
5. Jakumeit, E., et al.: A survey and comparison of transformation tools based on the transformation tool contest. Sci. Comput. Program. **85**, 41–99 (2014). https://doi.org/10.1016/j.scico.2013.10.009. https://www.sciencedirect. com/science/article/pii/S0167642313002803. Special issue on Experimental Software Engineering in the Cloud (ESEiC)
6. LinX4Rail: System architecture and Conceptual Data Model for railway, common data dictionary and global system modelling specifications, December 2019. https://projects.shift2rail.org/s2r_ipx_n.aspx?p=LINX4RAIL
7. Liu, J., Ulianov, C., Hyde, P., Ruscelli, A.L., Cecchetti, G.: Novel approach for validation of innovative modules for railway traffic management systems in a virtual environment. In: Proceedings of the Institution of Mechanical Engineers, Part F: Journal of Rail and Rapid Transit, August 2021. https://doi.org/10.1177/ 09544097211041879
8. OPTIMA: cOmmunication Platform for TraffIc ManAgement demonstrator, December 2019. https://projects.shift2rail.org/s2r_ip2_n.aspx?p=S2R_OPTIMA
9. Salih Dawood, O., Sahraoui, A.E.K.: From requirements engineering to UML using natural language processing - survey study. Eur. J. Ind. Eng. **2**(1), 44–50 (2017). https://doi.org/10.24018/ejers.2017.2.1.236. https://hal.laas.fr/hal-01703317
10. X2Rail-4: Advanced signalling and automation system - completion of activities for enhanced automation systems, train integrity, traffic management evolution and smart object controllers, December 2019. https://projects.shift2rail.org/s2r_ip2_n. aspx?p=X2RAIL-4

Acceleration Techniques for Symbolic Simulation of Railway Timetables

Rebecca Haehn[✉], Erika Ábrahám, and Niklas Kotowski

RWTH Aachen University, Aachen, Germany
{haehn,abraham}@cs.rwth-aachen.de, niklas.kotowski@rwth-aachen.de

Abstract. In this paper, we improve the scalability of an exact symbolic simulation method to compute the impact of stochastic delays in railway systems. We present transformation rules that allow minimizing the size of the system state representation (which train is where with which probability), without losing exactness. Based on these transformation rules, we propose two different approaches to decrease the simulation effort and thus the running time of the symbolic simulation method. One approach iteratively applies our transformation rules to the state representation, while the other encodes transformation steps logically and uses satisfiability checking tools to determine which rule combination leads to the strongest possible reduction. We evaluate the proposed improvements on realistic case studies and discuss further possible speed-up techniques that approximate the results.

Keywords: Simulation · Railway timetables · Delay propagation

1 Introduction

Railway systems play an important role in satisfying the increasing need for environmentally friendly transportation. However, it is not possible to increase the railway infrastructure's capacity according to the increased demand. Though the network structure can be extended, places where local conditions do not allow to build additional tracks become a bottleneck, such that the total network capacity cannot further increase. In addition to this, construction work to extend the infrastructure where this is possible is expensive and often protracted. This makes it necessary to optimally exploit the capacity of the existing infrastructure.

The problem that arises with increasing capacity utilization is *delay propagation*. If a network infrastructure element is highly utilized according to the train timetable then even a few slightly delayed trains might cause full exploitation, blocking other trains that want to use the element, which might again propagate their delays to further trains. Thus we can distinguish between *secondary* delays that are caused by other delays, and *primary* delays that have other sources.

This research is funded by the German Research Council (DFG) - Research Training Group UnRAVeL (RTG 2236).

© Springer Nature Switzerland AG 2022
S. Collart-Dutilleul et al. (Eds.): RSSRail 2022, LNCS 13294, pp. 46–62, 2022.
https://doi.org/10.1007/978-3-031-05814-1_4

Simulation allows to estimate the relation between primary and secondary delays. The most commonly used simulation approach is Monte Carlo simulation. It requires input probability distributions that model primary delays, allowing to iteratively sample primary delay values and simulate the network to compute the induced secondary delays. A statistical analysis of the results allows to draw conclusions about the stochastic properties of interest.

Several commercial software products implement Monte Carlo simulation. There are for example the systems RailSys [4,17] and OpenTrack [3,15], which apply *synchronous* simulation (i.e., all train rides are simulated simultaneously in a single run). Alternatively, the train rides could also be simulated sequentially one after another, starting with the trains with highest priority, in a so-called *asynchronous* simulation. This is the case in the system MOSES/WiZug [18], which is applied specifically for rail freight transportation. A combination of synchronous and asynchronous simulation is used in the system LUKS [1,14].

Unlike Monte Carlo simulation, the approach in [8] computes delay propagations using an *analytical* procedure. This approach is implemented in the system OnTime [2,11]. Another synchronous approach is our previous work [12], with the ability to simulate *all* possible primary delay configurations simultaneously, in contrast to the sequential simulation of individual primary delay configurations in Monte Carlo simulation. Thereby certain sets of possible primary delay configurations are represented abstractly in so-called *symbolic* representations, offering the chance to share simulation effort if the same computations need to be carried out for all contained configurations. This last approach is to the best of our knowledge the only one that can compute exact probability distributions for the train delays under consideration of stochastic dependencies. Though our symbolic representation allows a major reduction of the computational effort to get exact answers (compared to simulating each possible primary delay configuration independently), it is computationally still quite expensive, restricting its applicability to smaller networks and shorter time horizons. In this paper, we propose and evaluate methods to accelerate this symbolic simulation approach in order to achieve better scalability.

Outline. After providing some preliminaries and explaining our symbolic simulation method from [12] in Sect. 2, we present our novel reduction method in Sect. 3. We evaluate our reduction experimentally in Sect. 4 and draw some conclusion in Sect. 5.

2 Symbolic Simulation

In the following we abstract as much as possible from the details of the symbolic simulation presented in [12]. We only mention here the information needed to understand the acceleration approaches presented in this paper. First, we introduce primary delays. Then we proceed with recalling the symbolic representation for primary delay scenarios. Last, we give an overview over the symbolic simulation algorithm itself, before moving on to the acceleration approaches in the next section.

2.1 Primary Delays

A *railway system* is a pair, composed of

- an *infrastructure network* consisting of infrastructure elements and
- a *timetable* specifying how trains traverse through this network.

A train that drives later than stated in the timetable is *delayed*. There are two types of delays. *Primary delays* are caused by technical problems or external influences, while *secondary delays* of a train are caused by other trains fully occupying the capacity of its next needed infrastructure element. In the following we use $\mathbb{N}$ to denote the set of non-negative integers (including zero).

We model primary delays as discrete random variables p with sample space $\mathbb{N}$. We denote the probability that p has the value $v \in \mathbb{N}$ as $\mathbb{P}(p = v) \in [0, 1] \subseteq \mathbb{R}$ and its support as $\mathcal{D}(p) = \{v \in \mathbb{N} \mid \mathbb{P}(p = v) > 0\}$. Note that $(\sum_{v \in \mathcal{D}(p)} \mathbb{P}(p = v)) = 1$. In the following we will only consider random variables with finite support (modeling finitely many possible primary delay values).

In [12], we introduced stochastically independent random variables, one for each timetable train i and each infrastructure element x that i uses; their random values represent the number of time units the delay of the train i increases at x without the cause being another train's delay. For the sake of simplicity, here we only consider primary delays at start, represented by one random variable p_i for each train $i = 1, \ldots, n$, forming the set $P = \{p_1, p_2, \ldots, p_n\}$. The presented method can be extended to consider additional primary delays during train rides in a straightforward way.

2.2 Scenarios

A *primary delay value combination* (*PDC*) is a sequence $(v_1, \ldots, v_n) \in \mathbb{N}^n$ of initial primary delay values with $v_i \in \mathcal{D}(p_i)$ from the support of p_i for $i = 1, \ldots, n$. In a Monte Carlo simulation, each run corresponds to one PDC. In contrast, our symbolic simulation algorithm presented in [12] receives the set of discrete random variables P with their respective primary delay distributions as input and computes the corresponding secondary delay distributions as output, in one run. To achieve this, *sets* of PDCs are grouped together and represented symbolically by so-called *scenarios*.

Definition 1. *A scenario $S : P \to 2^{\mathbb{N}} \setminus \{\emptyset\}$ is a function, where $S(p) \subseteq \mathcal{D}(p)$ for all $p \in P$. The scenario S represents the PDCs from $repr(S) = S(p_1) \times \ldots \times S(p_n)$. We call S minimal if it represents a single PDC (i.e., if $|repr(S)| = 1$), and maximal (denoted S^{max}) if it represents all PDCs. Let $\mathbb{S}$ be the set of all scenarios.*

Let $S, S' \in \mathbb{S}$. We say that S refines S' (written $S \preceq S'$) iff $repr(S) \subseteq repr(S')$; we also say S' contains S. Equivalence $S \equiv S'$ requires mutual refinement (i.e., $repr(S) = repr(S')$). We call S and S' compatible iff $repr(S) \cap repr(S') \neq \emptyset$, and incompatible otherwise. For compatible S and S' we define the scenario $S \hat{\cap} S' : P \to 2^{\mathbb{N}} \setminus \{\emptyset\}, p \mapsto S(p) \cap S'(p)$ to represent their common PDCs.

In our examples we use for a scenario $S : P \to 2^{\mathbb{N}} \setminus \{\emptyset\}$ the notation $\{(p_0, S(p_0)), (p_1, S(p_1)), \ldots, (p_n, S(p_n))\}$ and silently skip tuples $(p_i, \mathcal{D}(p_i))$ for $i \in \{1, \ldots, n\}$ (i.e. the values of not listed random variables are not restricted).

Example 1. Let $P = \{p_0, p_1\}$, with $\mathcal{D}(p_0) = \{0, 1, 2\}$ and $\mathcal{D}(p_1) = \{0, 1\}$. The scenario $S = \{(p_0, \{0\})\}$ contains the minimal scenarios $\{(p_0, \{0\}), (p_1, \{0\})\}$ and $\{(p_0, \{0\}), (p_1, \{1\})\}$. S is incompatible with $\{(p_0, \{1, 2\})\}$ and compatible with $\{(p_1, \{0\})\}$.

2.3   Algorithm

The above defined scenarios are used to symbolically represent for each train, when it resides where under which PDCs. More formally, a *train instance* (*TI*) is a tuple (x, i, t, S) consisting of an infrastructure element x, a train id i, a time value t and a scenario S; it encodes that train i is currently (say at time point t') at x and plans to move to the next infrastructure element on its scheduled path at time t under all PDCs represented by S. If $t < t'$ then the train already wanted to move on in the past, but the capacities did not allow this yet. The difference between t (or t', if $t < t'$) and train i's arrival time at the next infrastructure element according to the timetable is this instance's current delay.

We say that (x, i, t, S) *represents* a PDC v if S represents v. The *probability* of a train instance (x, i, t, S) is the sum of the probabilities of its represented PDCs, computable as $\Pi_{i=1}^{n} (\sum_{v_i \in S(p_i)} \mathbb{P}(p_i = v_i))$.

For every time point in a timetable, for each train i we store a set of instances such that each PDC is represented by exactly one of them. From these, for each PDC we can uniquely determine the position of train i (namely the infrastructure element x of the instance (x, i, t, S) that represents the PDC). More importantly, we have all information we need to compute (e.g., the probability distributions for the current delay of train i). Furthermore, the stochastic contexts enable also combined information for the different trains, such that we can also compute probabilities for certain railway system states, for example that a set of trains are at the same time at a given infrastructure element.

In the symbolic simulation algorithm from [12], we iteratively compute for each time point in a timetable all currently possible states of the railway system in the form of a set of train instances for each train. We only explain the general concept of the algorithm needed to understand the modifications suggested in this paper. Therefore, we depict a slightly modified representation of the algorithm in Algorithm 1. The changes were made for better understandability of the parts relevant for our modifications and do no change the functionality.

Algorithm 1 first establishes the initial state of the railway system in line 2. Then iteratively for each relevant time point (i.e., each time point where some train plans to move to its next infrastructure element (those are collected during the simulation)), the state of the railway system is updated (lines 3–11). This is done for each infrastructure element separately (line 5). First all train instances that plan to move to the respective infrastructure element at the current time are collected in line 6. There $pre(x)$ is the set of all infrastructure elements

Algorithm 1. Symbolic simulation from [12] (slightly modified representation)

```
1: procedure SIMULATE( )
2:     INITIALIZE();                              // initial state of the railway system
3:     while times ≠ ∅ do
4:         t ← times.GETSMALLEST(); times ← times \ {t};        // current time value
5:         for each infrastructure element x do
6:             req ← {(y, i, t′, S) | y ∈ pre(x), t′ ≤ t};      // TIs planning to move to x
7:             occ ← OCCUPATION(x, t); // partition PDCs according to x's utilization
8:             while req ≠ ∅ do
9:                 r ← req.GETHIGHESTPRIORITIZED(); req ← req \ {r};
10:                S ← AVAILABLE(occ, r);          // scenarios where r can move to x
11:                UPDATE(x, r, t, S); // update TIs; cap updated accordingly (line 10)
```

from where x can be reached directly, without having to travel over another infrastructure element. Then its used capacity at the time is determined, see line 7. At last, the train instances are updated, one after another, starting with the train instance with the highest priority (line 9). A train instances' priority here depends on the corresponding trains' type (e.g., freight train, high-speed train) and its planned arrival time at the infrastructure element. In line 10 it is determined in which scenarios the respective train instance can move to the infrastructure element as planned. Afterwards the train instance is updated accordingly in line 11.

When a train instance is updated, it is split into multiple instances in case it can only move to its next infrastructure element in some of the PDCs represented by its scenario S (i.e., when in a proper subset of $repr(S)$ the infrastructure element is fully occupied). Thus during the execution of this symbolic simulation algorithm the number of train instances increases. This is to a certain extent unavoidable, in order to represent the possible states of the railway system exactly. However, additional train instances are created due to the way in which the algorithm works currently. We explain this with an example for the execution of the three methods OCCUPATION, AVAILABLE and UPDATE. Pseudocode for these methods is left out of this paper, as the relevant functionalities become clear from the example.

Example 2. Let $t = 10$ and $\mathcal{D}(p) = \{0, 5, 10\}$ for all $p \in P$. Assume we update infrastructure element x with capacity 2,

- train instances $(x, 1, 12, \{(p_1, \{5\})\})$ and $(x, 2, 12, \{(p_2, \{5\})\})$ and
- $req = \{(y, 3, 10, \{(p_3, \{0\})\})\}$ with $y \in pre(x)$.

OCCUPATION(x, t) is executed first and partitions the set of all PDCs (i.e., $\mathcal{D}(p_1) \times \ldots \mathcal{D}(p_n)$) into scenarios, where for each scenario holds that every train instance currently at x either represents every PDC represented by this scenario or none of them. Therefore, OCCUPATION(x, t) starts with $\{(S^{max}, 0)\}$, iterates over these train instances and partitions its current set of scenarios further if the condition is not satisfied. Additionally, for each scenario the number of train instances currently at x that represent all PDCs of it are counted. This results in the following set of tuples:

$$occ = \{(\{(p_1, \{5\}), \quad (p_2, \{5\}))\}, \quad 2),$$
$$(\{(p_1, \{5\}), \quad (p_2, \{0, 10\}))\}, \; 1),$$
$$(\{(p_1, \{0, 10\}), \; (p_2, \{5\}))\}, \quad 1),$$
$$(\{(p_1, \{0, 10\}), \; (p_2, \{0, 10\}))\}, \; 0)\}.$$

AVAILABLE(occ, r) with $r = (y, 3, 10, \{(p_3, \{0\})\})$ is executed next, to compute the scenarios in which x has available capacity for r to move there. For each tuple (S, c) in occ with c strictly smaller than the capacity of x and S compatible with the scenario $\{(p_3, \{0\})\}$ of r, r can move to x in the scenario $S \hat{\cap} \{(p_3, \{0\})\}$. In this example the resulting set of scenarios is the following:

$$S = \{\{(p_1, \{5\}), \quad (p_2, \{0, 10\}), \; (p_3, \{0\})\},$$
$$\{(p_1, \{0, 10\}), \; (p_2, \{5\}), \quad (p_3, \{0\})\},$$
$$\{(p_1, \{0, 10\}), \; (p_2, \{0, 10\}), \; (p_3, \{0\})\}\}.$$

In case req contains further elements, occ has to be updated accordingly. UPDATE(x, t, r, S) is executed last. There the train instance $(y, 3, 10, \{(p_3, \{0\})\})$ is replaced by the following train instances for the current time step:

$$(y, 3, 10, \{(p_1, \{5\}), \quad (p_2, \{5\}), \quad (p_3, \{0\})\}),$$
$$(x, 3, 12, \{(p_1, \{5\}), \quad (p_2, \{0, 10\}), \; (p_3, \{0\})\}),$$
$$(x, 3, 12, \{(p_1, \{0, 10\}), \; (p_2, \{5\}), \quad (p_3, \{0\})\}),$$
$$(x, 3, 12, \{(p_1, \{0, 10\}), \; (p_2, \{0, 10\}), \; (p_3, \{0\})\}).$$

The time value in the last three instances is the current time value 10 plus the time train 3 occupies x according to the timetable, here 2.

In the example above, the train's behaviour varies for different scenarios, in some it can move to its next infrastructure element, in some it can not. Thus at least two train instances are needed to represent the possible behaviour of the train. In this particular case at least three instances are needed, since each scenario (as defined in Definition 1) is syntactically restricted to represent a set of PDCs that can be expressed as a cross product. However, four are not necessary, for example the last two could be replaced by the following instance:

$$(x, 3, 12, \{(p_1, \{0, 10\}), \quad\quad\quad\quad\quad (p_3, \{0\})\}).$$

This brings us to the main part of this paper, where we present different techniques to reduce the number of train instances.

3   Reduction

As we have seen, our symbolic representation is not unique (i.e., two syntactically different sets of TIs might represent the same information). To reduce the number of train instances, we want to replace some set of train instances T_1 by another set T_2 with smaller cardinality $|T_2| < |T_1|$, but such that the represented PDCs remain the same (i.e., $repr(T_1) = repr(T_2)$). We make the following observations:

1. Each train has a unique train id, thus two TIs with different train ids cannot be merged and represented by a single train instance.
2. Similarly, each TI has a fixed infrastructure element, therefore, we are neither able to merge TIs with the same train id but different infrastructure elements.
3. The same argument holds for the time points when the train plans to move to its next infrastructure element, if these time points lie in the future. However, train instances with current or past time values could be combined, even if the time values are not equal: they will move on as soon as their next infrastructure element is available and thus the exact time values have no impact on their future.

Using these observations, we call two TI sets T_1 and T_2 *equivalent* at time t', written $T_1 \equiv_{t'} T_2$, iff for each infrastructure element x_0 and each train i_0:

$$\bigcup_{(x_0,i_0,t,S)\in T_1 \wedge t \leq t'} repr(S) = \bigcup_{(x_0,i_0,t,S)\in T_2 \wedge t \leq t'} repr(S)$$

$$\wedge \; \forall t'' > t'. \bigcup_{(x_0,i_0,t,S)\in T_1 \wedge t=t''} repr(S) = \bigcup_{(x_0,i_0,t,S)\in T_2 \wedge t=t''} repr(S) \; .$$

That means, two TI sets are equivalent if they represent the same trains at the same infrastructure elements that want to move on at the same time (either now if $t \leq t'$ or in the future if $t > t'$) under consideration of the same primary delays.

In the following we discuss possibilities to reduce a set of TIs to another, equivalent set that contains fewer train instances, by identifying a subset that we can reduce.

TI-REDUCE: Let $T_1 = \{(x,i,t_1,S_1),\ldots,(x,i,t_\ell,S_\ell)\}$ and $T_2 = \{(x,i,t'_1,S'_1),\ldots,(x,i,t'_k,S'_k)\}$ be two sets of TIs and t a current time point such that

$$\left[(\bigwedge_{j=1}^{\ell} t_j \leq t) \wedge (\bigwedge_{j=1}^{k} t'_j \leq t) \right] \vee \left[(\bigwedge_{j=1}^{\ell} t_j = t_1) \wedge (\bigwedge_{j=1}^{k} t'_j = t_1) \right] \wedge$$

$$\cup_{j=1}^{\ell} repr(S_j) = \cup_{j=1}^{k} repr(S'_j).$$

Then for all TI sets T we have that $T \cup T_1 \equiv_t T \cup T_2$.

3.1 Transformation Rules

We consider first how to replace two TIs with scenarios $S_1, S_2 \in \mathbb{S}$ by a single one with a scenario $S \in \mathbb{S}$ that represents the same PDCs. As illustrated in Example 2 in Sect. 2.3, this is possible only if the two scenarios agree on all but one random variable, formalized by the following transformation rule:

MERGE: For all TIs (x, i, t_1, S_1) and (x, i, t_2, S_2) and time point t, if either $t_1 = t_2$ or $t_1 \leq t \wedge t_2 \leq t$ and

$$\exists p \in P. \; \forall p' \in P \backslash \{p\}. \; S_1(p') = S_2(p')$$

then for all TI sets T and $S = \{(p, S_1(p) \cup S_2(p)) \, | \, p \in P\}$ we have that $T \cup \{(x, i, t_1, S_1), (x, i, t_2, S_2)\} \equiv_t T \cup \{(x, i, t_1, S)\}$.

The two suitable TIs are replaced by one whose scenario assigns to each random variable the union of the assignments from both original scenarios. This rule can be applied repeatedly to replace multiple scenarios and not just two. However, it is not always sufficient to only apply this rule to achieve a minimal set of scenarios.

Example 3. Let $P = \{p_1, \, p_2, \, p_3\}$ with $\mathcal{D}(p) = \{0, 1, 2\}$ for all $p \in P$. Assume the following set of four pairwise incompatible scenarios:

$$S = \{\{(p_1, \{0\}), \quad (p_2, \{1\}), \quad (p_3, \{1\})\},$$
$$\{(p_1, \{0, 1\}), \; (p_2, \{0, 1\}), \; (p_3, \{2\})\},$$
$$\{(p_1, \{1\}), \quad (p_2, \{1\}), \quad (p_3, \{0\})\},$$
$$\{(p_1, \{0\}), \quad (p_2, \{2\}), \quad (p_3, \{1, 2\})\}\}.$$

The MERGE rule can not be applied to the scenarios in this set. It is possible though to represent the respective PDCs with just three scenarios:

$$S' = \{\{(p_1, \{0, 1\}), \; (p_2, \{0\}), \quad (p_3, \{2\})\},$$
$$\{(p_1, \{1\}), \quad (p_2, \{1\}), \quad (p_3, \{0, 2\})\},$$
$$\{(p_1, \{0\}), \quad (p_2, \{1, 2\}), \; (p_3, \{1, 2\})\}\}.$$

Starting with a set of minimal scenarios (each representing exactly one PDC) the MERGE rule, applied in a certain order, is sufficient to achieve a minimal set of scenarios. Thus by applying the MERGE rule in combination with a rule that allows to split a scenario into two, a minimal set of scenarios can be reached.

SPLIT: Assume a TI (x, i, t, S) and $p \in P$ such that $|S(p)| \geq 2$. Let $S(p) = D_1 \cup D_2$ with $D_1 \neq \emptyset$, $D_2 \neq \emptyset$, $D_1 \cap D_2 = \emptyset$, and S_i with $S_i(p') = S(p')$ for all $p' \in P \setminus \{p\}$ and $S(p) = D_i$ for $i = 1, 2$. Then for each TI set T and time point t' we have that $T \cup \{(x, i, t, S)\} \equiv_{t'} T \cup \{(x, i, t, S_1), (x, i, t, S_2)\}$.

Splitting temporarily increases the number of TIs, but this is unavoidable to reach a minimal representation. We will use a special combination of SPLIT and MERGE that does not yet decrease the representation size but might enable further MERGE steps by shifting a part of the represented PDCs from one TI into another. This shift is possible if the scenarios in two TIs differ only for two random variables p and p', and to one of these random variables, say p', the second scenario assigns strictly more values D_2' than the first $D_1' \subsetneq D_2'$. In this case, we can first split the second TI in the dimension p' into the common part D_1' and the rest $D_2' \setminus D_1'$. Now, the first TI and the first half of the second one differ only for one variable and we can merge them.

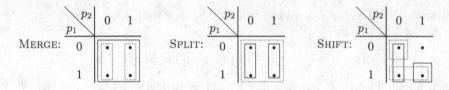

Fig. 1. Illustration of the transformation rules

SHIFT: Assume $p, p' \in P$ and two TIs (x, i, t_1, S_1) and (x, i, t_2, S_2) whose scenarios differ only for p and p', with $S_1(p') \subsetneq S_2(p')$. We define S_1' differing from S_1 only for p with $S_1'(p) = S_1(p) \cup S_2(p)$ and S_2' differing from S_2 only for p' with $S_2'(p') = S_2(p') \setminus S_1(p')$. Let t be a time point, such that either $t_1 = t_2$ or $t_1 \leq t \wedge t_2 \leq t$. Then for all TI sets T we have that $T \cup \{(x, i, t_1, S_1), (x, i, t_2, S_2)\} \equiv_t T \cup \{(x, i, t_1, S_1'), (x, i, t_2, S_2')\}$.

We illustrate all three rules for some examples in Fig. 1. There we restrict the scenario representations to two variables $p_1, p_2 \in P$ with $\mathcal{D}(p) = \{0, 1\}$ for $i \in \{1, 2\}$, as the assignments for all others need to be identical to apply each of the rules anyway. Each field in the matrix corresponds to one PDC, which is represented by the scenario that contains the respective field. Note that due to the form how scenarios are defined, each scenario has the form of a box. The scenarios before the transformation are denoted by dotted lines, the ones after the transformation by solid lines.

It is easy to see that our transformation rules preserve the set of represented PDCs and that they do not introduce any double representations of PDCs. It is also easy to see that a minimal representation can always be reached by applying a finite sequence of our three rules: if we know a minimal representation then we can just split all TIs down to minimal TIs and then merge them to achieve the known minimal representation. However, normally the minimal representations are not known, thus we need some heuristics in which order to apply these rules to have good chances to get small (and optimally even minimal) representations with little computational effort. It should be kept in mind though that our intention is to improve the scalability of the symbolic simulation in [12]. Thus slowing down the computations by protracted minimization of the number of train instances would be counterproductive.

3.2   Iterative Approach

Our first heuristic given in Algorithm 2 iteratively applies the MERGE and SHIFT rules from the previous section to a given set of scenarios. We do not apply the SPLIT rule alone, in order to assure that the representation size does not increase. This has the consequence that the proposed iterative approach does not guarantee optimal results. However, it might still lead to an overall improvement of the simulation algorithm's running time.

In each step one of the rules is applied to one pair of TIs. The selection of the rule and the TI pair can follow any criteria, but we need to prevent applying the

SHIFT rule in endless loops to ensure termination. In the extrem case, we can apply only the MERGE rule, omitting the grey parts of Algorithm 2. The rules are applied until there is no further suitable pair (lines 3–6).

Algorithm 2. Iterative Reduction Algorithm

1: **procedure** ITERATIVEREDUCTION($\mathcal{S}$)
2:     let set $R \leftarrow \emptyset$;
3:     **while** $(S_1, S_2) \in \mathcal{S}^2$ could be merged or shifted **do**
4:         **if** (S_1, S_2) can be merged **then** $R \leftarrow \{\text{MERGE}(S_1, S_2)\}$;
5:         **else** $R \leftarrow \{\text{SHIFT}(S_1, S_2)\}$;
6:         $\mathcal{S} \leftarrow (\mathcal{S} \setminus \{S_1, S_2\}) \cup R$;   // replace scenarios
7:     **return** $\mathcal{S}$;

3.3 Bounded Model Checking Approach

The iterative approach uses a heuristic to determine the rule applications and it does not provide any optimality guarantees. Our second approach aims to find the smallest representation achievable by a bounded number of rule applications. To identify a rule sequence whose application leads to such a smallest representation, we apply the technique of *bounded model checking* (*BMC*) [6,9]. First, for each train and infrastructure element, we group the scenarios of the corresponding TIs into sets, each set collecting the scenarios from the TIs that share the same planned time for the next movement. For each of the resulting scenario sets of size m, we encode that the application of at most k rules leads to a set with less than m scenarios by a propositional logic formula. We solve the corresponding *satisfiability checking problem* (*SAT*) [7] using the SAT solver MINISAT [5,10]. If the formula is unsatisfiable then no scenario set of size less than m can be achieved with at most k reduction steps. Otherwise, if the formula is satisfiable then the satisfying assignment encodes which sequence of at most k rules we need to apply to which scenarios in order to achieve a scenario set of size $m' < m$. We remember this solution and check the same formula but targeting less than m' scenarios in order to find the minimum.

In the following we use $[x..y]$ to denote intervals in $\mathbb{N}$ and write $\underline{x}$ for $[1..x]$. For better understandability, we use equivalence $\leftrightarrow$ and implication $\rightarrow$ in the depicted formulae. In the implementation we add auxiliary variables and transform the formulae to *conjunctive normal form* (*CNF*), which MINISAT expects as input.

Assume the initial set of scenarios $\mathcal{S} = \{S_1, \ldots, S_{m'}\}$ with $P = \{p_1, \ldots, p_n\}$, and let K be the upper bound on the number of rule applications. Since splits increase the number of scenarios, we extend the scenario set with some auxiliary "empty" scenarios $S_{m'+1}, \ldots, S_m$ to be able to store split results.[1] For each

---

[1] Worst-case, to reach an optimal result, m needs to be greater or equal to the number of PDCs represented by the input scenario.

scenario in this extended set, we encode $k+1$ instances (for the initial value and the values after each transformation step), to which we refer as $S_{k,i}$ for $k \in [0..K]$ and $i \in \underline{m}$.

We use Boolean variables $a_{k,i}^{v,d}$ for $k \in \underline{K}$, $i \in \underline{m}$, $v \in \underline{n}$ and $d \in \mathcal{D}(p_v)$ to encode whether after k rule applications it holds that $d \in S_i(p_v)$. By $\varphi^e(k,i) := \bigwedge_{v \in \underline{n}} \bigwedge_{d \in \mathcal{D}(p_v)} \neg a_{k,i}^{v,d}$ we encode that the kth instance of scenario i is "empty". We encode the initial set of scenarios $\mathcal{S}$ as:

$$I_0 := \bigwedge_{i \in \underline{m}} \bigwedge_{v \in \underline{n}} \bigwedge_{d \in \mathcal{D}(p_v)} \nu(i,v,d), \text{ with } \nu(i,v,d) := \begin{cases} a_{0,i}^{v,d} & \text{, if } i \leq m' \wedge d \in S_i(p_v) \\ \neg a_{0,i}^{v,d} & \text{, else.} \end{cases}$$

To encode the set of scenarios after the kth rule application, we encode the transformation rules for two arbitrary scenarios with $i,j \in \underline{m}$, $k < K$. The respective formulae consist of two parts each, one encoding whether the rule can be applied to the scenarios and the other encoding what the result would be. For the MERGE rule this is relatively straight forward:

$$\varphi_{\text{MERGE}}(k,i,j) := \Big(\bigvee_{v \in \underline{n}} \bigwedge_{v' \in \underline{n} \setminus \{v\}} \bigwedge_{d \in \mathcal{D}(p_{v'})} (a_{k,i}^{v',d} \leftrightarrow a_{k,j}^{v',d}) \Big) \; \Big\} condition$$

$$\wedge \, \varphi^e(k+1,j) \wedge \bigwedge_{v \in \underline{n}} \bigwedge_{d \in \mathcal{D}(p_v)} (a_{k+1,i}^{v,d} \leftrightarrow (a_{k,i}^{v,d} \vee a_{k,j}^{v,d})) \Big\} result$$

Note that the $(k+1)$th instance of scenario j is removed ("emptied") by setting all corresponding variables to false. Note furthermore that we do not exclude the possibility to merge two "empty" scenarios (we could easily do so, but it is not needed for correctness or completeness). To encode the SPLIT rule, we need cardinality constraints to restrict the number of variables in a set that are assigned true.

Definition 2. *A cardinality constraint $\varphi_{\sim x}(\mathcal{B})$ for a set of Boolean variables $\mathcal{B}$, with $\sim \in \{<, \leq, =, \geq, >\}$ and $x \in \mathbb{N}$, is a propositional logic formula, such that for all assignments $\alpha : \mathcal{B}' \to \{true, false\}$ with $\mathcal{B} \subseteq \mathcal{B}'$ it holds that $\alpha \models \varphi_{\sim x}(\mathcal{B})$ iff $|\{b \in \mathcal{B} \mid \alpha(b) = true\}| \sim x$.*

In our implementation we use for these constraints encodings presented in [16,19]. The SPLIT rule for splitting a scenario $S_{k,i}$ into two scenarios $S_{k+1,i}$ and $S_{k+1,j}$ is then encoded as follows:

$$\varphi_{\text{SPLIT}}(k,i,j) := \Big(\bigvee_{v \in \underline{n}} \varphi_{\geq 2}(\{a_{k,i}^{v,d} \mid d \in \mathcal{D}(p_v)\}) \Big) \wedge \varphi^e(k,j) \; \Big\} condition$$

$$\wedge \Big(\bigvee_{v \in \underline{n}} \Big[\Big(\bigvee_{d \in \mathcal{D}(p_v)} a_{k+1,i}^{v,d} \Big) \wedge \Big(\bigvee_{d \in \mathcal{D}(p_v)} a_{k+1,j}^{v,d} \Big) \wedge \bigwedge_{v' \in \underline{n} \setminus \{v\}} (a_{k,i}^{v,d} \leftrightarrow a_{k+1,i}^{v,d}) \wedge (a_{k,i}^{v,d} \leftrightarrow a_{k+1,j}^{v,d})$$

$$\wedge \bigwedge_{d \in \mathcal{D}(p_v)} (a_{k,i}^{v,d} \leftrightarrow (a_{k+1,i}^{v,d} \vee a_{k+1,j}^{v,d})) \wedge (\neg a_{k+1,i}^{v,d} \vee \neg a_{k+1,j}^{v,d}) \Big] \Big)$$

The first line encodes the enabling condition that $|S_{k,i}(p)| \geq 2$ at least for one $p \in P$, and that $S_{k,j}$ is "empty". The next two lines encode possible results. The second line encodes that both resulting scenarios are non-empty, and assign the same sets as the original one for all but one random variable p_v. The third line finally ensures that the value domain $S_{k,i}(p_v)$ of p_v before the transformation is the disjoint union of the domains in the resulting scenarios. We do not consider the SHIFT rule here, as it can be composed from a split and a merge, but in our implementation we do use also this rule (see Sect. 4).

To model the choice of rule applications, we define Boolean variables $merge_k^{i,j}$ and $split_k^{i,j}$ for $k \in [0..(K-1)]$, $i \in \underline{m}$ and $j \in \underline{m}\backslash\{i\}$, which are assigned true, if the respective rule is applied to the ith and jth scenario in step k. We define $s_{k,i} := \bigvee_{j \in \underline{m}\backslash\{i\}} (merge_k^{i,j} \vee merge_k^{j,i} \vee split_k^{i,j} \vee split_k^{j,i})$ for $k \in [0..(K-1)]$ and $i \in \underline{m}$, to encode that the ith scenario is used in the kth rule application. We will also use $split_k := \{split_k^{i,j} \mid i \in \underline{m} \wedge j \in \underline{m}\backslash\{i\}\}$, and analogously for MERGE. Now we are ready to encode a transformation step:

$$T(k, k+1) := \bigwedge_{i \in \underline{m}} \left(\neg s_{k,i} \rightarrow \left(\bigwedge_{v \in \underline{n}} \bigwedge_{d \in \mathcal{D}(p_v)} a_{k,i}^{v,d} \leftrightarrow a_{k+1,i}^{v,d}\right)\right) \wedge \varphi_{\leq 1}(merge_k \cup split_k)$$

$$\wedge \bigwedge_{i \in \underline{m}} \bigwedge_{j \in \underline{m}\backslash\{i\}} \left(merge_k^{i,j} \rightarrow \varphi_{\text{MERGE}}(k, i, j)\right) \wedge \left(split_k^{i,j} \rightarrow \varphi_{\text{SPLIT}}(k, i, j)\right)$$

Last, we encode the desired size of the resulting set of scenarios. Therefore, we define $E := \{E_i \mid i \in \underline{m}\}$, where each proposition E_i encodes whether the ith scenario is "empty" at the end of the reduction sequence. The final BMC encoding then looks as follows:

$$[\![M]\!]_{K,m,c} := I_0 \wedge \bigwedge_{k=0}^{K-1} T(k, k+1) \wedge \bigwedge_{i \in \underline{m}} (E_i \leftrightarrow \varphi^e(K, i)) \wedge \varphi_{\geq c}(E)$$

Note that this approach in general does not guarantee optimal results, only for suitable values for K, m and c. Let d be the number of PDCs represented by the scenarios in $\mathcal{S}$, assume $m = d$ and $K = d$. To reach an optimal result we let MINISAT solve $[\![M]\!]_{K,m,c}$ for increasing values for c. Let c' be the largest value for c for which the formula is still satisfiable. Then $m - c'$ is the size of the optimal result. The satisfying assignment found by MINISAT for the respective instance can be transformed to an optimal set of scenarios. In our implementation we also consider different values, as we abandon optimality for speed-up.

For the same reason, we could also only consider the MERGE rule here, by leaving out the grey parts in $T(k, k+1)$. Further attempts to reduce the solving times of MINISAT for our encoding include symmetry breaking by removing redundant constraints and additional constraints to guide the search or terminate it faster. The latter could for example be achieved by adding cardinality constrains for "empty" scenarios in all steps and propagating the scenarios without rule applications, if the desired size is reached for some $k < K$ already. We implemented some of these improvements and use an accordingly modified encoding for the experimental evaluation.

Table 1. Running times in *seconds*

input	version		[12]	I_R	I_{RS}	B_R	B_{RS}	B_{Split}	B_{all}
night	1h	72	1.71	1.75	1.83	1.73	1.74	1.73	1.89
	2h	112	14.54	5.83	6.12	5.89	5.78	5.80	5.81
	3h	143	23.05	11.88	11.98	11.65	11.64	11.79	11.58
morning	1h	281	5.95	5.71	5.24	5.19	5.24	5.16	5.31
	2h	427	13.16	12.23	11.53	11.52	11.51	11.62	11.58
	3h	550	51.56	20.52	21.01	20.65	20.40	20.60	21.01
day	1h	264	6.29	5.56	5.49	5.64	5.52	5.67	5.51
	2h	394	19.22	15.27	14.11	14.14	14.18	14.29	14.10
	3h	529	78.71	39.97	36.78	37.07	38.11	36.95	37.49

4   Experimental Evaluation

Our implementation of the above presented reduction approaches in C++ is available at [13]. We have run the experimental evaluation on a computer with a 3.60 GHz × 8 Intel Core i7 CPU and 32 GB of RAM. As input we used a part of the real-world railway infrastructure network in Germany that has been generated from confidential XML data, provided by DB Netz AG (German Railways). As we want to examine the impact of our proposed reduction approaches, we use the same infrastructure network for all experiments and only vary the considered time interval and the infrastructure utilization. The latter varies naturally in the course of a day, at night less trains drive, as opposed to rush-hours.

The input infrastructure network we use here has 2646 stations and junctions and 5622 tracks connecting them. We consider time intervals of different length, distributed over a day. The time intervals start at 12:00 am (night), 06:00 am (morning), and 12:00 pm (day). Time was as in [12] modeled in the unit of minutes with a day being modeled by $[0; 1440]$ with 0 representing 12:00 am. The different executable timetables we considered are based on the DB data, but slightly modified in order to match the network's level of detail as in [12]. The number of trains in those timetables is given in Table 1 in the input column, the last value in each cell.

For the symbolic simulation algorithm itself we use here the version described in Section "Experimental Results" of [12], also with the there specified parameter values. This symbolic simulation algorithm we then extend with our reduction approaches. We consider six different versions:

- iterative: using MERGE (I_R) or MERGE + SHIFT (I_{RS})
- bounded model checking: using MERGE (B_R); MERGE + SHIFT (B_{RS}); MERGE + SPLIT (B_{Split}) or MERGE + SHIFT + SPLIT (B_{all})

The symbolic simulation algorithm in combination with each of these versions (applied in each time step) is then compared with the one without reduction.

We depict the total running times of the different versions in Table 1, marking the shortest running times in grey. Except for the smallest inputs, where the reduction apparently causes too much overhead, all reduction approaches bring remarkable speed-ups for the longer time horizons. The best running time was for the given inputs never achieved by an approach using only the MERGE rule. However, in general the differences between the different versions are relatively minor.

Table 2. Running time improvement and share of reduction in %

input	night			morning			day		
	1h	2h	3h	1h	2h	3h	1h	2h	3h
Improvement	−1.3	60.2	49.8	13.3	12.5	60.4	12.7	26.7	53.3
Share of reduction in B_{RS}	11.9	14.9	16.2	19.1	25.0	27.8	17.0	20.5	19.7

The highest improvements of the running time were about 60% as shown in the first row of Table 2, where the changes of the running time from the original symbolic simulation to the fastest version with reduction are presented. A promising observation is that the improvements for the longest time interval of 3 hours were about 50% to 60% for all three daytimes. This is the case due to the continued reduced computational effort after reducing the number of train instances and thereby the interruption of the propagation of unnecessarily many train instances.

The second row in Table 2 shows the percentage of the running time that was spent on identifying and applying reductions for the approach B_{RS}; the values for the other approaches are very similar. The differences between the relative times spent on reduction are way smaller than the ones of the running time improvements. The time spent with reducing the state's representation varies from 11.9 to 27.8% of the total running time. While these two values correspond to the smallest, respectively largest improvement in the running time, there is no obvious correlation observable in general. For example for the morning input the share of the reduction increases from 1h to 2h time-frame, but the running time improvement slightly decreases. Still, the time spent on reducing the state's representation pays off, especially for inputs with longer time intervals.

This can be explained by the way the symbolic simulation works. Assume there are three train instances of one train at some time point during the simulation that could be represented by one train instance instead. Without reduction, the computations within the symbolic simulation are performed with three train instances as input rather than one. This is not only more time consuming but also more likely leading to even more train instances (e.g., if these train instances are split again even just in two train instances each, there would be six train instances instead of two). So the difference between the numbers of train instances increased even further.

To illustrate this effect, we visualize the number of train instances over time for the input timetable 'day' both for the 2 and the 3 hour time interval in Fig. 2. The figure shows that the number of instances indeed increases a lot towards the end of the simulated time interval of 3 hours without reduction. With reduction, the number of train instances even decreases in total. This happens when train instances representing a train being delayed initially eventually catch up with the punctual or less delayed instances of the same train. That is possible by driving faster and halting shorter than planned, where this is feasible. This observation speaks for the robustness of the input timetable, where it is apparently possible to make up for delays.

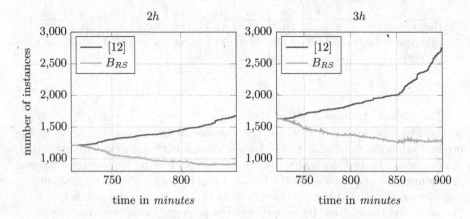

Fig. 2. Number of train instances over time for input timetable 'day'

As shown in the second row of Table 2, the time spent with reducing the current state's representation is a significant share of the total running time. Still, the reduction approaches greatly improve the symbolic simulation's running times making an important step towards scalability. The various approaches we proposed in this paper did not have significant differences as is, at least on the inputs we examined.

5   Conclusion

In this paper we presented several reduction approaches to speed up the symbolic simulation algorithm introduced in [12]. The experimental results show that reduction in general improved the running time of the symbolic simulation. However, the differences between the different approaches were insignificant on the used examples. We expected a more significant difference, though this might still be the case on larger inputs (i.e., inputs for a longer time interval).

We intend to work on further improvements of the scalability of the symbolic simulation approach, for example by examining further heuristics for finding reduction sequences, or developing an SMT encoding to identify optimal solutions as fixed-points (instead of the result of a sequence of reduction steps). Alternatively, it could be interesting to compute an over-approximation ("conservative" approximation) of the simulation results and refine it in a CEGAR (counterexample-guided abstraction refinement) framework. Also the parallelization of the symbolic algorithm would be an option.

Another area we are working on is the visualization of the obtained results, to make them more easily accessible for human users and help identify problematic issues in given timetables.

References

1. LUKS (2021). https://www.via-con.de/en/development/luks/. Accessed 28 Apr 2021
2. OnTime (2021). https://www.trafit.ch/en/ontime. Accessed 28 Apr 2021
3. OpenTrack Railway Technology (2021). http://www.opentrack.ch/opentrack/opentrack_e/opentrack_e.html. Accessed 28 Apr 2021
4. RailSys (2021). https://www.rmcon-int.de/railsys-en/. Accessed 28 Apr 2021
5. MiniSat (2021). https://github.com/niklasso/minisat. Accessed 8 Nov 2021
6. Biere, A., Cimatti, A., Clarke, E.M., Strichman, O., Zhu, Y.: Bounded model checking. Adv. Comput. **58**, 117–148 (2003)
7. Biere, A., Heule, M., van Maaren, H.: Handbook of Satisfiability, vol. 185. IOS Press (2009)
8. Büker, T., Seybold, B.: Stochastic modelling of delay propagation in large networks. J. Rail Transp. Plan. Manag. **2**(1), 34–50 (2012). https://doi.org/10.1016/j.jrtpm.2012.10.001
9. Clarke, E., Biere, A., Raimi, R., Zhu, Y.: Bounded model checking using satisfiability solving. Formal Methods Syst. Des. **19**(1), 7–34 (2001)
10. Eén, N., Sörensson, N.: An extensible SAT-solver. In: Giunchiglia, E., Tacchella, A. (eds.) SAT 2003. LNCS, vol. 2919, pp. 502–518. Springer, Heidelberg (2004). https://doi.org/10.1007/978-3-540-24605-3_37
11. Franke, B., Seybold, B., Büker, T., Graffagnino, T., Labermeier, H.: Ontime - network-wide analysis of timetable stability. In: 5th International Seminar on Railway Operations Modelling and Analysis, May 2013
12. Haehn, R., Ábrahám, E., Nießen, N.: Symbolic simulation of railway timetables under consideration of stochastic dependencies. In: Abate, A., Marin, A. (eds.) QEST 2021. LNCS, vol. 12846, pp. 257–275. Springer, Cham (2021). https://doi.org/10.1007/978-3-030-85172-9_14
13. Haehn, R., Kotowski, N., Ábrahám, E.: Symbolic simulation for railway timetables, December 2021. https://doi.org/10.5281/zenodo.5750431
14. Janecek, D., Weymann, F.: Luks - analysis of lines and junctions. In: Proceedings of the 12th World Conference on Transport Research (WCTR 2010), Lisbon, Portugal (2010)
15. Nash, A., Huerlimann, D.: Railroad simulation using OpenTrack. Computers in Railways IX, pp. 45–54 (2004). https://doi.org/10.2495/CR040051
16. Nguyen, V., Mai, S.T.: A new method to encode the at-most-one constraint into SAT. In: Proceedings of the Sixth International Symposium on Information and Communication Technology, SoICT 2015, pp. 46–53. Association for Computing Machinery, New York (2015). https://doi.org/10.1145/2833258.2833293

17. Radtke, A., Bendfeldt, J.: Handling of railway operation problems with RailSys. In: Proceedings of the 5th World Congress on Rail Research (WCRR 2001), Cologne, Germany (2001)

18. Schneider, W., Nießen, N., Oetting, A.: MOSES/WiZug: strategic modelling and simulation tool for rail freight transportation. In: Proceedings of the European Transport Conference, Straßbourg (2003)

19. Sinz, C.: Towards an optimal CNF encoding of Boolean cardinality constraints. In: van Beek, P. (ed.) CP 2005. LNCS, vol. 3709, pp. 827–831. Springer, Heidelberg (2005). https://doi.org/10.1007/11564751_73

Optimal Railway Routing
Using Virtual Subsections

Tom Peham[1]([✉]), Judith Przigoda[2], Nils Przigoda[2], and Robert Wille[1,3]

[1] Chair for Design Automation, Technical University of Munich, Munich, Germany
{tom.peham,robert.wille}@tum.de
[2] Siemens Mobility GmbH, Braunschweig, Germany
{judith.przigoda,nils.przigoda}@siemens.com
[3] Software Competence Center Hagenberg GmbH (SCCH), Hagenberg, Austria

Abstract. The design of railway systems has become a non-trivial task
which more and more demands for efficient design automation methods. Modern railway systems based on standards such as the *European
Train Control System* (ETCS) Level 3, the *Chinese Train Control System*
(CTCS) Level 3+/4, or the Indian *Train Protection and Warning System*
(TPWS) introduce new concepts such as virtual subsections which allow
for a much higher degree of freedom and provide significant potential
for increasing the efficiency in today's railway schedules. At the same
time, this substantially increases the complexity of determining efficient
solutions. The current state of the art addresses this complexity by discretizing the problem. In this work, we show that this, however, leads to
substantial problems, namely infeasible configurations, rounding errors,
and oversimplifications, that either harm the efficiency of the solving process or yield results which are significantly off from the actual optimum.
Motivated by that, we propose an alternative design automation method
that avoids discretization at all, overcomes the resulting problems, and
additionally allows to solve the problem magnitudes faster than before.

1 Introduction

Railways are an important part of today's infrastructure, whether it is for delivering goods and resources or as a part of the public traffic system. They prove to
be an environmentally friendly alternative to air traffic, road transport, and ship
traffic. It is therefore vital to increase the usage of railways in the future – a goal
which a huge number of societies has made one of their top priorities recently.
But expanding railway infrastructures is costly, difficult, and time-consuming.
The alternative is to increase the efficiency of existing railway infrastructure by
increasing its throughput.

This can be achieved by putting more trains on the tracks. But to ensure
the safe operation of them, railway networks are divided into *blocks*. A block
can only be occupied by one train at any given time, thus, preventing collisions.
To register trains moving in and out of blocks *Trackside Train Detection* (TTD)

© Springer Nature Switzerland AG 2022
S. Collart-Dutilleul et al. (Eds.): RSSRail 2022, LNCS 13294, pp. 63–79, 2022.
https://doi.org/10.1007/978-3-031-05814-1_5

hardware, e.g., axle-counters, are employed. The blocks connected by TTD hardware are often also called TTDs and we will follow this convention in this paper. A consequence of the resulting *block signaling* is that the throughput of a railway network is limited by the size of the blocks. Until a train has completely left a TTD, no other trains can enter the TTD. It is therefore sensible to decrease the size of TTDs in order to increase throughput. This entails installing new TTD hardware which requires maintenance and is not flexible when new layouts are required.

A solution to this problem is provided by the introduction of so-called *Virtual Subsections* (VSS). They are specified in modern railway traffic management systems such as the *European Train Control System* (ETCS) Level 3 [1,2] by the *European Railway Traffic Management System* (ERTMS) [3,4], the *Chinese Train Control System* (CTCS) Level 3+/4 [5], or the Indian *Train Protection and Warning System* (TPWS) [6]. VSS essentially are blocks, just as TTDs. But in contrast to TTDs, these blocks do not require hardware. Instead, the occupation of a VSS is tracked by a radio control center which exchanges position information with trains in the network. Because these blocks are purely virtual, layouts are easy to adapt if changing schedules or demands necessitate it.

However, the implementation and utilization of such schemes and, hence, of virtual subsections, is just at the beginning. In fact, researchers started formalizing the underlying concepts (using, e.g., iUML-B [7,8], Electrum [9], SysML/ KAOS [10], Event-B [11,12], or SPIN [13]), conducted corresponding case studies [14,15], or even presented first simulations [16,17]. But the main task, namely designing corresponding railway routings that exploit the extended degree of freedom provided by VSS in order to improve the travel times, remained an endeavor mostly tackled by manual labor thus far. Obviously, such a state of the art is not sufficient in order to address the upcoming challenges in extending the throughput of today's railway systems and, hence, *automatic* methods for railway routing using virtual subsections are urgently needed[1].

To the best of our knowledge, our previous approach recently introduced in [25] constitutes the first solution that generates (optimal) railway routings while, at the same time, using virtual subsections in order to minimize the sum of the travel times. To this end, we formulated the problem in terms of a satisfiability problem and, afterwards, used corresponding SAT solvers to determine a solution. This, however, requires a discretization of the problem which, on the one hand, makes the problem manageable for the solving engine, but also frequently leads to infeasible configurations, rounding errors, and oversimplifi-

---

[1] Please note that, due to the long history of railway systems, approaches for routing trains through networks are of course not new and research into determining optimal schedules and verifying their correctness with respect to block signaling constraints has been conducted for a long time (see, e.g., [18–24]). Such solutions are inadequate when dealing with VSS because these approaches assume a fixed block layout to begin with. Simply partitioning the network into many VSS is also not practical because that puts a lot of workload on the radio control center communicating VSS occupations with the trains on the network. Solutions taking virtual subsections under consideration hardly exist.

cations. Hence, while providing a first solution towards design automation for modern railway routing, this approach still has severe shortcomings (something which is discussed and illustrated in more detail later in Sect. 3).

In this work, we propose an alternative solution for the railway routing problem using virtual subsections that overcomes these drawbacks. To this end, an A*-based search scheme is proposed which works *without* discretization but still is capable of efficiently determining optimal railway routings. Experiments confirm that the proposed scheme spares the user the need to determine a proper discrete formulation, generates results of much higher precision, and additionally is orders of magnitudes faster than the currently available solution.

The remainder of this paper is structured as follows: Sect. 2 briefly reviews the railway routing problem with VSS and Sect. 3 discusses the shortcomings of the currently available solution – motivating our work. Afterwards, the proposed solution is described in Sect. 4. Experimental evidence for the efficacy of the proposed solutions and comparisons to the state of the art is presented in Sect. 5. Section 6 concludes this paper.

2   Railway Routing in ETCS Level 3

This section briefly reviews and illustrates the considered problem as well as the used notation. We start with the concept of a *rail network* which can be modeled as an undirected edge-labeled graph $G = (V, E, L)$, where the edges E describe track sections that are connected via vertices V. The vertices $v \in V$ represent *Trackside Train Detection* (TTD) hardware like axle-counters (also called *TDD points*). The blocks separated by this hardware are often called TTDs themselves and we follow this convention in this work, i.e., we refer to edges E of G as TTDs[2]. Finally, every TTD $e \in E$ has a label $L(e) = l_e$ defining the length l_e of this TDD.

Example 1. Figure 1 shows an example of a railway network with 4 TDD points and, hence, 7 TDDs labelled $e_1, e_2, \ldots, e_7$. The lengths l_e for all TDDs $e \in E$ are given by the labels annotated onto the respective blocks in Fig. 1.

To properly define train positions and train movements, we use the following terms: A *TTD interval* is a triple (e, a, b) with $e \in E$ and $0 \leq a < b \leq l_e$. A *range* is a sequence of TDD intervals $((e_1, a_1, b_1), \ldots, (e_n, a_n, b_n))$ such that, for all $1 \leq i < n$, e_i is connected to e_{i+1} via a TTD point in G and, for all $1 < i < n$, $a_i = 0$ and $b_i = l_{e_i}$. The length of a range rg is given by $l_{rg} = \sum_{i=1}^{n}(b_i - a_i) = (b_1 - a_1) + \sum_{i=2}^{n-1} l_{e_i} + (b_n - a_n)$. Then, a *train tr* is described by the tuple $tr = (l_{tr}, s_{tr}, start_{tr}, dest_{tr})$, where l_{tr} is the length of the train, s_{tr} its maximum speed, $start_{tr}$ its start position, and $dest_{tr}$ its destination position. A *position* p of a train tr is a range such that $l_p = l_{tr}$. Intuitively a train's position is the part of the track in the network that the train is standing on. The set of trains is denoted as Tr.

---

[2] We implicitly assumed here that the entire rail network being modelled is covered by TTDs. This is a reasonable assumption for modern rail network, however.

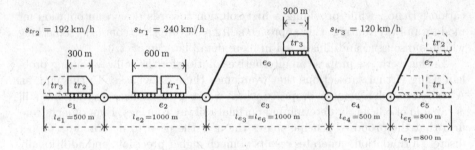

Fig. 1. Example network

Example 2. The railway network shown in Fig. 1 is used by three trains: The train denoted tr_1 occupies a part of TTD e_2, i.e., its position is described by the range containing a single TTD interval $((e_2, 200 \text{ m}, 800 \text{ m}))$. The position of tr_2 is $((e_1, 100 \text{ m}, 400 \text{ m}))$. The position of tr_3 is $((e_6, 650 \text{ m}, 950 \text{ m}))$. Note that the length of the positions is the same as the lengths of the trains. The respective maximum speeds $s_{tr_1}, s_{tr_2}, s_{tr_3}$ are given above the trains in Fig. 1. The start positions are depicted by the trains with solid lines and the destination positions are depicted by trains with dashed lines. Train tr_1 has destination position $((e_5, 200 \text{ m}, 800 \text{ m}))$, tr_2 has destination position $((e_7, 500 \text{ m}, 800 \text{ m}))$, and tr_3 has destination position $((e_1, 0 \text{ m}, 300 \text{ m}))$.

The *movement* m of a train tr is described by a range such that $l_{tr} \leq l_m \leq l_{tr} + s_{tr}$. Intuitively, a single movement is described by the parts of the track in the network the train moves over in one Because of that, a movement of a train is at least as long as the train itself (even if a train stands still in one time step, it still covers the part of the network its standing on). Furthermore, a movement covers the train's position before and after the movement. The direction of a movement is implicitly given by the sequence of TTD intervals. Then, a *route* R_{tr} of a train tr can be described by a sequence of movements $(m_1, \ldots, m_n)$ such that m_1 starts at $start_{tr}$ and m_n ends at end_{tr}. The *travel time* $|R_{tr}| = n$ of R_{tr} is the number of time steps it takes for train tr to reach its goal. The problem considered in this work is to determine routes of all trains $tr \in Tr$ in the given railway network G such that, e.g., the sum of travel times of all trains is minimal.

Note that there might be additional constraints on movements and routes imposed by the underlying railway network. Because TTD points may represent hardware such as switches, a train might not be able to move from one edge to another even if they are connected via a TTD point. In Fig. 1, for example, trains cannot move from e_3 to e_6. Also trains can of course not just change directions during a route.

Example 3. Consider again the layout and specification of trains given in Fig. 1. Figure 2 shows example movements for all trains in the network if we assume a time step of 15 s. The movement m_1 of train tr_1 is given by the range consisting of two TTD intervals $m_1 = ((e_2, 200 \text{ m}, 100 \text{ m}), (e_6, 0 \text{ m}, 600 \text{ m}))$. Similarly

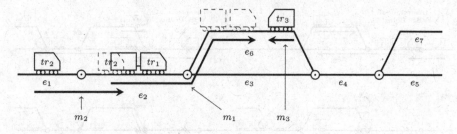

Fig. 2. Train movement

the movement m_2 is given by the range consisting of two TTD intervals $m_2 = ((e_1, 100 \text{ m}, 500 \text{ m}), (e_2, 0 \text{ m}, 400 \text{ m}))$. Train tr_3 remains at the same position. This is still considered to be a movement which is simply the position of the train (therefore, m_3 is set to $((e_6, 650 \text{ m}, 950 \text{ m})))$. Note that the lengths of the movements might be smaller than the length of the respective train.

Solving this problem for a single train is relatively simple (as reviewed later in Sect. 4.1). However, determining the fastest routes becomes significantly harder if multiple trains need to be considered because, then, collisions have to be avoided. More precisely, there are two types of collisions: (1) a *move collision* occurs if two movements overlap and (2) a *TTD collision* occurs if two movements contain the same TTD and no move collision occurs. Two routes R_1 and R_2 are then in collision if any of its movements are in collision.

Example 4. Consider again the movements depicted in Fig. 2. A move collision occurs between movements m_1 and m_2 since both movements overlap on the range $((e_2, 20 \text{ m}, 40 \text{ m}))$. A TTD collision occurs between movements m_1 and m_3 since both movements contain a TTD interval on TTD e_6.

Collisions substantially harden the railway routing problem and frequently lead to solutions with overly long travel times. Thus far, move collisions have been avoided by re-routing trains until no more move collisions occur. But using modern railway systems such as ETCS Level 3, CTCS Level 3+/4, or TPWS, TTD collision can also be resolved by introducing virtual subsections, i.e., VSS. Recall that a TTD collision only occurs when two trains occupy the same TTD, but would not occur if there would be a TTD point between the two trains. VSS basically introduces such (virtual) TDD points and, by this, can help resolving these TTD collisions without the need to re-route trains[3].

Based on all that, the railway routing problem considered in this work can be succinctly described as: Given a railway network $G = (V, E, L)$ as well as a

---

[3] Note that, for our purposes, blocks defined by TTDs and blocks defined by VSS are indistinguishable. We can therefore interpret a *VSS layout* of a railway network G as a graph G' that is obtained from G by splitting TTDs into VSS. This partitioned graph then simply defines a new railway network. There are in general an infinite number of VSS layouts for a given railway network. We will see in Sect. 4 how to handle this search space.

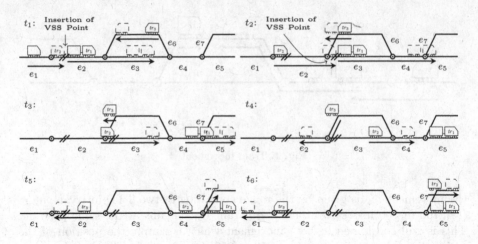

Fig. 3. Possible routes for Example 5

set of trains Tr with start and destination positions, determine a VSS layout $G' = (V', E', L')$ and a set of routes $\{R_{tr} \mid tr \in Tr\}$ on G' such that the objective $\sum_{tr \in Tr} |R_{tr}|$ (i.e., the sum of travel times) is minimized.

Example 5. Let's consider the layout specified in Fig. 1 again and assume time steps of 15 s as in Example 3. Possible routes for the three trains are shown in Fig. 3. Train tr_1 reaches its destination in time step t_3, trains tr_2 and tr_3 reach their destinations in time step 6. The sum of travel times is therefore 15 time steps, i.e., 225 s. In time steps t_1 and t_2, a TTD collision occurs between tr_1 and tr_2. These are repaired by introducing a VSS in TTD e_2 and e_3. Without these VSS, tr_2 would have to wait until tr_1 has left e_2 completely before it can enter. This would delay the route of tr_2 and tr_3 (because it has to wait until tr_2 has left e_2) by one time step. Hence, the introduced VSS indeed improved the train movements.

3   Motivation: The Problem of Discretization

Virtual subsections as introduced above provide a huge degree of freedom that allow for a more efficient railway routing. At the same time, they make the task of determining the best possible routes substantially harder. Because TTDs can be split up into VSS at arbitrary positions in the network, the resulting VSS layouts can be very complex. Techniques to solve the routing problem while simultaneously generating VSS layouts are still in its infancy. An existing solution tackling this problem is proposed in [25] where the problem is defined as a satisfiability problem and handed over to a reasoning engine. In that work, we model the search space of VSS layouts by discretizing the network. This is needed to model the possible positions of the trains on the network. While there are in theory an infinite number of positions, the discretization narrows this search space down such that it can be modelled using a finite number of Boolean variables.

To this end, a *spatial resolution* r_s is defined. Every TTD is then split into *segments* of length r_s. That is, with a spatial resolution of $r_s = 100$ m, a TTD of length 1 km would be split into 10 smaller segments. Such a discretized TTD can then no longer give rise to arbitrarily many VSS, rather VSS can only be composed of these segments.

Discretizing the network like this does not only simplify the search space for VSS layouts, but also the train movements. Similarly to VSS, train positions are described by the segments that are occupied by a train. For example, the trains in Fig. 4 occupy one and two segments, respectively. The trains might actually be much shorter than r_s but they are still considered to occupy an entire segment. Train speeds are therefore defined in terms of *segments traversed per time step*, i.e., a train tr with speed s_{tr} has a *discretized speed* of $s_{tr} \cdot \frac{r_t}{r_s}$, where r_t is the so-called *temporal resolution*, the duration of one time step. For example, with $r_t = 10$ s and $r_s = 100$ m a train with a speed of 200 km/h would have discrete speed of about 5.556.

Although this discretization yields a smaller search space, it also causes several problems.

- *Infeasible configurations:* Because train movement is described in terms of segments traversed per time step, the choice of temporal resolution depends on the spatial resolution. A fine temporal resolution combined with a coarse spatial resolution can lead to situations where trains can seemingly not move at all or move faster than they should be able to.
- *Rounding Errors:* An improper discretization can lead to incorrect solutions. Because the simulation proceeds in discrete steps, train speeds can only be integral values. Therefore sub-optimal routes may be found when speeds are rounded down; or impossible solutions may be found when speeds are rounded up. Even if constraints are added enforcing that resolutions must be chosen such that train speeds can be modelled accurately, this constraint becomes harder and harder to satisfy the more trains are to be considered.
- *Oversimplifications:* Imposing a spatial resolution leads to difficulties when finer details of the network should be accurately portrayed. This can be mitigated by choosing different resolutions for different parts of the network but opting to do this again increases the complexity of the network.

In addition to these issues the approach from [25] also requires the definition of the maximum number of time steps the trains can take to ensure a finite search space. All of the above combined makes it very hard for a designer to choose correct configurations in order to obtain a good solution. Controlling for all issues at the same time is highly non-trivial or might even be infeasible. It is also difficult to judge the quality of a found solution. Infeasible configurations and oversimplifications can lead to solutions that are better than what is possible in reality, whereas rounding errors lead to solutions that are worse than the "real" optimum.

Example 6. Consider the simple layout shown in Fig. 4 consisting of a single TTD with a length of 10 km and 2 trains tr_1 and tr_2 moving from left to right

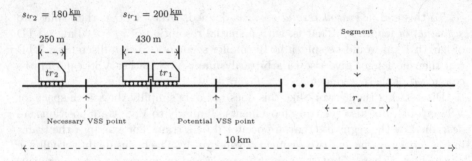

Fig. 4. Discretizing space

with maximal speeds of 200 km/h and 180 km/h as well as lengths of 430 m and 250 m, respectively. Now, the following problems may emerge when trying to choose proper values for r_s and r_t.

Choosing $r_t = 10$ s and $r_s = 1000$ m leads to tr_1 having a discretized speed of 0.556. If we round down, then tr_1 would not be able to move at all. If we round up, tr_1 takes 10 time steps to reach the other end of the track. Converting this speed back to real units gives a speed of 360 km/h which does not remotely reflect the actual speed of tr_1.

Choosing $r_t = 10$ s and $r_s = 100$ m leads to discretized speeds 5.556 and 5 for tr_1 and tr_2, respectively. Here, speeds are rounded down and, thus, tr_1 is treated as having an actual speed of 180 km/h. It is easy to see that, with the chosen temporal resolution, the optimal number of time steps for tr_1 to reach the right end of the TTD is 18 time steps. But with the rounded speed, the best solution that can be found takes 20 time steps. Moreover, since both trains are treated as having the same speed, more VSS have to be placed than necessary. Since the lengths of the trains are not multiples of 100 m, they take up more space of the network than necessary. More specifically, tr_1 would occupy 5 segments at any time step. This prevents tr_2 from moving as close to tr_1 as possible, yielding a suboptimal route for tr_2.

All these problems may be avoided by choosing $r_t = 10$ s and $r_s = 5$ m. Then, the trains have discretized speeds of 100 and 111 respectively, thus avoiding the impact of rounding errors as much as possible. But this would partition the TTD into 2000 segments, an unreasonably fine grained discretization.

These examples show that the problems described above already occur in very simple scenarios. Motivated by that, this work proposes an alternative approach that overcomes these problems by avoiding discretizing the network at all – while still being able to determine optimal railways routings.

4   Proposed Solution

This section describes the proposed alternative solution to the optimal railway routing problem described above. Its main approach rests on an A*-based search scheme which is described first. Afterwards, we explicitly describe how virtual subsections are utilized to resolve collisions. Using both, A* and the extended degree of freedom through those VSS eventually allow to generate optimal railway layouts.

4.1   Main Approach Based on A* Search

A* Search is a state-space search algorithm. That is, the search space is defined over states $s \in S$ (with S being the set of all possible states) and transitions between them. Starting from an initial state, the goal is to determine a route towards a goal state within that search space which satisfies a certain goal condition. By dedicated functions, the total costs of the current state are tracked while the remaining costs towards the goal state are estimated. By this, A* Search traverses through the search space – ideally only expanding towards states with the lowest cost and, by this, avoiding traversing parts of the search space that lead to no or overly expensive solutions.

In order to solve the problem reviewed in Sect. 2, we use the main concept of A* Search as a basis. More precisely, given a set of trains Tr, we model a state $s \in S$ at time step t as the set of positions of all trains, i.e., $s = \{pos_{tr}^{t_{tr}} \mid tr \in Tr\}$, where t_{tr} is the time step at which train tr has reached its destination or t if tr has not reached its destination yet. Two states s and s' are then connected if all trains can make a movement from their position in s to their position in s' within one time step and without causing any collisions. The initial state is then $s_{init} = \{start_{tr}^{0} \mid tr \in Tr\}$ and the goal states are defined by $s_{goal} = \{dest_{tr}^{t_{tr}} \mid tr \in Tr\}$.

Because trains do not move in discrete steps, there is an enormous number of successors for each state. While this is true in principle, most of these positions are redundant. The only branching points in the network are at TTD points. It is therefore superfluous to consider every possible position a train might have within a TTD and consider only movements that transport a train as far as possible within a TTD.

Example 7. Let's consider the start positions in Fig. 1 as an example for an initial state s_{init}. The successor states of s_{init} are derived by considering all possible combinations of movements the three trains in this example can make. As discussed previously, only those movements are considered that move the trains as far as possible within one TTD. In this example, there are 6 potential successor states $s_i, 1 \leq i \leq 6$, as shown in Fig. 5.

However, states s_3 and s_6 are not valid, because the movements of tr_1 and tr_3 are in collision (as indicated by ⚡ in Fig. 5). Similarly, s_4 and s_5 are not valid, because tr_1 and tr_2 are in collision. Therefore, s_{init} has only two real successor states, namely s_1 and s_2.

Recursively or iteratively searching through *all* possible states eventually would lead to several goal states. Out of those, we are then interested in the one with the smallest costs. These are provided by means of a function $g(s)$ which

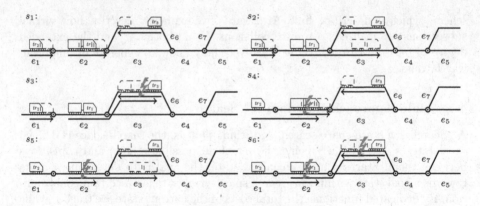

Fig. 5. A* search

gives, for a state s, the costs up to this state. In our case, the costs are defined by the sum of total travel times[4], i.e., for state $s = \{pos_{tr}^{t_{tr}} \mid tr \in Tr\}$ we have $g(s) = \sum_{tr \in Tr} t_{tr}$.

However, to avoid expanding towards non-promising states (i.e., states that will not lead to a goal state or only through substantially longer paths), a *heuristic function* $h(s)$ is additionally employed. This heuristic function assigns to each state s an *estimation* of the costs from s towards a goal state. If we knew the distances d_{tr}^s from the position of each train tr in state s to its destination position $dest_{tr}$, those costs can be estimated by $h(s) = \sum_{tr \in Tr} \frac{d_{tr}^s}{s_{tr}}$. These distances can easily be obtained for a train tr by precomputing a lookup table of distances from each TTD to the destination of tr via breadth-first search. To get the true distance from this lookup table, the offset of the train within the TTD has to be subtracted. Overall, this leads to a total costs of a state $s \in S$ defined as $f(s) = g(s) + h(s)$.

An important property of A* Search is that an optimal solution is guaranteed to be found if the heuristic function is *admissible*. A heuristic function is admissible if the heuristic function never overestimates the true cost to a goal state. It is easy to see that the heuristic function defined for our problem is admissible since trains can never arrive at their respective destinations faster than if they were traveling with maximum speed for the entire route.

Example 8. Consider again the example in Fig. 5. There are two possible successors of s_{init}, s_1, and s_2. In s_2, all trains are closer to their goal than in s_1. Therefore, the estimated sum of travel times is smaller in s_2 and, hence, s_2 would be expanded next by the search.

---

[4] Note that the cost function can, of course, accordingly be adjusted if the focus is put on other aspects such as the overall travel time.

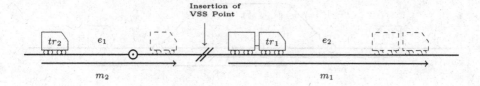

Fig. 6. Resolving TTD collisions with VSS

4.2 Resolving Collisions with VSS

Using A* Search as proposed above, we are looking for a path in the search space from the initial state s_{init} to one of the goal states s_{goal} with the smallest costs. But, thus far, possible paths are severely restricted since states are connected only if trains can reach them without causing any collisions. Using VSS, however, many collisions can be prevented – likely leading to faster routes. Recall from Sect. 2 that there are two types of collisions: move collisions and TTD collisions. Let's consider TTD collision first because resolving them is conceptually easier. A TTD collision occurs when two movements contain the same TTD but are not in a move collision. This kind of collision can be resolved by splitting the TTD into two separate VSS.

Example 9. Consider the situation in Fig. 6 involving two trains moving on a straight track. Movements m_1 and m_2 are in a TTD collision on TTD e_2. By splitting e_2 into two VSS at the point shown in the figure, the TTD collision is resolved.

For move collisions, we can identify three different cases:

- A *head-on-collision* occurs when two movements go in opposite directions in a TTD.
- An *overlap collision* occurs when two movements go in the same direction in a TTD that is not the start of either movement.
- A *rear-end-collision* occurs when the end of a movement collides with the start of another movement.

Head-on-collisions and overlap collisions can not be resolved. In these two cases, corresponding states cannot be connected and, hence, the A* Search needs to determine alternative routes. But rear-end-collisions can be resolved: If movement m_1 rear-end-collides with movement m_2, then a new movement m_1' can be obtained by truncating m_1 in such a way that no collision with m_2 occurs anymore. The movements m_1' and m_2 are then in a TTD collision. But as we have seen previously, these can be resolved.

Example 10. The three different types of movement collisions are depicted in Fig. 7. Figure 7a is an example of a head-on-collision. It is apparent that this situation cannot be rectified by introducing further VSS.

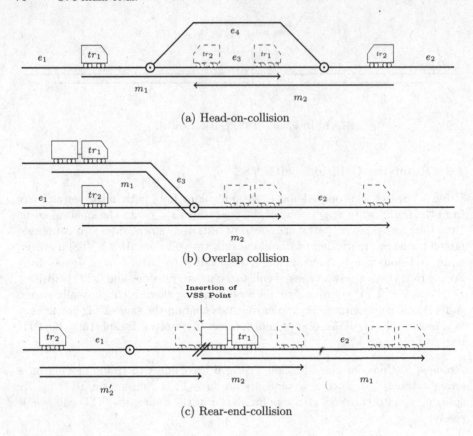

(a) Head-on-collision

(b) Overlap collision

(c) Rear-end-collision

Fig. 7. Move collision cases

Figure 7b is an example of an overlap collision. As it was in the case of a head-on-collision, the collision cannot be resolved by splitting TTDs into VSS. The conflict can only be avoided if one of the trains waits with their movement, possibly leading to a longer route.

Figure 7c is an example of a rear-end-collision. Movement m_1 and m_2 are in collision on TTD e_2. But by moving tr_2 with movement m_2' instead of m_2 the collision is avoided.

5   Experiments

The A*-based approach as described above has been implemented in C++ and was subjected to several benchmarks to evaluate its performance. Additionally, we also considered the solution described in [25] in order to compare the proposed solution to the current state of the art. Both implementations are part of the DA-ETCS toolkit available at https://iic.jku.at/eda/research/etcs/. All those experiments have been conducted on an Intel(R) Core(TM) i7-7700K machine using a 4.20 GHz processor with 32 GB of main memory running Ubuntu 18.04.4. In this section, the obtained results are summarized and discussed.

As benchmarks, we considered the railway layouts and tasks which have been used in the evaluations in [25] (namely, *Running Example*, *Simple Example*, *Complex Example*, and *Nordlandsbanen*) as well as further instances of representative use cases (namely, *Bottleneck*, *Bidirectional*, and *Train Station*). Here, *Bottleneck* refers to a track layout where all trains have to be funneled through a single TTD before their paths diverge again, while *Bidirectional* refers to a layout where trains are moving in both directions on a main track with occasional sidings to pass each other. Finally, *Train Station* refers to a track layout with several interconnected and branching paths for the trains to reach their goals. All these benchmarks represent frequent use cases that usually have many potential collisions to be avoided through the use of virtual subsections.

The obtained results are shown in Table 1. Here, for each considered benchmark, the generated results for both methods (as indicated in the first column) are provided in the respective lines of the table. As described in Sect. 3, the approach from [25] always needs a *configuration* in terms of the spatial resolution r_s and the maximum number of time steps t_{max} in order to generate a discrete formulation; these values are provided in the second and third column. Afterwards, the respectively obtained results are presented, i.e., the number blocks (both, TDDs and VSS combined), the number of *Time Steps* until all trains have reached their goal, and the sum of travel times of all trains $\sum t$ (the actual optimization objective which has been optimized). Finally, the required runtime is provided (note that, in case of the approach from [25], only the solving time is listed, even though also the runtime for generating the discrete formulation often is substantial).

The obtained results clearly confirm the shortcomings of the previously proposed approach as discussed in Sect. 3 and show how the approach proposed in this work addresses them. More precisely:

First, since the approach from [25] always requires a discrete formulation, the designers are urged to provide a configuration in terms of spatial resolution r_s and maximal number of timesteps t_{max}. This frequently pushes him/her to trade-off between accuracy (demanding a finer resolution) and performance (demanding a coarser resolution). These values require prior knowledge about the benchmark like an estimation of the time steps a solution might have. If no proper estimation can be made, multiple configurations have to be tried such that a satisfactory solution can be obtained in an iterative fashion (which is why, we present several configurations in Table 1). In contrast to all that, the proposed approach does not require a configuration and does not rely on a discrete formulation, which is why all these problems do not occur here.

Second, the precision of the approach from [25] highly depends on the respectively chosen configuration (and, hence, discretization). This explains the huge differences in the obtained results. In the worst case, choosing an improper configuration may yield a formulation out of which no solution can be generated at all. This is the case in the two instances marked *Unsatisfiable* where the maximum number of time steps is too small to allow a solution to be found with the given discretization (although the optimum from the A* Search shows that a solution indeed is possible). But even if solutions are determined, they are often significantly off and, hence, imprecise compared to the actual optimal value (obtained by the A* Search without discretization). All this basically confirms the discussions from Sect. 3 about the shortcomings of the discretization and shows that the A* Search proposed in this work nicely addresses these problems.

Finally, the runtime performance of both approaches confirms what could be expected. The coarser the resolution and, hence, discretization of the approach from [25], the better its runtime. In order to get precise results, however, this frequently leads to timeouts (in our evaluations of 1 h). In contrast, the proposed method's main drawback is an increased memory requirement – in particular in cases where the A* Search expansion leads to a huge number of possible states to consider (as in the case of the last instance in Table 1). These cases, however, usually also cannot be handled by the approach from [25] (at least, not with proper precision) and most likely constitute instances, where optimal railway routing probably reaches its limits due to the underlying complexity (in the worst case, both methods exhibit exponential time or space complexity). In all other cases, the A* Search clearly outperforms the state of the art and often yields magnitudes of better runtime – in particular compared to instances with proper precision.

Table 1. Obtained results

Method	Configuration r_s [m] t_{max}		TTD/VSS	Time steps	$\sum t$	Runtime [s]
Running Example (with 4 trains an total travel length of 7 km)						
Approach from [25]	500	11	5	7	23	0.1
A* Search	–		9	7	21	<0.1
Simple Example (with 4 trains and total travel length of 27 km)						
Approach from [25]	500	20	14	15	53	29.2
A* Search	–		26	15	50	<0.1
Complex Example (with 6 trains and total travel length of 148 km)						
Approach from [25]	1000	18	25	16	71	124.9
A* Search	–		42	14	58	138.3
Nordlandsbanen (with 3 trains and total travel length of 819.6 km)						
Approach from [25]	1000	140	–	–	–	>3600
A* Search	–		519	135	286	45.713
Bottleneck (with 4 trains and total travel length of 10 km)						
Approach from [25]	1000	20	13	18	60	0.6
	500	20	13	18	60	2.3
	100	20	16	15	54	84.9
	50	20	16	15	54	777.9
	50	15	16	15	54	866.5
A* Search	–		39	15	50	<0.1
Bottleneck (with 10 trains and total travel length of 2.6 km)						
Approach from [25]	1000	20	*Unsatisfiable*			1185.9
	1000	30	–	–	–	>3600
	100	15	–	–	–	>3600
A* Search	–		30	12	65	11.1
Bottleneck (with 12 trains and total travel length of 3 km)						
Approach from [25]	1000	20	*Unsatisfiable*			1275.1
A* Search	–		34	15	92	371.0
Bidirectional (with 6 trains and total travel length of 14.6 km)						
Approach from [25]	1000	30	16	30	124	50.6
	500	30	18	21	112	698.2
	100	30	–	–	–	>3600
	100	23	–	–	–	>3600
A* Search	–		53	22	105	1.6
Train Station (with 6 trains and total travel length of 7.1 km)						
Approach from [25]	1000	30	19	9	39	1.1
	500	30	19	9	39	1.1
	100	30	31	21	114	64.1
	50	30	31	22	117	1381.3
A* Search	–		58	22	110	17.7
Train Station (with 8 trains and total travel length of 7.3 km)						
Approach from [25]	1000	30	21	11	59	9.6
	500	30	21	11	59	9.6
	100	30	–	–	–	>3600
	100	23	33	23	159	564.1
A* Search	–		*Out of Memory*			–

6 Conclusion

In this work, we considered the automatic generation of optimal railway routings for modern railway systems such as the ETCS Level 3, CTCS Level 3+/4, or TPWS, which allow for virtual subsections. To this end, we first analyzed the major shortcomings, namely infeasible configurations, rounding errors, and oversimplifications, of the current state of the art which are mainly caused by discretization. We proposed an approach which addresses all these problems and, at the same time, even led to substantial runtime improvements (reaching several orders of magnitudes). Experiments and detailed comparisons confirmed these benefits.

Acknowledgments. This work has partially been supported by the BMK, BMDW, and the State of Upper Austria in the frame of the COMET program (managed by the FFG).

References

1. Pachl, J.: Besonderheiten ausländischer Eisenbahnbetriebsverfahren (2019)
2. Pachl, J.: Railway Signalling Principles, Braunschweig, June 2020
3. Set of specifications 1/2/3. https://www.era.europa.eu/content/ccs-tsi-annex-mandatory-specifications. Accessed 18 Sept 2020
4. Stanley, P.: Institution of railway signal engineers. In: ETCS for Engineers (2011)
5. Yang, Z.: Application and development of CTCs. In: UIC ERTMS World Conference, vol. 12 (2016)
6. Rail Analysis India: Implementation of ETCs and TPWs system over Indian railway network. Rail Analysis India (2019)
7. Dghaym, D., Poppleton, M., Snook, C.: Diagram-led formal modelling using iUML-B for hybrid ERTMS level 3. In: Butler, M., Raschke, A., Hoang, T.S., Reichl, K. (eds.) ABZ 2018. LNCS, vol. 10817, pp. 338–352. Springer, Cham (2018). https://doi.org/10.1007/978-3-319-91271-4_23
8. Dghaym, D., Dalvandi, S., Poppleton, M., Snook, C.: Formalising the hybrid ERTMS level 3 specification in iUML-B and Event-B. Int. J. Softw. Tools Technol. Transfer **22**, 297–313 (2020)
9. Cunha, A., Macedo, N.: Validating the hybrid ERTMS/ETCS level 3 concept with electrum. In: Butler, M., Raschke, A., Hoang, T.S., Reichl, K. (eds.) ABZ 2018. LNCS, vol. 10817, pp. 307–321. Springer, Cham (2018). https://doi.org/10.1007/978-3-319-91271-4_21
10. Tueno Fotso, S.J., Frappier, M., Laleau, R., Mammar, A.: Modeling the hybrid ERTMS/ETCS level 3 standard using a formal requirements engineering approach. In: Butler, M., Raschke, A., Hoang, T.S., Reichl, K. (eds.) ABZ 2018. LNCS, vol. 10817, pp. 262–276. Springer, Cham (2018). https://doi.org/10.1007/978-3-319-91271-4_18
11. Abrial, J.-R.: The ABZ-2018 case study with Event-B. In: Butler, M., Raschke, A., Hoang, T.S., Reichl, K. (eds.) ABZ 2018. LNCS, vol. 10817, pp. 322–337. Springer, Cham (2018). https://doi.org/10.1007/978-3-319-91271-4_22

12. Mammar, A., Frappier, M., Tueno Fotso, S.J., Laleau, R.: An EVENT-B model of the hybrid ERTMS/ETCS level 3 standard. In: Butler, M., Raschke, A., Hoang, T.S., Reichl, K. (eds.) ABZ 2018. LNCS, vol. 10817, pp. 353–366. Springer, Cham (2018). https://doi.org/10.1007/978-3-319-91271-4_24

13. Arcaini, P., Ježek, P., Kofroň, J.: Modelling the hybrid ERTMS/ETCS level 3 case study in SPIN. In: Butler, M., Raschke, A., Hoang, T.S., Reichl, K. (eds.) ABZ 2018. LNCS, vol. 10817, pp. 277–291. Springer, Cham (2018). https://doi.org/10.1007/978-3-319-91271-4_19

14. Hoang, T.S., Butler, M., Reichl, K.: The hybrid ERTMS/ETCS level 3 case study. In: Butler, M., Raschke, A., Hoang, T.S., Reichl, K. (eds.) ABZ 2018. LNCS, vol. 10817, pp. 251–261. Springer, Cham (2018). https://doi.org/10.1007/978-3-319-91271-4_17

15. Hansen, D., et al.: Using a formal B model at runtime in a demonstration of the ETCS hybrid level 3 concept with real trains. In: Butler, M., Raschke, A., Hoang, T.S., Reichl, K. (eds.) ABZ 2018. LNCS, vol. 10817, pp. 292–306. Springer, Cham (2018). https://doi.org/10.1007/978-3-319-91271-4_20

16. Jansen, J., Quaglietta, E., Bartholomeus, M., Pot, A., Goverde, R.: ETCS hybrid level 3: a simulation-based impact assessment for the Dutch railway network. 20 May 2019

17. Gill, D.: ETCS level 3 for metro-type mainline operation. In: Aspect (2017)

18. Ghoseiri, K., Szidarovszky, F., Asgharpour, M.J.: A multi-objective train scheduling model and solution. Transp. Res. Part B: Methodol. **38**(10), 927–952 (2004)

19. Cai, X., Goh, C.: A fast heuristic for the train scheduling problem. Comput. Oper. Res. **21**(5), 499–510 (1994)

20. Zhou, X., Zhong, M.: Bicriteria train scheduling for high-speed passenger railroad planning applications. Eur. J. Ope. Res. **167**(3), 752–771 (2005). Multicriteria Scheduling

21. Liebchen, C.: The first optimized railway timetable in practice. Transp. Sci. **42**(4), 420–435 (2008)

22. Lusby, R., Larsen, J., Ryan, D., Ehrgott, M.: Routing trains through railway junctions: a new set-packing approach. Transp. Sci. **45**(2), 228–245 (2011)

23. Goossens, J.-W., van Hoesel, S., Kroon, L.: On solving multi-type railway line planning problems. Eur. J. Oper. Res. **168**(2), 403–424 (2006). Feature Cluster on Mathematical Finance and Risk Management. https://www.sciencedirect.com/science/article/pii/S0377221704003169

24. Garrisi, G., Cervelló-Pastor, C.: Train-scheduling optimization model for railway networks with multiplatform stations. Sustainability **12**(1), 257 (2020)

25. Wille, R., Peham, T., Przigoda, J., Przigoda, N.: Towards automatic design and verification for level 3 of the European train control system. In: Design, Automation and Test in Europe (DATE) (2021)

Safety and New Technologies

Verification of Multiple Models of a Safety-Critical Motor Controller in Railway Systems

José Proença[1]([✉])(iD), Sina Borrami[2](iD), Jorge Sanchez de Nova[2],
David Pereira[1](iD), and Giann Spilere Nandi[1](iD)

[1] CISTER, Polytechnic Institute of Porto, Porto, Portugal
{pro,drp,giann}@isep.ipp.pt
[2] Alstom, Stockholm, Sweden
{sina.borrami,jorge.sanchez-de-nova}@alstomgroup.com

Abstract. Motor controllers, such as the ones used in signalling systems, include critical embedded software. Alstom is a company that produces such embedded systems, which must follow complex certification processes that require formal modelling and analysis. The formal analysis of these real-time systems have to balance between including enough details to be useful and abstracting away enough details to be verifiable.

This paper describes our work in the context of the European VALU3S project to integrate the analysis of such systems with the Uppaal model checker during the development cycle, involving both developers from Alstom and academic partners. We use special Excel tables to configure the underlying Uppaal models and requirements, bridging these two stakeholders. We follow Software Product Line Engineering principles, e.g., allowing features to be turned on and off and periodicities to be changed, and verify different properties for each of such configuration. We automate the instantiation and verification in Uppaal of a set of selected configurations via an open-source prototype tool named *Uppex*.

Keywords: Verification · Variability · Railway · Real-time automata

1 Introduction

In railway systems, motor controllers play a crucial and safety-critical role in point switch machines. Guaranteeing its correct design and development is a challenging but essential task to avoid catastrophic accidents that could cause severe damage to the environment and property, or even result in the loss of human lives. Most state of the art approaches address this safety concerns using formal modelling and verification, including abstract interpretation [15] and Event B [1,7], to enforce compliance with certification processes and railway-specific safety standards, such as EN-50126 [10], EN-50128 [11], and EN-50129 [12]. In these systems, safety means that faults are detected with very high probability, leading to a fallback state.

© Springer Nature Switzerland AG 2022
S. Collart-Dutilleul et al. (Eds.): RSSRail 2022, LNCS 13294, pp. 83–94, 2022.
https://doi.org/10.1007/978-3-031-05814-1_6

The design of motor controllers is usually performed by multidisciplinary teams composed of experts in hardware, embedded software, and verification. Guaranteeing that all stakeholders with different backgrounds have the same understanding of the critical aspects of the system development can be challenging. We model the behaviour of a railway motor controller using the Uppaal model checker [8], in the context of the European project VALU3S (https://valu3s.eu). This paper reports on how we integrate and automate the formal verification of this controller during its development by the rail manufacturer Alstom, while improving the trade-off between fine-grained details in the formal models and its verifiability, and efficiently involving all team members in this process.

Our use-case uses a controller with software components that interact with a dashboard and a circuit board (Fig. 1). Intermediate components are used to poll the circuit, to add and verify CRC error codes, etc. We compiled a set of safety requirements for the controller's software to be verified using model checking. However, when trying to build a network of automata to model the controller with enough details to cover all requirements, we concluded that it generated a state-space too large to be feasible when model-checking. For example, the requirement *"the controller component should take less than 100 ms to send a given command to the circuit"* should not need to consider all combinations of states involving the sending of messages to the dashboard. Similarly, the requirement *"if the controller component receives an error message it should go to a fallback state and the dashboard should be informed within 100 ms"* should not need to consider the mechanisms to interact with the circuit.

This lead to a family of formal models with different parameters and levels of detail, each targetting different requirements. This lead us to 3 challenges: **C1: maintain the model**, to kept it up-to-date with the system under development; **C2: manage variability**, as too many models with commonalities are needed; and **C3: improve the collaboration** between developers and modellers of the formal specifications.

Our approach uses a high-level representation of the configurations of the family of formal models for real-time systems. This representation consists of Microsoft Excel spreadsheets with parameters and requirements to be used in the formal models, read by our prototype tool *Uppex* that automatically generates and verifies the full family of models and requirements. These spreadsheets include, for example, the time-bounds of certain components, the size of buffers, and the initial values of certain variables. Furthermore, these values vary according to the set of active *features*; for example, by activating a feature named *SelfTesting*, a variable named TSelfTest is set to 200, otherwise it is set to 0. A special table compiles a set of *configurations*, each listing its active features. For example, a given configuration could activate *SelfTesting*, deactivate unrelated monitoring features, and activate its associated requirements.

Organisation of the Paper. Section 2 describes the motor controller use-case and its requirements, formalised in Sect. 3 using the Uppaal model checker. Section 4 describes how we configure and verify many variations of a Uppaal model. Section 5 summarises what we have learned during this process and the plans for future developments, and Sect. 6 concludes this paper.

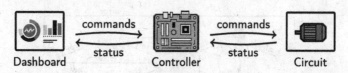

Fig. 1. Architecture of the motor controller system under verification

2   Use-Case: Motor Controller

Our running use-case consists of a motor controller, or controller for short, running in a resource constraint device with a Real Time OS. This controller is connected both to a physical circuit and to a dashboard, as depicted in Fig. 1. The circuit includes a DC motor that is being controlled, receives simple commands from the controller to turn left, turn right, or to stop, and sends back a status report, including the information of whether the limit of a rotation has been reached or if a problem has been found. The dashboard sends instructions to the controller, including commands to be sent to the circuit, which in turn informs the dashboard of internal state updates.

We focus on the behaviour of the software part of the controller, and on its formal verification via model-checking of timed-behaviour. This is complementary to other analysis and tests performed by other stakeholders involved in the same use-case, e.g., to inject faults in hardware and to generate batches of tests with enough coverage. We expect our underlying formalizations and tools to also benefit, directly or after repurposed, the other stakeholders in this use-case.

This paper includes behavioural details only of the core controller component, and the full Uppaal models are not publicly available since they are intellectual property of Alstom.[1] We believe that these descriptions, supported by our open-source prototype tool, are rich enough to convey our approach and its benefits.

Safety-Critical Behaviour. Hazard analysis for the controller has been performed to justify the desired criticality levels. This analysis guided the architecture of the software components deployed on the controller board. Most components are replicated and executed in two diversified processing units available in the selected board, to detect when their behaviour diverges. Also, CRC codes are applied to incoming and outgoing packages to ensure message consistency.

The replicated components are: a core controller, a monitor to check if the state of the controllers are consistent, a decoder to compare incoming messages against their CRC error code and against the messages from the neighbour decoder, a buffer to store messages to be sent to the dashboard, an encoder to add CRC codes to messages to be sent to the dashboard, and a reader of messages received from the circuit. Non-replicated components are: a scheduler to start runtime self-tests, a simulator of the dashboard, a simulator of the circuit, and a fault-injector to cause some components to fail. The simulators exist only on the formal models, to mimic the environment, while capturing the

---

[1] These can be made available to the reviewers if needed.

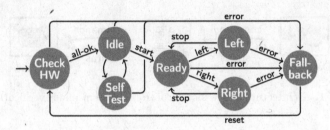

Fig. 2. General behaviour of the controller component

minimum information required to perform formal analysis, represented as pre-defined sequences of messages to be sent.

The behaviour of the core controller task is depicted in Fig. 2. The controller performs some initialisation in Check-HW, tests the interaction with the circuit in Self-Test, and can trigger the rotation of the motor to the left or to the right. At any moment, it can receive an error and go to a Fall-back state.

Parameterised Requirements. Following the hazard analysis, we compiled a set of requirements to be verified using model checking based on Uppaal. The most relevant ones are listed in Table 1. Requirements follow some syntactic structure to tighten the gap between formal and informal requirements, following the EARS approach [17]. For example, the 3rd requirement reads *"In Conf$_3$, **when** controller$_1$ fails **the** controller$_2$ **shall** go to a fallback state within 100 ms."* Configurations specify the parameters of the model when validating the requirement. This covers both general parameters of the system, such as the time to decode messages and the frequency of operation of monitors, and the scenario consisting of the messages sent by the dashboard, by the circuit, and by the fault-injector. In our example Conf$_3$ defines a scenario where the dashboard sends a start and a left command after 20 ms and 100 ms, respectively, and the fault-injector causes controller$_1$ to fail after 120 ms.

Table 1. Some functional and non-functional requirements for the motor controller

		State	Trigger	Comp.		Expected
In	Conf$_1$	controller$_1$ is ready	decoder receives a left command	controller$_1$	the	send a left command within 100ms
	Conf$_2$		monitor$_1$ or reader$_1$ fail	controller$_2$		go to a fallback state within 100ms
	Conf$_3$	while	controller$_1$ fails	controller$_2$	shall	go to a fallback state within 100ms
	Conf$_4$		controller$_1$ receives an error message	controller$_1$		send immediately a stop command to the circuit
	Conf$_4$		controller$_1$ receives an error message	encoder$_1$		notify the dashboard within 100ms
	Conf$_5$	dashboard can send messages		full system		never get stuck

When formalising requirements (c.f. Table 1) using the temporal logic supported by Uppaal, the notions of *state*, *component*, and *expected observation* followed in a relatively straightforward manner. Specifying the *triggers* often required manually enriching the model with new variables, since the logic does not express events. Specifying *configurations* were the most complex operations, and the core challenge addressed by this paper and our prototype tool. Traditionally for each configuration a new model would have to be specified, fine-tuning values of variables spread throughout the model, often deactivating some components to simplify the model-checking of more complex properties. Maintaining a collection of such models, in a context where neither the system specification nor the full set of requirements are fixed, quickly becomes infeasible. We provide support to specify all configurations and properties in a single Excel file, and to automatically use these with a single annotated Uppaal model.

3 Formal Specification in Uppaal

Uppaal [8] is a well-known model-checker for real-time systems, successfully used in many industrial applications and in the context of embedded systems [5]. Systems are specified as a set of timed-automata that interact both by using synchronisation on actions and by using shared variables. In a nutshell, each timed-automaton is a state machine whose edges are labelled by a guard and an update over shared variables, and by an optional action name used to synchronise with neighbour automata. Special variables named clocks capture the time that has passed since they were last reset, and are incremented automatically by the rules that guide the automata evolution.

The topology of the timed automata network used in the specification of our use-case is depicted in Fig. 3, one for each task mentioned in Sect. 2. This topology is built iteratively by both developers and formal modellers, during the development of the system. Each node depicts the timed-automaton of a component, and arrows depict interactions between nodes: $\longrightarrow$ denote synchronous interactions that block until both automata can trigger the associated action; $--\rightarrow$ and $\cdots\rightarrow$ denote synchronous interactions that do not block the sender – the former requires the receiver to be always ready and the latter discards data if the receiver is not ready; and $\Longrightarrow$ denotes asynchronous communication by atomic writes and reads to a shared variable.

The dashboard, circuit, and fault-injector components are parameterised by a scenario, i.e., a sequence of actions with timestamps. The dashboard sends commands to the encoders, the circuit sends reports to the readers describing if there are errors and if the motor reached a limit, and the fault-injector sends messages that cause some components to go to a faulty state with no behaviour. Furthermore, the circuit reports errors for a predefined time-window during the self-test phase, and the controllers validate that an error is indeed reported.

The behaviour of the components involved is expressed using Uppaal's notion of timed automata. We depict the automata of the controller's behaviour in Fig. 4. All the 5 states of Fig. 2 appear in this automata, extended with extra

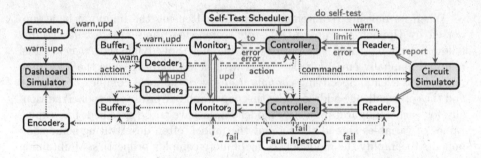

Fig. 3. Topology of the network of communicating timed-automata of the use-case

details. The arrows pointing to and from the Controllers in Fig. 3 appear in this diagram either as channels in the labels, represented by names prefixed with '?' or '!', or as shared variables such as limit, which is read to detect if the motor reached its target position. The non-blocking behaviour of the error and fail channels is captured by including an extra transition labelled by this channel in every node where time can pass.

Uppaal supports imperative code using a C-like language inside a global *Declarations* block, accessible by all automata in the network. These variables and functions can be used by the expressions in the timed-automata. For example, the concrete actions (e.g., goLeft), time-bounds ((e.g., TLeft[id][max])), shared variables (e.g., limit), and channel names (e.g., action) are declared in this block.

4   Parameterisation and Verification with Uppex

In order to cope with the multiple configurations of Uppaal's models, we developed **Uppex** to provide a mechanism based on annotations to customise many aspects, including channels, shared variables, data types, time-bounds, and requirements. Uppex is an open-source tool that uses the workflow depicted in Fig. 5: it reads both an Excel file with the configurations and an Uppaal file with annotations, and it creates a new Uppaal model for each configuration found. Either one of the new models is used to replace the original Uppaal file, or they are verified by Uppaal and a report is produced. Uppex is developed in Scala, uses the Apache POI libraries for Microsoft documents [13], and is available at https://cister-labs.github.io/uppex.

4.1   Annotating Uppaal Models

Declarations in the input Uppaal model are annotated with special blocks starting with "// @Name", which act as hooks that Uppex uses to inject and update the values that configure the model. XML blocks from "<Name>" until "</Name>" also act as hooks for annotations, which we use to inject and update the properties being verified in the <queries> block. We call these *@-annotations* and *xml-annotations*, respectively.

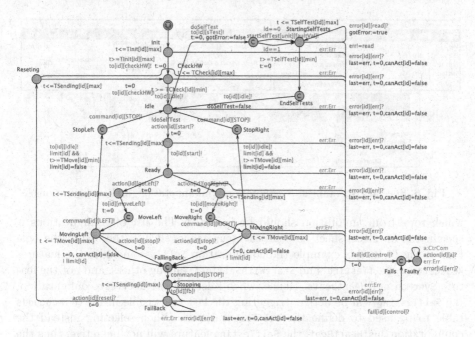

Fig. 4. Specification in Uppaal of the a controllers' timed-automata with identifier `id`

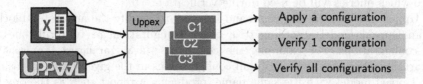

Fig. 5. Uppex workflow: updating and verifying models based on configuration tables

Each annotation can be defined in the Excel file in a sheet named with the same name (c.f. Fig. 6). The first line of these sheets describe the pattern used to produce code that will be injected for each line of the table, followed by a table with a *header* of names in row 2 and their values below. E.g., in the `@TimeBounds` table (Fig. 6), row 4 injects the line "`const int TCheck[Ids][Intrv] = {{4,4},{6,6}};...`" to the Uppaal code in the corresponding block. The first column acts as unique identifier: if multiple lines are found, the last one prevails. The column named `Features` associates feature names that must be *active*, otherwise the line is discarded. In our example, when the feature `SelfTesting` is active the variable for `SelfTest` is set to 200, otherwise it is set to 0. The `<queries>` table on the top-left of Fig. 6 depicts some of the requirements from Table 1.

4.2 Verifying Multiple Configurations

Using Uppex it is possible to specify a list of *configurations*, each regarded as a set of features that can be active or not. These feature selection guides

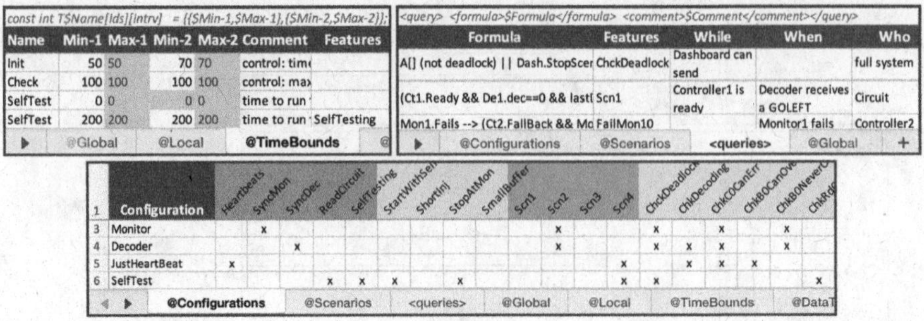

Fig. 6. Special Excel tables: @-annotation, xml-annotation, and configurations

which rows from annotation should be included. The list of configurations is specified in an Excel sheet named @Configurations, such as the one in the bottom of Fig. 6. In this example the configuration SelfTest includes the features ReadCircuit, SelfTesting, and StartWithSelfTest, among others, and not the feature SyncMon nor Heartbeats. Hence, when selecting the SelfTest configuration, the SelfTesting will be active, triggering the last row visible in the @TimeBounds table to be used to define the SelfTest variable. When selecting instead the configuration JustHeartBeat, the SelfTesting feature will not be active, thus the previous row will be used instead. Similarly, the selected features will also influence which queries will be used during verification.

Uppex can be used as a command line tool to modify the annotated blocks of an Uppaal model according to a given configuration, or to verify one or all configurations. For example, the command "java -jar uppex.jar -runAll motorController.xlsx" will verify all configurations in the given Excel file using the Uppaal model with the same name, producing a report such as the one in Table 2. This report states that 3 properties of configuration SelfTest passed and the verification timed-out while verifying the 4th property. This property would pass using a slighly larger timeout when calling Uppex. We write ellipsis '...' to omit parts of the report. Configurations Monitor and JustHeartBeat also passed and failed some properties.

Table 2. Report produced when verifying all properties and all configurations

```
> Reading Uppaal file 'motorController.xml'

--Verifying 'SelfTest'--

[OK] @SelfTest: the Controller1 shall be able to
     start the self-tests.

[OK] @ChkSelfTest1: when Self-test ends, the Reader
     shall have received some error.

[OK] @ChckDeadlock: while Dashboard can send
     messages, the full system shall not deadlock.

| Time-out. Missing 1 properties.
| Failed on property:
| "@SelfTest, StartWithSelfTest: the Controller1
     shall be able to end the self-tests."

--Verifying 'Monitor'--

[OK] @SyncMon: the Monitor1 shall be able
     to send a warning.

[OK] @ChkB0NeverOverflows: the Buffer1
     shall never overflow.
...

--Verifying 'JustHeartBeat'--

[OK] @ChkDecoding: the Decoder1 shall be
     able to send a warning.

[FAIL] @ChkB0NeverOverflows: the Buffer1
     shall never overflow.
...
```

5   Lessons Learned and Future Work

During the development of the motor controller system at Alstom in collaboration with ISEP and other academic partners, we iterated over core design architectural decisions and agreed upon different synchronisation mechanisms. Using the model-checking capabilities of Uppaal, we verified different properties, including the possibility of sending warnings, of buffer overflows, and of reaching deadlocks (or timelocks). These models are useful both to predict possible problems and bottlenecks, and to be used in certification processes. Our configuration-driven approach using Excel spreadsheets emerged as a solution to the growth in complexity of the underlying formal models, which typically must remain simple in order to be useful. We were able to find time-bounds that satisfy our requirements, e.g., the periodicity at which monitors and decoders check consistency, or the periodicity at which reports should be polled from the circuit, under different scenarios simulated by the dashboard.

Uppex adds a negligible overhead over the model-checking process, involving the parsing of the configuration tables and the Uppaal file, and the writing of an updated set of Uppaal files. In our use-case we use the 16 automata from Fig. 1 in a file with ~1.7K lines excluding queries. Our tables currently include around 25 requirements, 15 configurations, and 135 different entries (including scenarios, time parameters, data channels, and data constructors). Invoking Java to produce a concrete instance takes less than 5 s in our 1.4 GHz Quad-Core Intel Core i5 machine.

Related Work. The verification of complex embedded systems has been investigated, e.g., by Basten et al. [3] who generate Uppaal models (and Petri net models) using a model-driven approach with the Octopus toolset, focusing on design-space exploration and schedule optimisation. Gario et al. [14] and Dureja and Rozier [9] provide an exhaustive analysis of a large air traffic control, in a joint effort with NASA team of engineers, using 3 concrete models specified in the OCRA architectural language with SMV component models. They validate the 3 models using a combination of different techniques based on the property at hand, and analyse dependencies among properties to avoid the verification of unnecessary queries. In contrast to these approaches, Uppex allows the manual definition and fine-tuning of models in the host model-checker instead of using generated models, and provides mechanisms to control the variability of the models in a way that can be perceived by both tool- and formal-developers.

The variability in Uppex is given as a set of tables that inject code in the annotated specifications, but it is not reasoned upon. Other approaches, such as the formal framework by Kim et al. [16] in the context of embedded systems, can be used to analyse valid configurations based on feature models [4].

Future Work. We are pursuing the following two directions of work.

1. Valid Configurations. Currently one can specify any combination of features, sometimes leading to incorrect configurations because of missing dependencies or incompatibilities. These restrictions can be captured by a set of constraints, usually taking the form of a Feature Model [4] in the context of Software Product Lines. One could, for example, make the feature StartWithSelfTest dependent on SelfTesting, marking any configuration with only the first one as invalid. Following existing work in this community, we could further exploit these validity constraints over features, e.g., by considering all configurations that satisfy these constraints, or to aim at finding the *best* configuration using some cost function. In the context of this work, the properties validated by Uppaal could also play a role in the validity of a configuration.

2. Other Backends. Our work targets Uppaal models using a frontend for developers based on Excel spreadsheets. However, these tables can also be used with different backends besides Uppaal. For example, to generate configuration files used in the implementation, or to use a different model-checker for verification, such as Imitator [2] for real-time systems, which supports the optimisation of some parameters, or mCRL2 [6] that supports a temporal logic over events and can handle very large state-spaces. We are also working on an intermediate domain specific language that can generate Uppaal models, among other analysis, with a better support to reason over the architectural topology, such as the one in Fig. 3, which emerges only implicitly in Uppaal.

Uppaal is free to use only for non-commercial purposes. It is currently being used by academic partners, and our use-case is not being commercialised and is representative of other ongoing projects. This work may lead to the adoption of Uppaal in commercial projects of Alstom, or to a different backend supported by Uppex.

6   Conclusions

This paper presents our approach to formalise the timed-behaviour in Uppaal of a motor controller system, under development by the Alstom railway company, in the context of the VALU3S European project. We use parameterised configuration tables that adapt a core Uppaal model, facilitating the customisation of the model so it can better suit different requirements. This paper also describes how we integrated the usage of model-checking within the development cycle of a safety-critical system, involving stakeholders with different background, relying on intelligible tables and architectural topologies. We produced a prototype open-source tool Uppex to automatise the extraction of parameters and adaptation of the formal models, and to verify many configurations on a single run. In the future we plan to further exploit the validity of configurations and to experiment with different backends.

Acknowledgments. This work was partially supported by National Funds through FCT/MCTES (Portuguese Foundation for Science and Technology), within the CIS-

TER Research Unit (UID/CEC/04234); also by the Norte Portugal Regional Operational Programme (NORTE 2020) under the Portugal 2020 Partnership Agreement, through the European Regional Development Fund (ERDF) and also by national funds through the FCT, within project NORTE-01-0145-FEDER-028550 (REASSURE); also by COMPETE 2020 under the PT2020 Partnership Agreement, through ERDF, and by national funds through the FCT, within project POCI-01-0145-FEDER-029946 (DaVinci); also by FCT within project ECSEL/0016/2019 and from the ECSEL Joint Undertaking (JU) under grant agreement No. 876852 (VALU3S). The JU receives support from the European Union's Horizon 2020 research and innovation programme and Austria, Czech Republic, Germany, Ireland, Italy, Portugal, Spain, Sweden, Turkey.

References

1. Abo, R., Voisin, L.: Formal implementation of data validation for railway safety-related systems with OVADO. In: Counsell, S., Núñez, M. (eds.) SEFM 2013. LNCS, vol. 8368, pp. 221–236. Springer, Cham (2014). https://doi.org/10.1007/978-3-319-05032-4_17
2. André, É.: IMITATOR 3: synthesis of timing parameters beyond decidability. In: Silva, A., Leino, K.R.M. (eds.) CAV 2021. LNCS, vol. 12759, pp. 552–565. Springer, Cham (2021). https://doi.org/10.1007/978-3-030-81685-8_26
3. Basten, T., et al.: Model-driven design-space exploration for embedded systems: the octopus toolset. In: Margaria, T., Steffen, B. (eds.) ISoLA 2010. LNCS, vol. 6415, pp. 90–105. Springer, Heidelberg (2010). https://doi.org/10.1007/978-3-642-16558-0_10
4. Benavides, D., Segura, S., Ruiz Cortés, A.: Automated analysis of feature models 20 years later: a literature review. Inf. Syst. **35**(6), 615–636 (2010)
5. Bourke, T., Sowmya, A.: Automatically transforming and relating Uppaal models of embedded systems. In: de Alfaro, L., Palsberg, J. (eds.) EMSOFT 2008, pp. 59–68. ACM (2008)
6. Bunte, O., et al.: The mCRL2 toolset for analysing concurrent systems. In: Vojnar, T., Zhang, L. (eds.) TACAS 2019. LNCS, vol. 11428, pp. 21–39. Springer, Cham (2019). https://doi.org/10.1007/978-3-030-17465-1_2
7. Comptier, M., Leuschel, M., Mejia, L.-F., Perez, J.M., Mutz, M.: Property-based modelling and validation of a CBTC zone controller in Event-B. In: Collart-Dutilleul, S., Lecomte, T., Romanovsky, A. (eds.) RSSRail 2019. LNCS, vol. 11495, pp. 202–212. Springer, Cham (2019). https://doi.org/10.1007/978-3-030-18744-6_13
8. David, A., Larsen, K.G., Legay, A., Mikučionis, M., Poulsen, D.B.: Uppaal SMC tutorial. STTT **17**(4), 397–415 (2015)
9. Dureja, R., Rozier, K.Y.: More scalable LTL model checking via discovering design-space dependencies (D^3). In: Beyer, D., Huisman, M. (eds.) TACAS 2018. LNCS, vol. 10805, pp. 309–327. Springer, Cham (2018). https://doi.org/10.1007/978-3-319-89960-2_17
10. Railway Applications. The Specification and Demonstration of Reliability, Availability, Maintainability and Safety (RAMS). Generic RAMS Process. Standard (N), CENELEC, December 2017
11. Railway applications. Communication, signalling and processing systems - Software for railway control and protection systems. Standard (N), CENELEC, July 2020
12. Railway applications. Communication, signalling and processing systems. Safety related electronic systems for signalling. Standard (N), CENELEC, November 2018

13. Apache Software Foundation. Apache POI - the Java API for Microsoft documents (2021). https://poi.apache.org. Accessed 30 Nov 2021

14. Gario, M., Cimatti, A., Mattarei, C., Tonetta, S., Rozier, K.Y.: Model checking at scale: automated air traffic control design space exploration. In: Chaudhuri, S., Farzan, A. (eds.) CAV 2016. LNCS, vol. 9780, pp. 3–22. Springer, Cham (2016). https://doi.org/10.1007/978-3-319-41540-6_1

15. Kästner, D., Ferdinand, C.: Applying abstract interpretation to verify EN-50128 software safety requirements. In: Lecomte, T., Pinger, R., Romanovsky, A. (eds.) RSSRail 2016. LNCS, vol. 9707, pp. 191–202. Springer, Cham (2016). https://doi.org/10.1007/978-3-319-33951-1_14

16. Kim, J.H., Legay, A., Traonouez, L.-M., Acher, M., Kang, S.: A formal modeling and analysis framework for software product line of preemptive real-time systems. In: Ossowski, S. (ed.) SAC 2016, pp. 1562–1565. ACM (2016)

17. Mavin, A., Wilkinson, P., Harwood, A., Novak, M.: Easy approach to requirements syntax (EARS). In: RE 2009, pp. 317–322. IEEE Computer Society (2009)

Learning to Learn HVAC Failures: Layering ML Experiments in the Absence of Ground Truth

Carlos E. Budde[1]([✉])(iD), Duncan Jansen[2], Inka Locht[3], and Mariëlle Stoelinga[2,4](iD)

[1] University of Trento, Trento, Italy
carlosesteban.budde@unitn.it
[2] University of Twente, Enschede, The Netherlands
[3] Dutch Railways (NS), Utrecht, The Netherlands
[4] Radboud University, Nijmegen, The Netherlands

Abstract. Passenger comfort systems such as Heating, Ventilation, and Air-Conditioning units (HVACs) usually lack the data monitoring quality enjoyed by mission-critical systems in trains. But climate change, in addition to the high ventilation standards enforced by authorities due to the COVID pandemic, have increased the importance of HVACs worldwide. We propose a machine learning (ML) approach to the challenge of failure detection from incomplete data, consisting of two steps: 1. human-annotation bootstrapping, on a fraction of temperature data, to detect ongoing functional loss and build an artificial ground truth (AGT); 2. failure prediction from digital-data, using the AGT to train an ML model based on failure diagnose codes to foretell functional loss. We exercise our approach in trains of Dutch Railways, showing its implementation, ML-predictive capabilities (the ML model for the AGT can detect HVAC malfunctions online), limitations (we could not foretell failures from our digital data), and discussing its application to other assets.

1 Introduction

Heating, Ventilation, and Air-Conditioning units (HVACs) are in charge of air circulation, filtering, heating, and cooling, not only in smart buildings and houses but also in every modern transport system, including trains [5]. At the same time, HVACs traditionally lack the data monitoring quality enjoyed by mission-critical systems, such as air-compressors for break release [8]. Moreover, climate change and higher ventilation standards—enforced by authorities to mitigate airborne diseases—have put HVACs in the foreground [5]. In this scenario where uninterrupted HVAC operation becomes essential, detecting their (even partial) malfunctions rapidly gains on importance. However, the need to automate failure detection is at odds with the reality of sub-optimal data coverage.

This work was partially funded by EU grants 830929 (H2020-CyberSec4Europe), and 952647 (H2020-AssureMOSS), and NWO grant NWA.1160.18.238 (PrimaVera).

© Springer Nature Switzerland AG 2022
S. Collart-Dutilleul et al. (Eds.): RSSRail 2022, LNCS 13294, pp. 95–111, 2022.
https://doi.org/10.1007/978-3-031-05814-1_7

As a result, HVAC malfunctions can remain unnoticed for long time periods. This occurs even with sensorially noticeable functions, provided they are not used to perceptible levels. Consider a gas compressor used for cooling, damaged during autumn, whose failure is noticed in summer when it is needed the most.

Silent failures are not rare: Dutch Railways (NS) handles hundreds of service requests for HVACs in trains, precisely in the first months of the year with temperatures above 25 °C. Periodic maintenance is the traditional mitigation technique for such cases, adjusted for the application domain via field-data studies [4,11]. More modern approaches use physical, failure, and Machine Learning (ML) models to implement predictive- or condition-based maintenance [2,3,10].

Whichever the underlying model, an ideal failure-prevention system would deploy self-diagnosis fed by live data streams, that notify a control unit as soon as threats are detected. Unfortunately this is overall unrealistic because (a) the shelf life of HVACs can surpass 15 years, so many units used today were manufactured even before the Internet of Things began; (b) in any case it is not possible to detect, let alone diagnose every subcomponent and its possible failure causes.

In this scenario, *ML can provide smart solutions that build up to a business case with current assets* [1]. This involves processing large amounts of data, searching for patterns correlated to functional loss. However, *this is hindered by suboptimal data collection, specially if no ground truth is available*, namely when confirmed HVAC failures are not part of the input data.

In this work we propose a simple yet effective supervised ML solution to this pressing challenge, tested in industry and consisting of two steps:

1. human-annotation bootstrapping, to detect functional loss on a fraction of in-coach temperature readings, used to build an ML model capable of creating an artificial ground truth (AGT) for the entire dataset;
2. digital-data failure prediction, that uses the AGT to train an ML model based on failure diagnose codes, and can be used to foretell functional loss.

We define our approach for both steps, including ML features and data pre-processing, applied to generic train coaches with two HVACs each. The outcome of step 1 is a linear and lightweight ML model, pivotal in the construction of the AGT, that extrapolates a minimal human-annotated input. A by-product of such interface between steps 1 and 2 is a software program, that can detect HVAC functional failure online based on temperature readings. Then step 2 uses an independent (digital) dataset—of HVAC components diagnostics—to train another ML model on the AGT. We aim to find patterns in the digital data that can be correlated to later functional loss, thus revealing HVAC silent failures.

1.1 Scientific Approach with Practical Applications

Setting and Challenges. *The general goal is to detect and if possible foretell functional failures of HVACs in trains, when there is no ground truth to mark such failures.* By functional failure we mean that a specific function does not perform as needed, e.g. an HVAC should cool down the interior of a coach, but the temperature remains above the one desired. This goal is particularly challenging given our choice of a data-driven approach: detection and prediction must be solely based on a company's data stream[1]. Here, *the historical information available for each HVAC are temperature readings and subcomponent diagnose codes.* Both are time series: the former has continuous data; the latter digital data, i.e. a diagnose code in an HVAC (e.g. "high pressure in valve V_{A2}" or "no power in compressor") is either ON or OFF at each point in time.

We define our ML approach in Sects. 2 and 3, demonstrating its applicability in Sects. 2.3 and 3.3 by means of a study on the rolling stock of NS. Thus we showcase our work in a real-world scenario, and stress-tests the ML paradigm in a situation with high-volume but low-information data. Furthermore, the study with NS shows that our approach can be implemented in large-stock companies (with standard data streams) by a team of 2–4 computer-technical personnel.

Concrete Objectives:

(O1) Build an ML model, whose input are the historical temperature readings of all HVACs in a train, that estimates the probability of cooling malfunction of each such HVAC currently in operation.

(O2) Build an ML model, whose input are the diagnose codes of an HVAC in operation, that estimates its probability of having a cooling malfunction.

(O3) Extrapolate objective O2 forward in the time series, to estimate the probability of malfunction before the next scheduled periodic maintenance.

We focus on cooling malfunctions as these are more critical for passenger comfort (the temperature in a coach raises with more people) and they are more abundant in our datasets than heating malfunctions. In objective O3 we use the diagnose codes for prediction, and not the temperature readings, because this dataset is richer (an HVAC has several components, each with possibly more than one code) and we expect it to be more likely to show patterns that can be correlated to silent failures. In contrast, patterns occurring in the temperature readings are susceptible to be sensed by train personnel, thus not leading to silent failures.

ML Models. The proposed approach involves two supervised ML models, the second built on top of the results of the first, keeping explainability in mind.

- Supervision: Although default solutions in the absence of a ground truth point at unsupervised learning, our objectives involve classification and regression, which require labelled datasets for supervised learning. We label data manually to overcome this for objective O1: simple rules allow non-experts to detect too-high temperatures indicative of cooling failures. To make the process manageable we label small independent data subsets, then extrapolate to the whole time series, and cross-validate the results; full details are in Sect. 2.

- Layering: In contrast, non-experts cannot interpret how diagnose codes from subcomponents indicate functional HVAC failure. But these HVACs are the same units whose malfunctions were labelled for the temperature-based model. Thus we use the result of the process performed for the temperature-based model, as labelled dataset on which to train the diagnose-code-based model.

---

[1] Besides being COVID-friendly, this is less cost- and time-consuming (although arguably less flexible) than mechanical experiments by technicians and engineers.

- **Explainability:** On top of suitability and performance, we select ML techniques to reach our objectives with the highest amount of transparency. White-box approaches like this are key for the acceptance of data-based solutions, specially in industrial sectors such as railways where processes are traditionally expert-driven. Objective O1 uses temperature: this is linear data, which partly motivated our choice of a logistic regression (LR) solution. We use LR also for Objective O2 and O3, but this can only estimate the likelihood of malfunction of a set of diagnose codes. It is of additional interest to tell how each individual code contributes to that estimation: we use decision trees (DT) for this purpose.

Main Results. On the one hand, • *our LR model for objective O1 can detect HVAC failures in real-time.* On the other hand, • *we could not find evidence of correlation between our HVAC diagnose codes for objective O2 and O3, and HVAC cooling malfunctions.* As a further result, • *our data features (for all ML models) could be used to study other types of failures and systems.*

2   Learning HVAC Failures from Temperature Readings

To reach objective O1 we use the readings of temperature sensors inside train coaches to detect malfunctioning HVACs. This Sect. 2 introduces our steps for data preprocessing, and for manual data labelling, to bootstrap the entire work. We also define the features used for LR, and the training and testing steps. The Sect. 2 ends showing our empirical studies done in the trains of NS.

2.1   Data Preparation

Input. This step works on continuous-valued data, formatted as a time series of HVAC temperatures. So for each time point and for each HVAC, the input indicates the temperature inside of the coach that HVAC is responsible for.

Preprocessing. Temperature values outside the range $[-20\,°C, 60\,°C]$ are considered outliers, and replaced by NaN in data imputation. Moreover, data streams may have interruptions that appear as missing values in the time series, which must also be imputed or discarded. If the missing data spans for less than 90 min we use linear interpolation to fill the gap—this was always the case for our NS studies—; else we impute by filling with NaN.

Those two steps remove or replace values that will later be used for LR. In addition, the desired temperatures must be computed, since the LR model of this step will be trained on human-annotated data, which must be created by comparing in-coach (actual) temperatures to set (desired) temperatures.

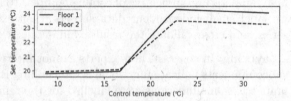

Fig. 1. In-coach temperature set by control temp.

More in detail, the automatic operation of an HVAC is typically regulated by a thermostat and a set of rules, that use a control temperature—e.g. from outside the train—to dictate the temperature desired in-coach: see Fig. 1. These so-called *set temperature values* are computed from the (time series of) control temperature values, using functions defined by the temperature-regulation rules.

Data Labelling. Supervised learning algorithms, such as LR, require labelled data. One contribution of this work is how to perform these studies on unlabelled data, i.e. when there is no ground truth indicating the moments in which an HVAC is malfunctioning. For that, we note that cooling failures can be spotted by (non-expert) human inspection, by comparing the desired and achieved temperatures inside of the train coaches. Thus we propose a bootstrapping process based on a manual labelling of 1–5% of the available data as follows.

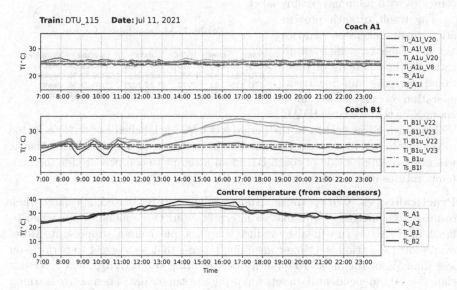

Fig. 2. Temperature plots used in the manual-labelling bootstrap process

Humans interpret images better and faster than numeric values, so the temperature time series should be plotted as in Fig. 2. In particular our plots show two values per HVAC because each coach has two decks, and an HVAC controls the temperature of both decks in one side of a coach. *For instance in coach A1, HVAC V20 controls the temperature of the lower and upper deck of the back side.*

These plots of internal temperatures must be time-aligned to the control temperatures, so it is visually straightforward to match high internal values with control values. Observing such high values suggests a cooling failure in the HVAC. *For instance in coach B1, the HVAC V23 shows such positive deviation.*

However, temperature deviations might also be explainable as data anomalies. If false positives are undesired (bringing trains to maintenance is costly) a conservative approach is suggested, where labels are applied iff other HVACs show correct performance during the same time period than the offending unit. *For instance in Fig. 2, this is the case for V23 in coach B1 after 15:00. But from 7:00 to 12:00 both V23 and V22 exhibit oscillatory values that are less easy to interpret as a malfunction, and thus we omit labelling that time period.*

Also periods of HVAC correct operation must be labelled, so the model learns to tell them apart from potential silent failures. *This is the case of both HVACs in coach A1, that keep the temperature at their set values despite the high control temperatures.* Thus in our case, a **true positive** is when the ML model tells an HVAC is failing, and this coincides with a human hot label. Instead, a **true negative** is when the ML model tells an HVAC is operating correctly, and this coincides with a human healthy label.

The result of such process are human-generated entries as in Table 1, which indicate the time periods of functional correct- and incorrect-operation of an HVAC in a train. Note that we label HVAC

Table 1. Manual labels for Fig. 2

train	coach	HVAC	date	period	symptom
DTU_115	A1	V20	11.07.2021	07:00-23:50	healthy
DTU_115	A1	V8	11.07.2021	07:00-23:50	healthy
DTU_115	B1	V22	11.07.2021	15:00-23:50	healthy
DTU_115	B1	V23	11.07.2021	15:00-23:50	hot

V22 in coach B1 as healthy in the period when V23 is labelled as hot. This is due to the low temperatures observed for V22 in that time period, indicating that it was over-cooling its side of coach B1, in an attempt to compensate for the high temperatures on the other side.

Practicality vs. Correctness. Human labels can be biased, specially when coming from images susceptible to interpretation. Our guidelines on when to label an HVAC as (un-)healthy reduce this bias, but cannot suppress it. Moreover, plots inspection is a time-consuming process that we suggest to perform on less than 5% of the data. To quantify the resulting subjectivity, $N > 1$ persons should label independent data sets following the same rules. Then active learning can be used to compute the inter-rater reliability: create training data from the sets labelled by e.g. $\lfloor \frac{N}{2} \rfloor$ persons, and then validate the data of the rest [9]. This allows using metrics such as the area under the receiver operating characteristics curve, to validate whether the different and independent manual labellings are consistent. A concrete example of such procedure is shown in Sect. 2.3.

2.2   Machine Learning Experiment

Our feature engineering process defines four data features to perform LR for objective O1. If data volume is too large because the frequency of the time series is high, e.g. a data point per second, the averages of a rolling window can be used. This involves defining the window size and the step used to discretise the time series. We do this to define four features over a rolling window of N steps.

Set Point (SP). This feature compares the coach temperature to the set temperature. More specifically, $SP_{c,v,d}$ is the average of the differences between the in-coach temperature on deck d of coach c in the side corresponding to HVAC v $\left(TI_i^{c,d,v}\right)$, and the desired (set) temperature on that deck of the coach $\left(TS_i^{c,d}\right)$, for each time step i in a rolling window of N steps. We use c to indicate both a coach and its train. We also define a feature $\overline{SP}_{c,d,v}$ that compares $TS_i^{c,d}$ to the temperature kept by the HVAC $\overline{v}$ that is on the opposite side of v in coach c (this feature is omitted for coaches with a single HVAC):

$$SP_{c,d,v} = \frac{1}{N} \sum_{i=1}^{N} TI_i^{c,d,v} - TS_i^{c,d} \qquad \overline{SP}_{c,d,v} = \frac{1}{N} \sum_{i=1}^{N} TI_i^{c,d,\overline{v}} - TS_i^{c,d}.$$

The sign of SP is informative: for cooling malfunctions only positive values are relevant. The magnitude of the difference should be positively correlated to the (cooling) malfunction probability. Similarly, the magnitude and sign of $\overline{SP}$ are related to possible compensations of HVAC v for failures in $\overline{v}$.

Compensation Behaviour (CB). This feature is a specialisation of $\overline{SP}$, that compares directly the temperature on opposite sides of a coach. $CB_{c,d,v}$ is the difference between the in-coach temperature of HVAC v and of $\overline{v}$, telling the degree to which v must compensate for the possible lack of cooling of $\overline{v}$:

$$CB_{c,d,v} = \frac{1}{N} \sum_{i=1}^{N} TI_i^{c,d,v} - TI_i^{c,d,\overline{v}}.$$

Comparison to Other Coaches (COC). The set-point temperatures among all coaches in a train should be almost equal. $COC_{c,v}$ compares the average temperature on both decks of a coach $TI_i^{c,v} = \frac{1}{2}\left(TI_i^{c,1,v} + TI_i^{c,2,v}\right)$ against the corresponding median over all other coaches:

$$COC_{c,v} = \frac{1}{N} \sum_{i=1}^{N} TI_i^{c,v} - \underset{c' \neq c}{\mathrm{median}}\left(TI_i^{c',v}\right).$$

This helps to spot inactivity: if the train is in standby, the HVACs could be inactive and let temperatures raise, but this should happen in all coaches similarly.

Defective Control Sensor (DCS). This feature tries to determine whether the control sensors in a coach are defective, which would result in an incorrect set temperature value. DCS_c compares the temperature measured by the sensor TC^c of coach c against the median over all other coaches:

$$DCS_c = \frac{1}{N} \sum_{i=1}^{N} TC_i^c - \underset{c' \neq c}{\mathrm{median}}\left(TC_i^{c'}\right).$$

ML Model. These features can be used to train a Logistic Regression classifier. We choose LR over other ML solutions because temperature data is unidimensional, so a linear classifier should suffice to divide HVAC malfunctions from their normal operation. Indeed, linear models can be high-accuracy detectors of HVAC availability [3,10]. Furthermore LR is known to be computationally fast, resistant against overfitting, and it can produce probabilistic values (indicating failure likelihood), as opposed to a binary output (defective/healthy).

After training and assessing this ML model, the features and permutation importance can be extracted, to determine which features contribute the most to the generalisation power of the model. As minimal-detection boundary a *random binary feature* can be introduced, which contains no information and hence no detection power. Computing the importance of this random feature helps to understand the relative importance of the other features.

2.3 Study on Rolling Stock of NS

We used the approach defined above to detect HVAC failures in the historic data for 2 months of operation (in summer) of 176 double-deck trains of NS.

Data. A sample in this experiment is a 1 h window corresponding to one HVAC, for which all features were computed. The time step was 30 min. The resulting class distribution had an imbalance of ratio 5:1 in favour of the healthy-label class, which we balanced via class weights as is common practice [7].

Assessment. The performance of the resulting LR classifier was measured via the Receiver Operating Curve (ROC), summarised with the area under the ROC (AUC); and also with the Precision Recall Curve (PRC), summarised with the average precision score (PRS). For this we used a 4-repeated stratified 4-folded cross validator [6]; we also grouped samples per HVAC, to avoid comparisons of temperature readings (human-labelled vs. ML-predicted) across different units. For stratification we added an indicator of whether the groups contain samples of the hot or healthy class, with the resulting distribution 17 (hot) vs. 71.

Main Result. Figure 3 shows how the data samples are automatically labelled by the resulting LR model. The probability of cooling failure of either of the HVACs in a coach is indicated by the value of the colour on a bar below the temperature lines: darker red indicates higher malfunction probability.

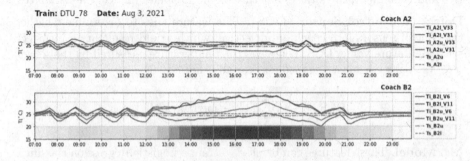

Fig. 3. Detection of HVAC malfunctions by LR model from temperature readings

Model Performance. Figure 4a and 4b show respectively the ROC and PRC for this model. The dashed green lines are the ROC (and PRC) for the splits on either the test or train data; the solid blue line is their mean. The AUC of the ROC is 1.00 on average for both test and train sets, *denoting an approximately perfect score of the LR model, to detect both healthy and malfunctioning HVACs.* The PRC points in the same direction, with PRS values of 1.00 and 0.99 on average resp. for the train and test sets, which further indicates that *the model is not overfitting on the training data.*

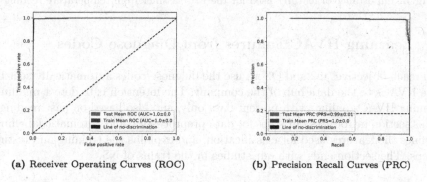

(a) Receiver Operating Curves (ROC)   (b) Precision Recall Curves (PRC)

Fig. 4. Performance of the LR classifier from temperature readings

Inter-rater Reliability Performance. We also computed the ROC and PRC to validate the human-labelled sets as indicated in Sect. 2.1. There were 191 samples (1% of the data available) distributed randomly and labelled independently by two authors of this work. The resulting AUC and PRS values were 0.99 on average for both cases, again denoting an excellent classification and a *negligible bias in the bootstrapping used as artificial ground truth.*

Feature Importance. Figure 5 shows the features and permutation importance of the LR model. The average feature importance (across all splits) is visualized with horizontal light-blue bars; the blue whiskers are their 95% confidence intervals. Figure 5 shows that features COC1 (Comparison to Other Coaches) and CB2 (Compensation Behaviour for the upper deck) are consistently ranked as the most predictive features, in that order. In contrast, DOS1 (Defect Control Sensor), SP3, and SP4 (Set Point for the complementary sides of the coaches), are the least useful features. Furthermore, the ranks for train and test sets in the permutation tests are equal, indicating that the model is not overfitting; and only features with very similar importance change among ranks.

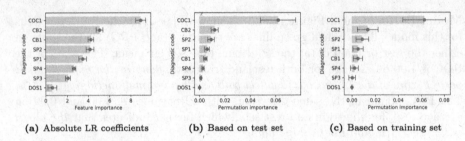

(a) Absolute LR coefficients   (b) Based on test set   (c) Based on training set

Fig. 5. Importance of features used for the LR classifier from temperature readings

3   Learning HVAC Failures from Diagnose Codes

To reach objectives O2 and O3 we use the diagnose codes automatically sent by the HVACs to the data hub of the company. The intention is to detect malfunctioning HVACs online: with present data only, and also based on past readings. This section introduces our steps for data preprocessing and automatic labelling, defines the features used for classification, and explains the training and testing steps. The section ends with our studies in the trains of NS.

3.1   Data Preparation

Input. This is digital data: a diagnose code (e.g. "high pressure in valve V_{A2}") identifies an event triggered by an HVAC component, including its activation and deactivation time, e.g. $x = (id : 333, start : 658210639, end : 658216644)$. We format this input data as a time series of codes corresponding to HVAC components. So for each time point and for each HVAC, we are able to know whether diagnose code x is ON or OFF.

Preprocessing. Code IDs must be chosen or computed s.t. an ID matches a type of symptom, regardless of the unit where it occurred. For example if the label of a code includes the HVAC or train numbers where it happened, this must be stripped from the label used as unique ID, e.g. by grouping. Diagnose codes without an ID or activation time must be discarded. Instead, missing deactivation times can be imputed if there is a standard deactivation time of all HVACs, e.g. when the trains are shut down for the night. We observed missing deactivation times on less than 1% of the data analysed from NS, for which we inserted the deactivation time corresponding to the end of the working day.

Data Labelling. We apply the proposed ML layering: use the LR model from the previous step, to build an artificial ground truth of HVAC malfunctions used in this step for training and testing. Therefore, unlike the previous step where the main input was human-generated and covered 1–5% of the data, here the AGT is automatically generated (via the previous LR model) and covers the whole dataset. We highlight that this scheme hinges on obtaining high-quality extrapolations in the previous step, such as those presented in Sect. 2.3.

Technically, this requires to match the discretisation used for the temperature time series, to that of the diagnose code time series. The work-day window of a train is too coarse: although an HVAC might be broken, the functional failure is only noticeable when cooling is needed, e.g. in the afternoon when the outside temperature rises. Moreover the windows and labels chosen must permit feature extraction: for the digital input in this step, all features are based on the presence of codes during the time periods when HVACs fail (or are deemed healthy).

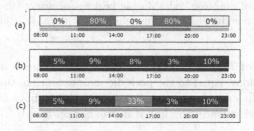

Fig. 6. An example of windows that divide the work day in 5 sections, for which we show the aggregated probability of HVAC malfunctions coming from the AGT. Periods that are labelled healthy (green ▪), defect (red ▪), or none (gray ▪), are indicated by colours in the narrow bar under the windows. (Color figure online)

A generic solution is to split the work day in windows, labelled as healthy or defect (or none) using the AGT, i.e. the aggregated failure probabilities. This can be parameterised with thresholds $0 < T_\ell < T_h < 1$ such that the window corresponding to an HVAC is healthy if its probability of failure is below T_ℓ; if it is above T_h the window is labelled defect; and if the probability falls in $[T_\ell, T_h]$ no label is applied. Further logical conditions include e.g. no healthy labels for HVACs whose failure probability is above T_ℓ at any point of the day.

3.2 Machine Learning Experiment

For objective O2 we define one feature that indicates whether a code is present during a healthy- or defect-labelled period. For O3 we define three features that quantify the occurrence of the code in the time before a labelled period. Thus all features need to match codes to labelled HVAC periods, which we do as follows.

The i-th occurrence of diagnose code x is given by a time interval $[x_i^{ON}, x_i^{OFF}]$. Similarly, for an HVAC period p labelled healthy or defect we have $[p_{start}, p_{end}]$ (an HVAC period p is implicitly linked to a specific train and coach). We say that *code x is present during period p* if there is an occurrence of x in which these time intervals overlap: $\exists i \,.\, [x_i^{ON}, x_i^{OFF}] \cap [p_{start}, p_{end}] \neq \emptyset$, as illustrated by the red segments in Fig. 7.

Code During Period (CDP). This is the Boolean feature used for objective O2. It determines, for each (time window of each) healthy/defect period p, whether diagnose code x was present during p:

$$\mathrm{CDP}_{p,x} \equiv \exists i \,.\, (x_i^{ON} \leqslant p_{end}) \wedge (x_i^{OFF} \geqslant p_{start}).$$

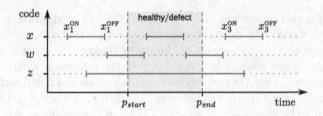

Fig. 7. Occurrence of diagnose codes during healthy- or defect-labelled periods of an HVAC. In practice, p is divided into time windows as in Fig. 6. (Color figure online)

Code: Number of Days (CND). This integral feature is used for objective O3. For a time window equal to the periodic maintenance of the HVACs, T, and backwards from the end of a period p, it counts the number of days since code x was last observed, introducing NaN if it was not observed:

$$\mathrm{CND}_{p,x} = \mathrm{CDP}^{T}_{p,x} \ ? \ \mathrm{days}\big(p_{end} - \max_i\{x_i^{\mathrm{OFF}} \mid x_i^{\mathrm{OFF}} \geqslant p_{end} - T\}\big) : \mathrm{NaN},$$

where $(\alpha\,?\,tt:\mathit{ff})$ is the ternary operator on condition α, true case tt, and false case ff, and $\mathrm{CDP}^{t}_{p,x}$ is the CDP feature bounded from below in time by $p_{end} - t$.

Code: Number of Occurrences (CNO). This feature is similar to CND, but counts the number of occurrences of code x in the interval $[p_{end} - T, p_{end}]$:

$$\mathrm{CNO}_{p,x} = \mathrm{CDP}^{T}_{p,x} \ ? \ \#\{x_i \mid x_i^{\mathrm{OFF}} \geqslant p_{end} - T\} : \mathrm{NaN}.$$

Code: Cumulative Time (CCT). This floating-point feature counts the total time that code x was active in the time window $[p_{end} - T, p_{end}]$:

$$\mathrm{CCT}_{p,x} = \mathrm{CDP}^{T}_{p,x} \ ? \ \sum\{x_i^{\mathrm{OFF}} - x_i^{\mathrm{ON}} \mid x_i^{\mathrm{OFF}} \geqslant p_{end} - T\} : \mathrm{NaN}.$$

ML Models. These features can be used to train different kinds of classifiers. For objective O2 we use logistic regression (as with O1), to check whether the full set of diagnose codes has good detection capabilities of HVAC malfunctions.

However, the components of an HVAC produce different codes, which could have different importance to predict a general failure. It would be useful to learn how each code contributes to the failure probability of the whole HVAC. This is in the best interest of companies, whose data streams already contain these codes, and thus could implement simple predictive maintenance rules such as "if codes x and w are seen together, send the HVAC to maintenance within n days".

For this purpose we also train a Decision Tree model (DT) for both objectives O2 and O3. Besides learning to estimate malfunctions, DTs can unfold the estimate to indicate how much each feature contributes to the total probability.

3.3   Study on Rolling Stock of NS

We apply this approach to the same trains used in Sect. 2.3. However, the features for objectives O2 and O3 are computed from two inputs: the diagnose codes, and the AGT computed from temperature readings in the previous step.

Data and Assessment for Objective O2. Only periods that contained a maximum ("outside") control temperature above 24° were used, to ensure that the HVACs had to cool down the train. On top of that, periods without active diagnose codes were discarded, since the source of information for CDP (the feature used for objective O2) is the intersection between diagnose codes and healthy/defect periods. The resulting data set contained 294 points, distributed with an imbalance ratio of 2:1 in favour of the healthy class. This data was used to train an LR model, and also a DT model. These were assessed via the ROC and PRC, equivalently to what was done for the LR model of the temperature readings. Data was stratified by grouping samples by HVAC, and adding an indicator on whether these groups included samples of the healthy class (66% of the total), defect (20%), or both (14%). Also here we added a random binary feature with no detection power, to draw the line of useful codes when we build the ranking based on feature importance.

Data and Assessment for Objective O3. The scheduled maintenance for the fleet under consideration occurs approximately every 3 months. Therefore we chose $T = 12$ weeks, which results in a large dataset on which to compute the features CND, CNO, CCT defined for this objective. To alleviate computations we randomly selected 1000 healthy periods, but kept all (625) defect ones: this reduced the data imbalance without hindering our intention to foretell members of the defect class. From this set we also filtered out periods with max temperature below 24 °C, and which did not coincide with any diagnose code (in their $[p_{end} - T, p_{end}]$ time window). This resulted in a balanced data set, with 499 members of the healthy class and 496 of the defect class. We used this to train a DT classifier, but omitted the LR classifier since the data was too sparse and we expected no further gain w.r.t. DT. Assessment was performed as for the previous objective: in this case the groups including samples of the healthy class added up to 61% of the total, and defect was 24%.

Performance of the LR and DT Models for Objective O2. Figures 8a to 8d show the ROC and PRC curves obtained for the two models trained on the CDP feature for objective O2. As before, the blue lines are the average of different splits between train and test sets. The intention was to use the diagnose codes to detect HVAC failures, i.e. determine which codes occur during functional loss of these units. The corresponding curves in Fig. 8 show that the correlation between the features and the defect (or healthy) periods of the HVACs is very low. The AUC for the ROC of the LR model is 0.6 on average, and the PRS for the PRC is 0.43. These low values suggest that the codes in our dataset, or the CDP feature used here, cannot detect HVAC failures in real time. However, the low values can also be linked to issues with the previous step, e.g. the AGT built with the LR classifier could be inaccurate. We discuss this further in Sect. 4.2.

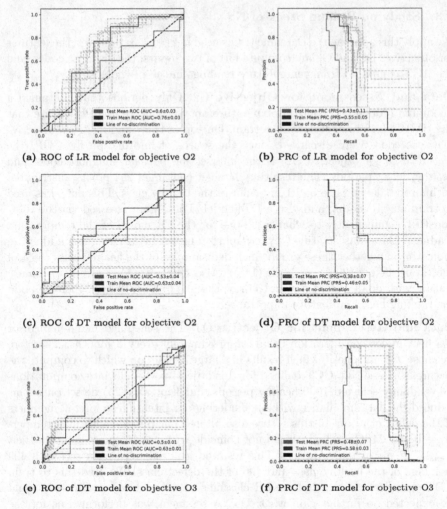

(a) ROC of LR model for objective O2

(b) PRC of LR model for objective O2

(c) ROC of DT model for objective O2

(d) PRC of DT model for objective O2

(e) ROC of DT model for objective O3

(f) PRC of DT model for objective O3

Fig. 8. Performance of ML models from different features of diagnose codes (Color figure online)

Performance of the DT Models for Objective O3. Figures 8e and 8f show resp. the ROC and PRC curves for the decision tree model built on features CND, CNO, and CCT. These use past information, which was expected to help the DT classifier. However Fig. 8 shows differently, as the resulting ROC and PRC are 0.5 and 0.48 resp. As above, this suggests that the diagnose codes, or all features used to interpret them, cannot be faithfully used to detect HVAC failures *for the given dataset used*. In that sense it is important to highlight that our data covered only two (summer) months, which might well be insufficient to discover the correlations sought. We touch upon this point again in Sect. 4.2.

Feature Importance. The rankings of feature importance (not included here) are another indicator of the low detection/prediction capacity of the dataset and features used for objectives O2 and O3. For the LR model, the permutation tests always place the random feature among the 10 most important codes. For the DT models of both feature sets (CDP on one side, and {CND, CNO, CCT} on the other) this does not happen, but the best-ranked code is an HVAC self-test, which is not expected to have true predictive capability of HVAC failures.

4   Final Discussion and Perspectives

4.1   Temperature Readings to Detect HVAC Failures

The results of the LR classifier in Sect. 2.3 make it clear that **it is possible to identify HVACs with cooling failures based on temperature readings.**

We note that the performance of our model could be experiencing a positive bias, related to the conservative rules applied to manually label hot or healthy periods. This could have resulted in relatively easy predictions for the NS input, as we intentionally ignored anomalies, and focused on data with high probability of coming from a defective (or healthy) HVAC.

To further improve the capabilities and scope of application of this model, one could use ground-truth labels of HVACs malfunctions (if available), to reduce any potential bias introduced by our manual annotation process. If that is not feasible, then manually labelling more data and employing multiple human annotators—as we show in Sect. 2.3—should also reduce any bias.

Regarding feature rankings, the COC feature (Compare to Other Coaches) is clearly the most relevant to determine HVAC malfunctions. Its importance seems nearly high enough to base all predictions on it alone. However there are scenarios where the SP (Set Point) and DCS (Defect Control Sensor) features are required, e.g. if the control sensors of the coaches have a manufacturing failure. Moreover, defects in the outside temperature sensor are interesting on their own, since they require different maintenance than HVAC systems, and may cause misbehaviour of any train component that depends on their data.

Other features for this dataset appear less important and could be removed without deteriorating the quality of the resulting LR model. We note however that another practical solution to remove features is to count with information that indicates when the HVAC is actively heating/cooling. In that case it should be possible to work with the SP features alone.

4.2   Diagnose Codes to Detect and Predict HVAC Failures

The results of Sect. 3.3 show that **we could not find strong evidence of correlation between diagnose codes and HVAC failures**, given our limited dataset and choice of LR and DT classifiers.

Further analysis revealed that no codes are present in 97% of the periods labelled as healthy by our LR model from the previous step. This could indicate good data quality, but also no codes are present in 80% of the periods labelled as defect. In fact, the tables built for the features (of intersections between healthy/defect periods and diagnose codes) were very sparse, e.g. 85% of the total data was purely zeroes for the CDP feature computed for objective O2.

This shows few intersections between HVAC malfunctions and codes in general, despite the high accuracy of the LR model that built the AGT. Such lack of intersections could be explained by a relative absence of codes, that in turn might have two explanations: the HVACs may be sending more events than the ones received, with messages being lost in the data stream; or the diagnose system of the HVACs could have limitations, thus sending less codes than required.

Nevertheless, we highlight that the diagnose codes are designed to identify specific errors in subcomponents of the HVAC. It may be that, contrary to our initial hypothesis, the codes in our dataset do not cover failures in components that can be related to cooling failures in the HVACs. Overfitting is yet another explanation for this result, since a few samples (i.e. independent cases of broken HVACs) are trying to be classified with many dimensions (i.e. diagnose codes). Moreover, the AGT used for this step comes from ML extrapolation of human-labelled data. However good the accuracy of the resulting LR model, it remains to be proved that the defect-labelled periods truly correspond to defective HVACs.

4.3   Perspectives

In Sect. 4.1 we indicate two ways to improve the usability of the LR model based on temperature readings: add ground-truth data regarding HVAC malfunctions; and add activation data regarding HVAC cooling/heating.

Regarding features and their importance, **the outcome of our feature engineering process—see Sect. 2.2 and 3.2—could be generalised to other rolling stocks or systems**. These features can be used on any train, or vehicle, or building, whose architecture is similar to those of this study. That is: having a main unit (train/building), divided in connected adjacent compartments (coaches/rooms), each with an HVAC and one or more temperature sensors. In particular, even though our studies are focused on cooling, the same can be done for heating, and also for ventilation e.g. using CO_2 sensor readings.

Another promising extension would be to use the temperature readings to foretell a malfunction. For instance, in our rules for manual labelling we disregard zigzag patterns as those observed in Fig. 3. It could be possible to build an ML model capable of finding correlations between these (or other) temperature patterns in time, that serve to estimate a probability of the HVAC failing before the next scheduled maintenance. For this we foresee the use of neural networks and frequency analysis, which are more complex (and more opaque, but also more powerful) than the simple and explainable LR approach followed here.

Regarding the diagnose codes, a first attempt to improve our results should use a larger dataset, e.g. covering several years. Also, the same features could be used in other sets of codes, e.g. from other train types, to determine whether it is the feature engineering process (and not the dataset) that requires revision.

Beyond HVAC cooling failures, diagnose codes are promising to guide the first steps of maintenance. For this, maintenance data serves as ground-truth to indicate the cause behind an HVAC failure. Further data analyses would reveal the preceding diagnose codes, which could be used in future failures to indicate to technicians where to look first, as a new broken HVAC arrives for repair.

Acknowledgement. The authors thank Nick Oosterhof, who contributed with invaluable discussion and feedback that helped to carry out and shape this work.

References

1. Aslansefat, K., Kabir, S., Gheraibia, Y., Papadopoulos, Y.: Dynamic fault tree analysis: state-of-the-art in modelling, analysis and tools, pp. 73–112. Taylor & Francis (2020). https://doi.org/10.1201/9780429268922-4
2. Catelani, M., Ciani, L., Guidi, G., Patrizi, G., Galar, D.: Estimate the useful life for a heating, ventilation, and air conditioning system on a high-speed train using failure models. ACTA IMEKO **10**(3), 100–107 (2021)
3. Daniel, R., et al.: Filtration understanding: FY10 testing results and filtration model update. Technical report, Pacific Northwest National Laboratory (2011)
4. Hale, P., Arno, R.: Survey of reliability and availability information for power distribution, power generation, and HVAC components for commercial, industrial, and utility installations. In: IEEE Industrial and Commercial Power Systems Technical Conference (Cat. No.00CH37053), pp. 31–54 (2000). https://doi.org/10.1109/ICPS.2000.854354
5. Lin, N., Du, W., Wang, J., Yun, X., Chen, L.: The effect of COVID-19 restrictions on particulate matter on different modes of transport in China. Environ. Res. (2021). https://doi.org/10.1016/j.envres.2021.112205
6. Ojala, M., Garriga, G.C.: Permutation tests for studying classifier performance. J. Mach. Learn. Res. **11**, 1833–1863 (2010)
7. Pedregosa, F., Varoquaux, G., Gramfort, A., et al.: Scikit-learn: machine learning in Python. J. Mach. Learn. Res. **12**, 2825–2830 (2011)
8. Ruijters, E., Guck, D., Drolenga, P., Peters, M., Stoelinga, M.: Maintenance analysis and optimization via statistical model checking. In: Agha, G., Van Houdt, B. (eds.) QEST 2016. LNCS, vol. 9826, pp. 331–347. Springer, Cham (2016). https://doi.org/10.1007/978-3-319-43425-4_22
9. Settles, B.: Active Learning. Synthesis Lectures on Artificial Intelligence and Machine Learning (2012). https://doi.org/10.2200/S00429ED1V01Y201207AIM018
10. Tehrani, M.M., Beauregard, Y., Rioux, M., Kenne, J.P., Ouellet, R.: A predictive preference model for maintenance of a heating ventilating and air conditioning system. IFAC **48**(3), 130–135 (2015). https://doi.org/10.1016/j.ifacol.2015.06.070
11. Wong, D.: A knowledge-based decision support system in reliability-centered maintenance of HVAC systems. Ph.D. thesis, University of Newfoundland (2000)

Safety

Enhancing Autonomous Train Safety Through A Priori-Map Based Perception

Ankur Mahtani[1]([✉])(ID), Nadia Chouchani[1](ID), Maxime Herbreteau[2],
and Denis Rafin[3]

[1] FCS Railenium, 180 Rue Joseph-Louis Lagrange, 59300 Famars, France
{ankur.mahtani,nadia.chouchani}@railenium.eu
[2] Thales Services Numériques SAS, 290 Allée du Lac, 31670 Labège, France
maxime.herbreteau@thalesgroup.com
[3] SpirOps, 8, passage de la bonne graine, 75011 Paris, France
denis.rafin@spirops.com

Abstract. Autonomous driving tends to increase use of perception as a tool for analyzing the environment before making a decision that could impact driving. However, recent techniques based on machine learning do not provide the necessary interpretability to ensure sufficient driving safety. Combining multiple sources, deterministic or not, allows results to be cross-referenced and therefore more reliable. In this paper, we propose a novel methodology that aligns an infrastructure mapping system and point cloud analysis for railway tracks and catenaries perception to ensure autonomous train's safety. By using a deep learning model to recognize and classify rails with the implicit knowledge of the railway infrastructure, we exceed in performance all previous systems of infrastructure: 60.9% in mIoU for tracks segmentation and 9.27 points mMink for points alignment with ground-truth, at an interesting runtime of 20 Hz. Moreover, we propose an embedded solution for automatic monitoring which avoids hours of maintenance traffic on the railway tracks. This solution is used as acquisition system feeding map and perception in real-world data for autonomous trains.

Keywords: Autonomous train · Railway map · Point cloud · 3D semantic segmentation · Deep learning

1 Introduction

Autonomous trains are safety critical systems and require a robust environment perception. This task refers to the ability to collect data from the environment, classify it by their semantic meanings and then extract contextual knowledge; such as track geometry, obstacle positions and even location of hazardous areas.

This research work is funded by the French program "Investissements d'Avenir" and is part of the French collaborative project TASV (Train Autonome Service Voyageurs), with SNCF, Alstom Crespin, Thales, Bosch, and Spirops.

Indeed, perceiving the surroundings and the near field context are crucial for safe navigation. The challenge of this paper is to improve the train's localization on the track with the additional input of perception. One of the main issues is rails detection, which correspond to the surface enabling the trains to roll upon depending on their wheels. It has been an exhaustive research topic, similarly to road detection in the fields of autonomous cars and advanced driver assistance systems. However, some challenging scenarios such as long distance detection or multi-modal computer vision solutions are not fully addressed. Indeed, the railway environment is non deterministic. For instance, illumination and weather conditions can influence the detection performance. In fact, the sensing provides collections of data based on cameras, lidars, radars or other sensors, which are affected by the outdoor conditions. How to leverage the whole available on-board data to improve the detection performance?

On one hand, the required data for environment perception can be captured using embedded sensors or a fusion of them. On the other hand, autonomous trains hold an on-board mapping system describing the whole railway infras-tructure to precisely localize themselves and to navigate safely on the tracks. The railway infrastructure information comprises plans of track constructions, geographic characteristics such as curves and gradient of lines and other func-tional network entities such as signs and panels. Does using maps enhance the performance of perception systems and then the safety of autonomous trains? Trains autonomy is subject to a SIL 4 (Safety Integrity Level) safety level accord-ing to the EN 50129 norm in order to ensure train driving safety, compliance with signaling, localization, transmission of information and speed regulation [17]. In this paper, we propose a new solution for environment perception based on the embedded mapping system. The obtained results confirm that the use of the cartographic information as input to the perception function improves the performance of detection. These results enhance the environment perception functions of autonomous trains which can facilitate its certification according to SIL 4.

The remainder of this paper is structured as follows. Section 2 provides an overview of related research work. The proposed methodology and solution are detailed in Sect. 3. Section 4 details the obtained results. The final section presents conclusions and future work.

2   State of the Art

In this section, we present an overview of the related work and our motivations.

2.1   Infrastructure Modelling

Research and industrial knowledge management initiatives have proposed differ-ent conceptual models for railway infrastructure. Some have become standards adopted by several actors in the field.

RailSystemModel. Based on ISO 19148 for Linear Referencing, RailSystemModel (RSM) is a UML conceptual model that aims to describe the whole objects of the railway infrastructure [18]. This description is independent of uses, structured in levels, and open to future developments. Ultimately, it covers all the subsystems of the rail industry, at all stages of design, construction, operation and maintenance. This model is a description of the railway infrastructure basically the topology of the tracks. The latter is represented by objects in the Topology package which are the carriers of other information. This description concerns on the one hand an operational breakdown of the network infrastructure in the Network package and on the other hand, positioning of these objects on the earth's geode through association with concepts from the PositioningSystem package. The information attached to the topology can be geometric in the context of the Location package and/or functional in the context of the NetEntity package.

IFC Rail. The Industry Foundation Classes (IFC) standards allow the Building Information Modelling (BIM) description of an infrastructure [19]. Modelling efforts, which have mainly focused on civil engineering, building construction and road infrastructure, have recently turned to the railway. The IFC 4 standard sees the appearance of a whole section dedicated to the description of railway infrastructure. Under the new version of the IFC Standard, a paradigm shift on the high-level model (migration from STEP/Express to UML) brings the BIM community to look at the models existing in the various fields.

EULYNX. It deals with modelling a format to allow the exchange of signaling information between infrastructure managers and signaling system providers [20]. The selected format is XML, generated from an UML model which is being aligned and linked with RSM. It includes a large set of signaling objects (signals, locks, etc.) and related concepts (routes, needle protection, etc.).

2.2 Perception and Segmentation

The 3D segmentation task can be divided into three types: semantic, instance and part segmentation. Semantic segmentation aims to predict object class labels such as catenaries and tracks. Instance segmentation additionally distinguishes between different instances of the same class labels. Part segmentation aims to decompose instances further into their different components such as armrests, legs and backrest of a same chair. Compared to 2D segmentation, 3D segmentation gives a more comprehensive understanding of a scene thanks to 3D data (e.g. RGB-D, point clouds, projected images, voxels, and mesh) contain richer geometric, shape, and scale information with less background noise.

Our perception task can be summarized as a 3D semantic segmentation work for catenaries and railway tracks. Segmentation of 3D scenes is a fundamental and challenging problem in computer vision. The objective of 3D segmentation is to build computational techniques that predict the fine-grained labels of objects in a 3D scene for a wide range of applications such as in autonomous driving. Using state of the art deep learning models on the SemanticKITTI benchmark

[3,15] whose labels can be used in our case (persons, traffic lights, vegetation, etc.), we evaluate models on our railway dataset and then analyze impact of adding map data as input.

Points convolution semantic segmentation networks procure most accurate results for catenaries and track diagnosis. Pointwise Multi-Layer Perception (MLP) networks such as PointNet [5] and PointNet++ [4], graph convolution based such as Attention-based Graph Convolution Networks (AGCN) [13] or 3DContextNet [12], or voxel based segmentation concepts of 3D semantic segmentation are described in [14].

Point convolution-based methods perform convolution operations directly on the points and on their neighboring points (like RSNet model [11]): the input can be a single object from the part region segmentation or a small part of 3D scene from the Object region segmentation. Points can be arbitrarily sorted in specific orders [10], through dilated KNN search [9] or with KD-tree like PCNN [8] to learn local features before points convolutions. (AF)2S3Net [6] consists of an end-to-end 3D encoder-decoder CNN network that combines the voxel-based and point-based learning methods into a unified framework. RandLA-Net [1] introduces a lightweight neural architecture that can process large-scale point clouds because it only relies on random sampling within the network and hence requires much lesser memory and computation. The local feature aggregator [1] obtains successively larger receptive fields by considering local spatial relations and point features. The entire network contains shared Multi-layered Perceptrons without relying on graph construction and kernelization and hence is efficient. KP-FCNN model [7] introduces spatial weighted-convolution on all points of a neighborhood given (KPConv), reducing the computation cost by the size of the neighborhood. Furthermore, a deformable version of this convolution operator was also introduced that learns local shifts to make them adapt to point cloud geometry. The ease with which the KP-FCNN model can be adapted and identified by the geometry of the scene is the characteristic that made the model a viable choice (it also has real-time performance and good compromise in terms of mean intersection over union on public benchmarks) for the first part of the proposed 3D semantic segmentation framework introduced in this paper.

3   Methodology

Figure 1 presents the overall architecture of our scientific contributions for the railways sector community. We develop a fusion-framework that processes perception data of lidar's sensors and simultaneously geo-localization and map information. This paper focuses on pointcloud processing and the fusion with map data for better railway track segmentation.

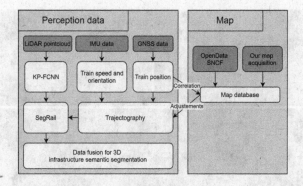

Fig. 1. Overall architecture of the combination use of perception and map data for 3D railway infrastructure semantic segmentation.

3.1   Our Database

Pointcloud Database. Collection of rich annotated dataset of lidar data in the railway environment is a very meticulous work that can open novel tasks of 3D detections and segmentations. We used a 64 layers lidar with multiple reflections to ensure robustness in the acquired points. These points contains depth data, useful for object localization or object volume measurement. Acquisition is made manually using 2 synchronized solid-state lidars to combine 550 000 points for each scan, accumulating over one million points per scan. The scans contains colorized points by RGB camera synchronization (see Fig. 2) and are geolocated. Acquisition were made in the region Hauts-de-France in France, and our privileged line of test is between Aulnoye-Aymeries and Busigny stations. As an example, there are around 300 scans on the Aulnoye-Busigny railway line. The dataset is annotated for these classes of interest: ground, vegetation, buildings, catenaries, catenary poles, railway tracks, infrastructure (tunnels, bridge, walkways, etc.). Some difficult points to annotate are classified as noise or non-classified. Each point vector contains these types of data, in addition to 3D spatial position: reflection intensity, number of deflection and deflection number, edge of flight line, classification value, RGB colorization of the point. These different types of data give crucial and rich information which help for pointwise segmentation. In this work, we do not work with the RGB camera and hence, with no point colorization data.

Fig. 2. Combined scan examples of the pointcloud dataset (with colorization information) for railway perception.

Map Database. The mapping system provides a topological and geometric description of the railway network. This system is based on RSM. It is fed by processed Lidar dataset to have a description of the infrastructure objects, their absolute positions as well as their types. SNCF-R[1] data are also used to supplement these data sets. In the Fig. 3, a track is described using a set of geometric coordinates in the form of track segments.

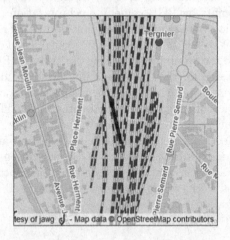

Fig. 3. Excerpt from OpenData SNCF

---

[1] https://ressources.data.sncf.com/pages/accueil/.

3.2 Our Approach

Based on the state of the art deep learning technique for 3D semantic segmentation KP-FCNN [7], we propose a novel architecture of data fusion between perception data from multiple sensors: lidar, Inertial Measurement Unit (IMU) and Global Navigation Satellite System (GNSS) sensors added to an embedded infrastructure map. 3D pointcloud datasets, which are more and more available, are compulsory for applying our method. Nowadays, SNCF-R the manager of the French national rail network, is making lidar acquisition campaigns to complete their infrastructure databases. In a nutshell, laser points are processed through KP-FCNN model, then predictions are improved by a set of segmentation rules made upon the infrastructure geometry, explained below. They were specified by experts of the railway domain. These assumptions led to processes we named the SegRail method. The lidar scan is synchronized with the IMU and GNSS sensor, making possible real-time correlation between data. Inertial and geo-localization data are used to calculate crucial information of train's run such as train position for example. This position data is used to request the online map information upon close and incoming railway infrastructure context data. This map data is then correlated with prediction's output of SegRail and allows performance increase and therefore, safety improvement for autonomous trains. Our approach is summarized in Fig. 1.

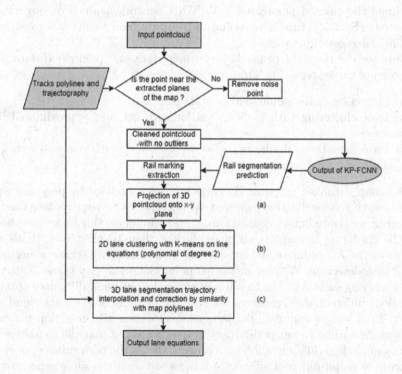

Fig. 4. SegRail method for rail segmentation correction.

We built a SegRail module based on the following geometry assumptions on the railway infrastructure tracks:

- The width of the rail is fixed;
- The separation between the rails is constant (1435 mm) for each physical installation;
- The rail is constant (always visible in front of a train);
- The overall appearance is always consistent (usually no deformation).

These rules are strong high level assumptions and allow the establishment of rules for optimizing the "perceived" trajectory of the rails in relation to the ground truth trajectory given by the infrastructure mapping.

Taking into account these geometrical rules, we build the SegRail module presented in Fig. 4. This module aims to correct 3D rails segmentation by matching map data with perception data. To do this, we correlate the polyline equations of the tracks recorded in the map with the polylines predicted by the segmentation model.

Firstly, we preprocess the input pointcloud by denoising all outliers points that are too far from threshold planes extracted from map database. These threshold planes are calculated by linear planes issued from arbitrary limits around tracks. This step allows to remove all points that are not in the range of the railway tracks in front of the train. We perform KP-FCNN network in inference upon the cleaned pointcloud. KP-FCNN network, trained on our dataset presented in Sect. 3.1, runs in real-time and outputs good results of segmentation on rails and vegetation labels.

Next step is the data fusion between map data and pointcloud data. It is composed of three steps (Fig. 4):

- (a) Projection of the pointcloud in a 2D plan x-y
- (b) Lane clustering with K-means on lanes to get best approximated lines equations
- (c) Lines equations similarity between predicted equations and extracted polylines of map database

Our map database proposes 2D trajectography modeled by polylines equations for each geo-localization captured. As polyline fitting requires lane marking clustering, we study light-weighted clustering techniques. Our first conclusion is that 2D clustering is simpler and more efficient than 3D clustering, that's why we remove the Z coordinate and consider the Z coordinate difference as negligible for 3D lane detection. We project the 3D point cloud onto x-y plane (a) to conduct clustering such as in Fig. 5. Without using the per-point difference obtained by various differentiable renderers, we cast the learning of 3D point cloud generation from images containing objects silhouette as a 2D projection matching problem. According to our preliminary results, we found that the consistency of points sampled on different silhouette objects affects the performance, since the 2D projections on different silhouette images are from the same generated 3D point cloud. Although this issue can be alleviated by sampling very dense points

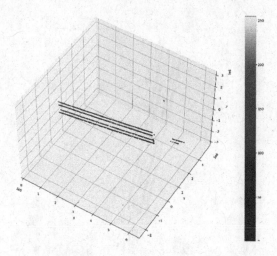

Fig. 5. Prediction output of KP-FCNN model (a), after 2D projection on (x, y) axis. Color scale reflects confidence score on predictions (the lighter the lower confidence score).

within each silhouette with many different sampling methods, it would make the loss calculation more costly.

This 2D projection now allows us to analyze features by region of interests or pointwise using point neighborhood. As written before, pointwise operations are computationally heavy and most of the time they cannot run in real-time. Other factor, traditional clustering methods are bad at closely positioned or elongated structures such as railway tracks. Then, we apply 2D lane clustering with K-Means algorithm on line equations (b). The problem with the normal implementation of K-means clustering is that we need to know how many clusters exist in the data. This is not available in the case of continuous lane detection. So we get around that particular problem by comparing the cluster means that we obtain from the K-means algorithm with the railway dataset. Moreover, experiments show that usual K-means is better initialized by building parallel structure into the clustering process. We apply the clustering algorithm inside each group of line segments (split according to y-axis threshold, see Fig. 6). The basic idea of clustering line segments is to find the "Average" of all the segments inside a cluster. In the case of point data, K-Means clustering involves finding clusters of point data. Thus, the algorithm provides us with the means of the clusters (centroids). By using K-means algorithm, we simplify the task of non-ending line equation similarity into local similarity.

Finally, we achieve 3D lane segmentation trajectory interpolation and correction by similarity with map polylines (c). Once we process the map database to extract and compute railway tracks equations and clusters, we can plot them on the same image as our clustered lanes segmentation (see left image of Fig. 7). We observe a mismatch between the detected geometric points and the drawn ground truth curves from the map. These imprecisions may be due to sensor

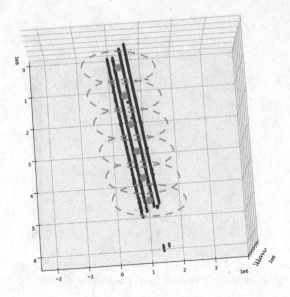

Fig. 6. Pointwise clustering illustration (b). Red dots are the position of the centroid and red dotted circles are examples of clusters. (Color figure online)

precision, train vibrations or KP-FCNN low confidence threshold. Our objective is to reduce as much as possible these imprecisions by combining map curves equations (which we consider ground-truth) with predicted lanes. We compute a similarity score and with a threshold, the farthest points are brought together inside similarity-accepted threshold. We use Minkowski distance calculation between each points of a cluster of the extracted map and the clustered pointcloud (c): we are achieving cluster-to-cluster feature comparison. We can calculate Minkowski distance only in a normed vector space, which means: "in a space where distances can be represented as a vector that has a length". Map database provide vector space and distances between cluster centers which are normed vector space (absolute value are used). These distances give us a metric to compare similarity in real-time between ground-truth (a-priori map knowledge) and segmentation predictions such as in Fig. 7. In this figure, we show the interpolations made with the Minkowski distance calculation. Minkowski gives a threshold circle of accepted points to correct. We interpolated each point to the nearest location under the Minkowski threshold. We named that step 2D point interpolation (c). Figure 7 illustrates an example of results we obtained: right image shows the corrections made on points after 2D point interpolation.

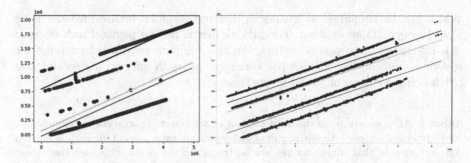

Fig. 7. Correlation results of map lanes with predicted lanes (c). **Left image** shows the predicted lanes before similarity correction with lines equations, and **right image** is the output lanes after 2D point interpolation.

4   Results and Analysis

This section describes the results and analysis made in this work.

Experimental Parameters. For this work, we acquired data with a mechanical lidar: Hesai Pandar64 with 64 layers of lasers reflection, embedded in a French Regional train. Concerning computational capacity, we use a Nvidia Quadro RTX6000 GPU for training and tests purposes. The number of operations performed during a forward pass of our network depends on the number of points of the current batch (mostly 15 000 points per batch), and the maximum number of neighbors of these points. Other hyper-parameters are similar as [7]. We use 6 as number of clusters to segment for the K-Means algorithm. We used Elkan algorithm to optimize convergence of the K-Means clustering.

Metrics of Performance. For the 3D semantic segmentation task, we use mean Jaccard or so-called intersection-over-union (mIoU) [3] over the railway class, i.e.,

$$mIoU = \frac{1}{C} \sum_{c=1}^{C} \frac{TP_c}{TP_c + FP_c + FN_c} \tag{1}$$

where TPc, FPc and FNc correspond to the number of true positive, false positive, and false negative predictions for class c, and C is the number of classes. This metric indicates the rate of close predicted points to ground-truth.

We use Minkowski distance as a distance metric between railway track points in map database and predicted railway tracks points. This distance is averaged (mMink) for all points of the class "railway tracks" of a scan. Minkowski formula is as follows:

$$mMink = D(X,Y) = \left(\sum_{i=1}^{n} |x_i - y_i|^p \right)^{(1/p)} \tag{2}$$

Which can be simplified as Euclidean distance formula, because we are using $P = 2$ in our 2D application. The mMink metric has no physical unit because it is calculated upon points vectors. We also compare runtime of inference for real-time applications. This metric is number of batch inferred per second, one batch being one scan of the 64 layers lidar.

Table 1. Ablation study on the improvement of 3D lane segmentation on pointclouds. Mean-Intersection over Union is calculated upon all rails present in each scan. Up Arrow indicates that higher values are better and down arrow indicates that lower values are better.

Method	Experiment	Dataset	mIoU(%) ↑	mMink ↓	Runtime (Hz)↑
KP-FCNN	Pretrained [7] (baseline)	KITTI [3]	58.8%	–	17.5
KP-FCNN	Transfer learning	Railway	46.4%	–	14
KP-FCNN	Trained from scratch	Railway	54.3%	35.1732	14
SegRail (base)	Preprocessed dataset	Railway	60.9%	34.7636	20
SegRail (a)	2D projection	Railway	60.9%	21.6333	20
SegRail (b)	Unparallel lines clustering	Railway	60.9%	26.8967	20
SegRail (b+)	Parallel lines clustering	Railway	60.9%	17.1452	20
SegRail (c)	Map correlation	Railway	60.9%	9.2753	20

Ablation Study. We conducted an ablation study to analyze each step (a), (b) and (c) of our approach. See Table 1 for quantitative results and Fig. 5(a), 6(b) and 7(c) for illustration. The experimental results obtained in Table 1 show that on the railway dataset, we improved KPconv model performances with SegRail (c) (after line 3 of the table) by 6.6% mIoU and mMink by 25.8979 points.

Finally, we obtained line equations on our test dataset, based on the output of (c) experiment. They are the mean equations calculated over 300 scans.

$$Y + Z = 3.91e - 4X^2 + 1.86X - 35.38 \tag{3}$$

$$Y + Z = 1.87e - 4X^2 + 1.88X - 13.08 \tag{4}$$

$$Y + Z = 5.01e - 6X^2 + 1.90X + 8.69 \tag{5}$$

$$Y + Z = -4.28e - 06X^2 + 1.90X + 13.19 \tag{6}$$

Equations (3) and (4) refers to usual left railway tracks when having only 2 tracks and Eqs. (5) and (6) refers to right tracks.

We conducted this ablation study based on previous experiments and continuously added features that improved performance. Our objectives are multiples: keep the mIoU high and confident on point segmentation prediction, drop the mMink score to lowest in order to comply with the map database, and keep runtime high enough for real-time inferences.

Performance on the Railway Dataset. For comparative and extension of this work purposes, we provide a table of performances on each class of the railway dataset (Table 3). We evaluate different existing models based on mIoU and runtime metrics. We trained these models with same hyper-parameters and same train/test split of the dataset, for fair comparison between models (Table 2). Table 1 shows that modules (a), (b+) and (c) corrected line predictions and improved KP-FCNN segmentation.

Table 2. Benchmark of state of the art models on the railway dataset. This benchmark justifies our choice of KP-FCNN model for the semantic segmentation task.

Model	mIoU ↑	Runtime ↑
PointNet++ [4]	25.3%	11.5
RandLA-Net [1]	41.4%	**22**
Cylinder3D [2]	44%	10
KP-FCNN [7]	**54.3%**	14

Table 3. IoU results of our implementation from Table 1 for each class of the railway dataset.

Model	mIoU ↑	Tracks	Ground	Vegetation	Building	Catenary	Pole	Infrastructure
SegRail (c)	54.3	60.9	55.7	65.3	41.5	58.8	76.8	21.4

Main results on each class of the railway dataset presented in Table 3 on the railway dataset show that our implementation is well adapted for railway tracks and catenaries segmentation as they can be represented in the form of polylines. However, the model is weak against other forms of objects such as ground, building and infrastructure which are more likely to closed polygons or other forms. These results outperform the state of the art. Indeed, our method tend to accomplish more competitive performances in order to reach SIL 4.

Safety Enhancement. Improving safety is essential for driverless systems, especially for autonomous trains. This would allow them to avoid accidents which can be caused by different factors such as derailment. The latter caused 32 deaths and 19 injuries in 2009, according to the report by Eurostat, the European center responsible for statistical information [16]. To define an industrial solution for increasingly secure autonomous trains, we propose a perception approach based on computer vision through the processing of lidar point clouds and images, combined with on-board mapping system, with the objective of improving derailment prevention through reliable rails detection. This solution also makes it possible to ensure a perception of the environment located at the front of the train by means of sensors in order to detect and monitor the objects of the infrastructure and the obstacles located on and near the tracks. Thanks to the consistent detection results, we also ensure a reliable train localization and correct information transmission. Achieving these performances ensures that SIL 4 criteria for the safety of autonomous trains can be reached.

5   Conclusion

The 3D segmentation model developed proved its robustness to the SemanticKITTI dataset and for the railway dataset. We used the network KP-FCNN as a robust baseline to benchmark our approach, with the SegRail proposed method which improved KP-FCNN performances by 6.6 points in mIoU on the railway dataset and by pre-processing data, improved runtime frequency to 20 Hz. In the same time, to make the model know the a priori railway infrastructure, we added map data as additional input to confirm predictions of KP-FCNN. By showing improvements in performance, we proved that map data is a must-have in autonomous driving systems to ensure high confidence in predictions, and so, increase safety of the AI-based system. Our approach is expandable to other use-cases such as level crossing, train stations monitoring that may need metrological pointwise perception and any other referenced map objects. The proposed algorithm can be improved by using sensor fusion with a RGB-camera for example. Technological redundancy between AI-based systems for monitoring has very high confidence rates and can lead to reliable systems for all inter-actors of the autonomous train.

References

1. Hu, Q., et al.: RandLA-Net: efficient semantic segmentation of large-scale point clouds. In: Proceedings of the IEEE/CVF Conference on Computer Vision and Pattern Recognition, pp. 11108–11117 (2020)
2. Zhu, X., et al.: Cylindrical and asymmetrical 3D convolution networks for LiDAR segmentation. In: Proceedings of the IEEE/CVF Conference on Computer Vision and Pattern Recognition (2021)
3. Behley, J., et al.: SemanticKITTI: a dataset for semantic scene understanding of LiDAR sequences. In: IEEE/CVF International Conference on Computer Vision (ICCV) (2019)
4. Qi, C.R., Yi, L., Su, H., Guibas, L.J.: PointNet++: deep hierarchical feature learning on point sets in a metric space. In: Neural Information Processing Systems (NeurIPS) (2017)
5. Qi, C.R., Su, H., Mo, K., Guibas, L.J.: PointNet: deep learning on point sets for 3D classification and segmentation. In: IEEE Conference on Computer Vision and Pattern Recognition (CVPR) (2017)
6. Cheng, R., Razani, R., Taghavi, E., Li, E., Liu, B.: (AF)2-S3Net: attentive feature fusion with adaptive feature selection for sparse semantic segmentation network (2021)
7. Thomas, H., Qi, C.R., Deschaud, J.-E., Marcotegui, B., Goulette, F., Guibas, L.J.: KPConv: flexible and deformable convolution for point clouds. In: Proceedings of the IEEE International Conference on Computer Vision, pp. 6411–6420 (2019)

8. Wang, S., Suo, S., Ma, W, Pokrovsky, A., Urtasun, R.: Deep parametric continuous convolutional neural networks. In: Proceedings of the IEEE Conference on Computer Vision and Pattern Recognition, pp. 2589–2597 (2018)

9. Engelmann, F., Kontogianni, T., Leibe, B.: Dilated point convolutions: on the receptive field size of point convolutions on 3D point clouds. In: International Conference on Robotics and Automation, vol. 1 (2020)

10. Hua, B., Tran, M., Yeung, S.: Pointwise convolutional neural networks. In: Proceedings of the IEEE Conference on Computer Vision and Pattern Recognition, pp. 984–993 (2018)

11. Huang, Q., Wang, W., Neumann, U.: Recurrent slice networks for 3D segmentation of point clouds. In: Proceedings of the IEEE Conference on Computer Vision and Pattern Recognition, pp. 2626–2635 (2018)

12. Zeng, W., Gevers, T.: 3DContextNet: KD tree guided hierarchical learning of point clouds using local and global contextual cues. In: Proceedings of the European Conference on Computer Vision (ECCV) (2018)

13. Xie, Z., Chen, J., Peng, B.: Point clouds learning with attention-based graph convolution networks. Neurocomputing **402**, 245–255 (2020)

14. He, Y., et al.: Deep learning based 3D segmentation: a survey. arXiv: 2103.05423 (2021)

15. Geiger, A., Lenz, P., Urtasun, R.: Are we ready for autonomous driving? The KITTI vision benchmark suite. In: IEEE Conference on Computer Vision and Pattern Recognition (CVPR), pp. 3354–3361 (2012)

16. EURO NCAP. EURO NCAP advanced: Autonomous Emergency Braking, September 2013

17. Commission Européene. Norme Européene NF EN 50126 Applications ferroviaires - Spécification et démonstration de la fiabilité, de la disponibilité, de la maintenabilité et de la sécurité, May 2003

18. UIC. Railtopomodel homepage. https://www.railtopomodel.org/en/

19. Eastman, C., Teicholz, P., Sacks, R., Liston, K.: BIM Handbook: A Guide to Building Information Modeling for Owners, Managers, Designers, Engineers and Contractors. Wiley, Hoboken (2008)

20. EULYNX Homepage. https://www.eulynx.eu/

Assigning Safe Executed Systems to Meanings

Lilian Burdy[✉], David Deharbe, and Denis Sabatier

CLEARSY, Aix-en-Provence, France
{Lilian.Burdy,David.Deharbe,Denis.Sabatier}@clearsy.com
http://www.clearsy.com

Abstract. The B method is a formal method to design software components and to prove that they are compliant with some formalized requirements, giving a way to build safety-critical programs. However, the correctness of the obtained programs obviously rely on the correctness of those formalized software requirements. Using the CLEARSY Safety Platform, a vital processing solution developed by CLEARSY (SIL4 certified, Certifer 9594/0262) with native B capabilities, we demonstrate here a method to develop vital software with formal proofs directly attached to the key system properties. For instance, a train localization system is proven regarding the property stating that the computed location interval shall always contain the actual train. Such proofs become possible by combining software variables with variables representing physical entities and their timed evolution, thanks to the guaranteed time and deadlines of the CLEARSY Safety Platform. Thus, we avoid the problem of ensuring the correctness of a complex set of formalized software requirements by directly ensuring the wanted system properties. Assumptions and properties for the non-software parts are included in the same B model used to develop the software on the CLEARSY Safety Platform.

Keywords: Formal modelling · System reliability

1 Introduction

Formal methods with proof support are a mean to specify the expected properties of a system, to describe the behavior of this system and to verify that the behavior description satisfies the properties [13].

Formal methods have long been applied in the railways. In particular, the B method [1] has been used to develop safety-critical software components for more than 20 years [3] and is still in use nowadays, e.g. in CBTC systems. In such applications, the goal is to produce a software implementation of a specification of the intended behaviour, expressed in terms of software entities. So its scope is completely within the realm of the software. For instance, a requirement for a train tracking function in a CBTC could be that the software representation of the position of every train must be continuous.

© Springer Nature Switzerland AG 2022
S. Collart-Dutilleul et al. (Eds.): RSSRail 2022, LNCS 13294, pp. 130–142, 2022.
https://doi.org/10.1007/978-3-031-05814-1_9

CLEARSY has also been applying the Event-B method [2] to model whole systems composed of interacting software and physical entities and to prove system-level properties involving those [6,8,11,12]. Such system-level models and proofs rely upon assumptions on the different sub-systems (including human behavior). For example, a system-level requirement for a CBTC could be the absence of train derailments; its proof would rely on assumption such as the train-tracking function guarantees that, for every train, the software representation of its position must cover the track portion it occupies.

Such assumptions involve both real, physical, entities (trains) and software entities (the representation of the position of trains in the tracking function). Again, formal methods may be applied to verify such assumptions. One approach, following the system-level approach, is to formalize both physical and logical entities and their behaviour in a single model and to prove that the assumed property holds [5,7,10].

In this paper, we present a second approach where assumptions made at system-level are part of the formal specification of the software and are guaranteed to hold on its implementation thanks to the correct-by-construction approach of the B method and by guarantees provided by the underlying executing platform, namely the CLEARSY Safety Platform[1] (CSP).

The CSP is briefly presented in Sect. 2. Next, Sect. 3 presents accompanying real-time constructs, describes how they are to be used to program real-time constraints, and justifies the obtained guarantees. Section 4 presents the principles to apply these constructs to specify and verify system-level timed properties provides two illustrating examples. Finally, conclusions are drawn in Sect. 5.

2   CLEARSY Safety Platform

CLEARSY has developed and certified the CLEARSY Safety Platform (CSP), a solution to develop safety critical real-time embedded systems certified up to SIL4. CSP provides a framework, based on the formal method B, to guarantee software-level safety properties.

The CLEARSY Safety Platform is made of:

- A software library called CLEARSY Safety Platform library (CSPlib).
- A compatible single board vital computer ($72.5 \times 45 \times 12$ mm) based on a composite safety architecture (CS0).

The hardware consists of two low power 32bits micro-controllers that continuously cross-check. The software library contains a set of routines which help to address the common challenges of a composite vital computing architecture.

The safety properties of the application are formalized in dedicated specifying modules. The modules also embed the software implementation of their specification. Thanks to the B method, such implementations can be formally proved to comply 100% with their specification. The CSP includes a library, also developed in B, providing the elements to express rich safety properties on software execution.

---

[1] https://www.clearsy.com/outils/clearsy-safety-platform/.

The CSP IDE provides a fully automatic dual compilation process that generates a binary executable and uploads it on the CSP platform. This executable is guaranteed to execute faithfully the developed software or to fall back to a stable vital state, as soon as the conditions of a safe execution cannot be guaranteed. Part of the safety is guaranteed thanks to a replicated execution of the vital software. Each replica is generated by a different compilation tool chain.

The safety of the CSP has been established and certified (SIL4 level). The purpose of this paper is *not* to discuss this safety: the topic here is the B formal proof of an application program. So, we request the reader to take the CSP safety for granted, i.e., that any application program developed for the CSP with the CSP toolkit and according to the requested conditions will always perform as defined in its B0 code, or a shutdown will ensure the absence of any permissive output. B0 is the programming language included in the B method, featuring standard programming constructs: scalar and array variables, IF, CASE, WHILE constructs, etc.

Figure 1 sketches how the safety is ensured in CSP. Each micro-controller runs the safety program twice, once for each of two replicas compiled independently. Replica variables are compared using the CSPLib services. Those services also provide timing, watchdog and liveness checks, interlocked with the application replicas in such a way that any disappearance of any part whose timely processing is required leads to shutdown of the affected micro-controller and ensures the shutdown of the other one. In the safety proof, we demonstrated that any compiling error, variable upset, clock drift, interrupt failure, ram or flash failure, etc., even common mode PIC32 instruction processing error all lead to shutdown before any wrong permissive output can be produced.

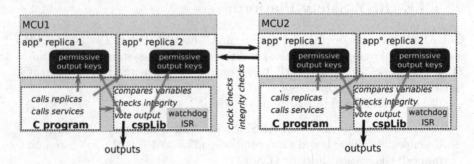

Fig. 1. Overview of the CSP safety architecture.

To develop an application program, the user writes the safety part in B0 (automatically replicated by the CSP toolkit) and the conventional parts in C. Provided that the keys to produce permissive outputs remain "hidden" in the B0 parts (as requested in the safety conditions), only binaries produced by the CSP toolkit can upload with read-back check-sums matching the certificate and run to produce permissive outputs without shutdown. No operating system is provided: the PIC32 micro-controllers run code either from the flow started at initialization or started from interrupts.

B0 was chosen as the input programming language firstly to favor the use of the B method to prove an application program, but also because we easily developed the B0 to PIC32 assembly independent compiler. One could sketch the B method as:

- Writing the specifications in B abstract language;
- Writing the program in B0;
- Using the tools from the B theory to prove that the program matches the specifications.

A B0 program can be written with empty B specifications, leading to no proof. Our topic in this paper is to present how to write meaningful B specifications for a CSP application program. In particular, the B proof paradigm is state based, assuming that operations change variables one at a time and in a one-shot manner, which does not directly match the PIC32 context where interrupts occur (as the watchdog services from the CSPLib). The proof scheme in this context is studied below, leading to the possibility to introduce abstract variables denoting the state over time of physical objects and ultimately to perform system level proofs from a software model.

3   CSPLib

CSP comes with a software library, called CSPLib, that provides services to the end-users so that they can formalize safety properties and implement software. In this section, only time-related interfaces are described and explained.

3.1   Timing Support

The CSPLib library defines services that shall be used to fulfill the CSP safety-related application requirements (SRACs) [4], notably methods vitalClock_check Accuracy and watchdogLiveness_testDeadline allowing guaranteed time measurement.

The library also provides read access to some state variables:

- v_watchdogLiveness_clock: guaranteed time from last boot expressed in 125 μs ticks with a specific accuracy;
- v_watchdogLiveness_watchdogIsAlive: Boolean flag indicating if a default has been encountered, notably concerning time, forcing outputs to become restrictive.

These CSPLib variables are updated automatically using the hardware interruption mechanism, in particular during the execution of user project operations.

Actually, the variable v_watchdogLiveness_clock contains a controlled approximation of the real time since start. CSP guarantees that as soon as a fault would potentially jeopardize the value of its clocks, it is safely shut down. Real time is measured in $125\,\mu s$ period from last boot, with a guaranteed precision: the period is between $125\,\mu s \times (1 - \varepsilon)$ and $125\,\mu s \times (1 + \varepsilon)$, where $\varepsilon = 0,000105$. There is no precise definition of when the clock is started, but it is not a problem as soon as the clock is used to time-stamp events and these measures are then compared. So, CSP furnishes a concrete variable v_watchdogLiveness_clock that is really implemented and maintained up to date by the CSPLib and that is effectively guaranteed to store a real clock value at a given accuracy whenever the CSP is not shutdown.

Note that variable v_watchdogLiveness_clock shall not be directly used in user code. Indeed, as code execution is duplicated, and as this variable is updated during execution, each replica may get different values when reading it. If the code directly depends on the clock value, the replicas will legitimately exhibit divergent behavior, which would be detected by the CSP safety mechanisms and force a shutdown. To avoid this pitfall, the CSPLib library provides the *checkAccuracy* service that validates that a clock value is recent enough. With this function, user code can test the validity and the freshness of a given clock value.

From such time measurements, the program can measure time differences as being sufficiently long. However, there is no guarantee that operations are called, and that an action is scheduled early enough.

Even though the CSP cannot be guaranteed that an action takes place early enough, it provides a mechanism to guarantee that it cannot be called too late. The function user_watchdogTimer is called whenever the clock is incremented. The user must define user_watchdogTimer and shall insert calls to testDeadline in user_watchdogTimer to test that a designated deadline is not missed. A failed testDeadline enforces immediately a shutdown in a safe fall back mode.

In summary, the CSPlib provides a mechanism to guarantee that actions cannot happen after their deadline.

3.2   Proof of Timing Properties

This paragraph describes how the reasoning framework B-method can be used to prove timing properties of the CSP execution of the designed software.

We have seen that v_watchdogLiveness_clock evolves with each call of the reserved operation user_watchdogTimer. Such calls happen thanks to underlying hardware interrupts and may occur at any time, including while executing other B operations.

Let us consider first that B operations do not take any time so the calls to user_watchdogTimer do not interrupt other B operations.

Also the clock variable is incremented whenever user_watchdogTimer is called. But as user_watchdogTimer has no access to this CSPLib variable, this information is not available in the proof. Let us suppose nevertheless that we could bring this fact to the knowledge of proof and discuss about proof of timing properties in this simplified framework.

Maximum Time. If the user needs to establish that an action A takes place at the latest T_{max} after a source event E, it is enough to specify with B variables and conditions that the state where E has taken place but not yet action A does not exist on more previous values of the clock than what corresponds to T_{max}. Since user_watchdogTimer increments the clock, thus extending the series specified as limited, and since only testDeadline can establish the post-condition that the clock stays below the deadline, the user is then forced by proof to call testDeadline in user_watchdogTimer. Of course, such deadline value must be less than T_{max} from the most recent clock value where the "E without A" state has occurred. To characterize this deadline variable with respect to the most recent clock value where this "E without A" state occurred, the user must call *checkAccuracy* to establish that the measured clock is before the current clock, since this is the only function allowing to establish a post-condition between the clock and a user variable. The proof thus establishes that, if the shutdown did not take place, action A happened less than T_{max} after the event E.

Minimum Time. To ensure a minimal delay T_{min} from event E1 to event E2, it is sufficient to specify that the successive values of clock separating the two actions correspond to a duration always greater than T_{min}. To establish the correctness, calls to the E2 require to prove that a time measurement (validated by checkAccuracy as less than clock, and sufficiently fresh) has indeed exceeded a limit establishing the delay T_{min}. To calculate this limit, T_{min} must be summed to a time measurement validated as not too old compared to clock at the time of E1 (taking into account this precision).

One can therefore specify all the temporal constraints with B and rely on the proof to guarantee them. It is sufficient to express these constraints with the states of the B project at each value of the clock variable of CSPLib.

Nevertheless, it remains to eliminate the previous simplifying assumptions.

3.3 Lifting Simplifying Hypotheses

We have so far made the simplifying assumption that the operations were of zero duration and that calls to user_watchdogTimer do not occur in the middle of other B operations. Of course, this is not true and we informally justify why this is not an issue.

For any B operation, at any time, at most one replica is executing it, and the other replica is stopped outside the execution of a B operation (this is guaranteed by the CSP safety mechanism). We believe that, thanks to this "stable" replica, the proof is valid despite the interrupt calls. There is also the problem that clock is incremented together with user_watchdogTimer. As we express in the main B project links between clock and project variables, can calls to user_watchdogTimer from an interrupt raised every 125 µs invalidate the proof?

Example: In a B program, the user sets an output S to permissive during a long operation, and sets it back to restrictive at the end of the operation. In the specification, the user defines $S(t)$ for t between 0 and now, proving that S remains restrictive whatever t is.

Seen from the B proof (between every operation execution), this output is always restrictive. In this example, we must consider the two replicas r_1 and r_2. With r_1 executing the operation, an interrupt may occur, the value of $r_1.S$ may be permissive (breaking the invariant). But we have the guarantee, by proof, that in the stable replica r_2, the output $r_2.S$ is restrictive. By SRAC, $r_1.S$ and $r_2.S$ must be combined to produce the output of the CSP. Since the safe combination of restrictive and permissive is restrictive, the output S will be restrictive, as specified.

By defining $S(t)$, the user "seems" to note in the sequence $S(t)$ the value of S at each time increment. The sequence $S(t)$ is a purely theoretical object, related to the states of S stable between r_1 and r_2, always restrictive in our example. The proof is therefore valid: $S(t)$ is always restrictive.

More generally, the clock variable and the variables that the user can attach to it (like $S(t)$ in the above example) remain purely abstract in the user's B project. When they are linked to implemented variables (like $S(t)$ linked to S) they refer only to the stable values ($r_1.S = r_2.S$) of these variables. We strongly believe that the safety invariants (i.e., properties that are true whenever outputs are restrictive) verified by proof are effectively established by the CSP framework.

> Result: in a CSP user B project, the user can specify all the temporal constraints with B and rely on the proof to guarantee them. To do this, it is sufficient to express these constraints with respect to the states of the project at each value of the clock variable of CSPLib. The effective respect of specified temporal constraints is then guaranteed by proof.

4 Proving Reality

4.1 Guidelines

With B, specifications are written on abstract variables linked to programming variables by gluing invariants; the proof establishes for each operation that there is an instance of the specified evolution that corresponds to what the concrete operation does. For instance:

- Specification: the system receives a sequence of samples $s(n)$, and shall produce a result which is a certain function F of this sequence. The abstract variable $s(n)$ represents the sequence, potentially unbounded (no limit of duration) of samples received since the beginning. The specification requires that the result is equal to $F(s)$.
- Real B0 program: let's imagine that to compute $F(s)$, it is sufficient to maintain up to date a restricted number of variables $v_1, ..., v_N$, updated at each new sample received. For example, F could be a sliding average or a theoretical Kalman filter.
- Proof: the proof will establish that there exists a sequence s such that the result produced by the program is $F(s)$. If we have made the necessary links

so that s always corresponds to the received samples, the proof establishes that the subroutine using $v_1, ..., v_N$ produces a result strictly equivalent to $F(s)$. If these links are absent, any result R is suitable, as long as there is a sequence s such that $R = F(s)$.

This defines the meaning of the refinement link, "satisfying the specification".

As explained above, the abstract variable that represents the received samples $s(n)$ must be related to the real inputs received by the B0 program. This link is done by successive gluing invariants; if one is missing the proof has no longer the wanted meaning. In the same way it is necessary to make sure that the output R (specified as equal to $F(s)$) corresponds to the real output of the B0 program: this is directly the case when this output is the return parameter of an externally visible B operation. More generally, one must ensure the correct link between the abstract variables representing the outputs and these real outputs.

Therefore we can say:

- If the specification indicates what is intended ($R = F(s)$ in our example);
- If the inputs are well represented ($s(n)$ related to the actual inputs in our example);
- If the outputs are well represented (R linked to the actual output in our example);
- If the B project is correct (100% proof, rules added OK, project check OK);
- Then the software is guaranteed to be correct with respect to systematic errors (no bugs). There is no need to review the code or to test the behavior of the software itself (which does not dispense with testing the environment).
- If it also runs on CSP, if the CSP SRACs and the B-CSP conditions are satisfied, then the execution is compliant.

Nevertheless, there is no guarantee that the operations are called (the calculation of $R = F(s)$ in our example) nor how often these calls will take place. In practice, this limits the abstract variables used for the specification to notions that can be deduced from the variables of the concrete program.

With the CSP, we now have a notion of time including call guarantees (in fact shutdown is guaranteed in case of call failure). As we have seen, this makes it possible to express timing constraints in the B specification, in the form of conditions on the successive states depending on successive values of clock. We can thus use abstract real time variables.

4.2   A Simple Example: Safety Flasher

The CSP is delivered with an simple example: the "Safety Flasher" [9]. In this system, there is only one output S with the following condition: If $S(t_0) = ON$, then there is t_1 in the interval $[t_0 - 2s; t_0]$ such that $S = OFF$ on $[t_1; t_1 + 1s]$.

This requires that the output cannot remain ON for more than one second, and that there are always OFF (cooling) periods of at least one second between. Using the previous constraints:

- If this specification is correct (let us assume it is);
- If the inputs are well represented: no input, OK;
- If the output S corresponds to the real output of the program;
- If the B project is correct;
- If the CSP SRACs and the B-CSP conditions are satisfied;
- Then the real output will behave according to this law, or the CSP falls back to failsafe mode (and then the desired law is still true: the output is OFF).

So, we can now express and prove timing properties on the real outputs.

4.3   Full Example: Train Location and Kinematics

This example is based on on-board localization function of the Rail-Map project[2], funded by ADEME. The objective is to measure the position of a train on an embedded calculator using the CSP. More precisely, let us suppose that we want to establish that the position and the real speed of the train were within the recently calculated intervals. This condition is sufficient, because then with the minimum/maximum accelerations of the train one can limit its position and speed during the whole interval between two measurements or two calculations, or for use within a given time period.

For this, we assume that the program reads inputs periodically, thus defining a cycle. These inputs can correspond to the reading of beacons, mats, other track markers, and/or wheel rotation sensors. Of course, these inputs must be safe, so it must always be possible to detect the presence of faults that make these inputs unsafe: this is achieved by introducing redundancies, creating composite or injection-testable inputs on which the program can apply tests (and avoid the accumulation of failures by ensuring the fallback). So if some checks are successfully performed, then these inputs correctly denote the evolution of the train position. To clarify things further, we will assume that the software is made of a single entry point called periodically: inputs are read, calculations performed producing the speed and position intervals I_{calc} as output, all within a single computation cycle.

We will assume that the knowledge of the guaranteed time between two cycles is obtained by specifying temporal constraints in B as presented previously:

- Time between 2 cycles less than T_{max};
- Time between 2 cycles greater than T_{min}.

To respect T_{max}, a deadline must be managed and tested in user_watchdogTimer. The program shall also guarantee T_{min}; thanks to checkAccuracy, this is possible. The B model then contains the property that the time difference between the present cycle and the previous cycle is between T_{min} and T_{max}. The entry-point function realized in B is launched at each cycle by the non-vital layers, but fallback is guaranteed in case of an incorrect time difference.

---

[2] https://www.ademe.fr/sites/default/files/assets/documents/rail-map.pdf.

We can define, in the B specification, the position and the speed of the real train for each computation cycle: $P(t)$, $V(t)$. These are abstract functions denoting the real position/velocity for a sequence of instants separated by $D_{cycle} \in [T_{min}; T_{max}]$. More precisely, these instants are also shifted in the past by the time of propagation in the measurement circuits. This propagation is necessarily safely bounded on the validated inputs (otherwise an indefinite buffering would be possible, contradicting the hypothesis of secure inputs after validation). The evolution of $P(t)$, $V(t)$ is also bounded according to the limits of acceleration of the train, thanks to a physical model of evolution which can be directly expressed in the B specification.

On the other hand, if the desired tests have been done, the cycle inputs correctly denote the movement of the real train during the cycle: we therefore have a link between these inputs E and the new position/speed of the train, according to its previous position and speed: $Link(E, P(t_N), V(t_N), P(t_{N-1}), V(t_{N-1}))$. This link can also be expressed in the B specification.

For example, validated inputs can provide a direct safely approximated measure of the distance traveled between t_{N-1} and t_N. It can then be stated that the position has progressed by this distance, while the speed has evolved according to the physical model with this constraint.

To ensure that the desired tests on the inputs are performed, we can also specify them in B: the proof and the CSP will guarantee their correct execution.

We have thus obtained a physical model of evolution directly represented in the B model of the software cycle function. The calculated position and speed intervals are also represented in this model, taking care as before that the corresponding abstract variables are well linked to the real outputs. It then becomes very easy to express a link indicating that $P(t_N), V(t_N)$ must belong to the calculated intervals.

What is the significance of such a specification? Of course there is no divination, even if $P(t)$ and $V(t)$ are supposed to represent the real position and speed of the train we cannot know this reality. But considering the meaning of the refinement link "satisfy the specification" recalled above, the proof will establish that given a real position $P(t_N)$ and a real speed $V(t_N)$, constrained only by the modeled physical model and the link with the cycle inputs, $P(t_N)$ and $V(t_N)$ are in I_{calc}. In other words: I_{calc} (software/logical entity) contains at least all positions and velocities (physical entities) actually reachable according to the past, the evolution laws and the inputs. This is exactly what needs to be shown to ensure that the system is correct.

Note that the fact that I_{calc} contains *only* these attainable positions/speeds is a functional problem of optimization and performance. If we reach this optimum, then the program exploits all the information it has at its disposal. But this is generally not achievable, even less provable.

The physical model expressed in B at the abstract level and the physical link on the validated inputs does not need to be detailed at the abstract level: one can for example use abstract constant functions. Further down, the software will have to use calculation functions that respect the laws of these models:

it is at this level that the correspondence with the real physical laws and the real laws resulting from the validated inputs will have to be established. We thus have physical laws (defined outside B, which must correspond to reality) represented in the form of anonymous abstract constants, and computational functions specified in B as corresponding to these constants. We have to check (outside B) that these computational functions are strictly compliant with these physical laws.

In particular, the connection of continuous physical laws with discrete calculations must be done carefully, so that the actual continuous values are within valid bounds of the discrete results.

In summary:

- If the inputs are well represented;
- If these inputs have been tested and the model that asserts that their frequent testing ensures their validity is correct;
- If the physical model of the train evolution (as provided in B specification) constrained by the validated inputs is correct with respect to the physical world;
- If I_{calc} corresponds to the real output of the program;
- If the B project is correct;
- If the CSP SRACs and the B-CSP conditions are satisfied;
- Then I_{calc} contains the real position/speed of the train at each cycle, or else the CSP is in fallback (and then no more localization is provided).

As long as the CSP has not shut down, we have valid I_{calc} bounds for $P(t_N)$ and $V(t_N)$, the true position and velocity of the train at time t_N whose deviation from the present can obviously be bounded.

B specification of the CSP program then guarantees by proof the correctness of the complete collection system. There are indeed "imported" external models:

- The physical evolution model (from the continuous physical model);
- The probabilistic model of failures or disturbances of the capture (represented by the specification of the tests to be performed on the inputs and by the laws $Link(E, P, V(t_N), P, V(t_{N-1}))$.

But it is the B CSP model that organizes the proof of the whole.

5   Conclusion

We have seen how it is possible to prove with a B formal proof the correctness of a system like the train localization example, directly establishing the key properties like "the computed localization shall contain the actual train". It relies on the possibility to express abstract variables denoting actual objects like the train's real position and speed, thanks to the guaranteed time and deadlines provided by the CLEARSY Safety Platform. Using these guaranteed time and deadlines, the evolution of the actual position and speed can be bounded in relationship with the validated sensors inputs.

Of course, proving the correctness at system level based on assumptions on the sub-systems properties with formal proofs is nothing new. But such system level proofs can easily become uncorrelated to what is actually done in the final subsystems, in particular in the software parts, because formalized assumptions must be transferred to the concerned parts in a mostly manual way. With the method described above, this pitfall disappears as the software formal specifications are directly included in the global B model and their correctness regarding the key system properties is proven. In fact, the problem of the correctness of the software specifications is purely eliminated, thus avoiding the difficulties that caused so many projects to encounter safety pitfalls, not because of low level software bugs, but because the utterly complex detailed software specifications contained the pitfalls from the start.

This method is presented here using the CLEARSY Safety Platform, that has natively formalized B objects to denote the guaranteed time and deadlines. Any vital computer platform normally provides such guarantees in some way, so the method should be adaptable to such random vital platform and, more generally, to any formal proof system. This remains prospective however, as our experience here is limited to the CSP and the B method.

References

1. Abrial, J.R.: The B-Book: Assigning Programs to Meanings, vol. 1. Cambridge University Press, Cambridge (1996)
2. Abrial, J.R.: Modeling in Event-B: System and Software Engineering. Cambridge University Press, Cambridge (2010)
3. Behm, P., Benoit, P., Faivre, A., Meynadier, J.-M.: Météor: a successful application of B in a large project. In: Wing, J.M., Woodcock, J., Davies, J. (eds.) FM 1999. LNCS, vol. 1708, pp. 369–387. Springer, Heidelberg (1999). https://doi.org/10.1007/3-540-48119-2_22
4. CLEARSY: CLEARSY Safety Platform – C_D720 User manual, v01.02, December 2020
5. Comptier, M., Déharbe, D., Fournier, P., Molinero-Perez, J.: Property-driven software analysis. In: ter Beek, M.H., McIver, A., Oliveira, J.N. (eds.) FM 2019. LNCS, vol. 11800, pp. 746–750. Springer, Cham (2019). https://doi.org/10.1007/978-3-030-30942-8_44
6. Comptier, M., Deharbe, D., Perez, J.M., Mussat, L., Pierre, T., Sabatier, D.: Safety analysis of a CBTC system: a rigorous approach with Event-B. In: Fantechi, A., Lecomte, T., Romanovsky, A. (eds.) RSSRail 2017. LNCS, vol. 10598, pp. 148–159. Springer, Cham (2017). https://doi.org/10.1007/978-3-319-68499-4_10
7. Comptier, M., Leuschel, M., Mejia, L.-F., Perez, J.M., Mutz, M.: Property-based modelling and validation of a CBTC zone controller in Event-B. In: Collart-Dutilleul, S., Lecomte, T., Romanovsky, A. (eds.) RSSRail 2019. LNCS, vol. 11495, pp. 202–212. Springer, Cham (2019). https://doi.org/10.1007/978-3-030-18744-6_13
8. Lecomte, T., Comptier, M., Molinero, J., Sabatier, D.: Ensuring safety with system level formal modelling. In: Margaria, T., Steffen, B. (eds.) ISoLA 2020. LNCS, vol. 12478, pp. 393–403. Springer, Cham (2020). https://doi.org/10.1007/978-3-030-61467-6_25

9. Lecomte, T., Lavaud, B., Sabatier, D., Burdy, L.: A safety flasher developed with the CLEARSY safety platform. In: ter Beek, M.H., Ničković, D. (eds.) FMICS 2020. LNCS, vol. 12327, pp. 210–227. Springer, Cham (2020). https://doi.org/10.1007/978-3-030-58298-2_9

10. Parillaud, C., Fonteneau, Y., Belmonte, F.: Interlocking formal verification at alstom signalling. In: Collart-Dutilleul, S., Lecomte, T., Romanovsky, A. (eds.) RSSRail 2019. LNCS, vol. 11495, pp. 215–225. Springer, Cham (2019). https://doi.org/10.1007/978-3-030-18744-6_14

11. Sabatier, D.: Using formal proof and B method at system level for industrial projects. In: Lecomte, T., Pinger, R., Romanovsky, A. (eds.) RSSRail 2016. LNCS, vol. 9707, pp. 20–31. Springer, Cham (2016). https://doi.org/10.1007/978-3-319-33951-1_2

12. Sabatier, D., Burdy, L., Requet, A., Guéry, J.: Formal proofs for the NYCT line 7 (flushing) modernization project. In: Derrick, J., et al. (eds.) ABZ 2012. LNCS, vol. 7316, pp. 369–372. Springer, Heidelberg (2012). https://doi.org/10.1007/978-3-642-30885-7_34

13. Woodcock, J., Larsen, P.G., Bicarregui, J., Fitzgerald, J.: Formal methods: practice and experience. ACM Comput. Surv. **41**(4), 1–36 (2009)

Generating and Verifying Configuration Data with OVADO

Frédéric Badeau[1]([⊠]), Julien Chappelin[2], and Joris Lamare[3]

[1] Systerel, Aix-en-Provence, France
`frederic.badeau@systerel.fr`
[2] Alstom, Aix-en-Provence, France
`julien.chappelin@alstomgroup.com`
[3] RATP, Paris, France
`joris.lamare@ratp.fr`

Abstract. This article presents a novel use of OVADO, a data validation tool for railway systems configuration, and its application in an industrial setting. We describe how OVADO usage evolved from data validation to generation of equipment configuration data, and report on the application of this technique in a real industrial context: the deployment of the OCTYS VTPA system by Alstom on Line 6 of the Paris metro, operated by RATP. While this new method requires some adaptation in industrial processes in order to retain compliance with a SIL4 safety level, it improves translation quality and factorizes data generation and verification activities.

Keywords: Railway systems · CBTC · Data validation · B language · Ovado

1 Introduction

The OVADO[1] tool has been used for more than a decade to formally check whether system configuration data comply with their rules in the context of railway systems [1]. OVADO is currently deployed in SIL4 processes compliant with the safety requirements of the CENELEC EN50128 standard [2]. In these processes, it is considered a T2-class tool since it only helps to verify the system. This article describes how the OVADO tool has been used, for the first time, by Systerel to formally generate equipment configuration data derived from the system configuration data. This innovative use has been applied in a real industrial context, the deployment of the OCTYS VTPA system by Alstom on Line 6 of the Paris metro operated by RATP. The industrial process had to be adapted in order to remain compliant with a SIL4 safety level of the EN50128 standard. The OVADO tool is considered a T3-class tool for this new purpose since it now produces system configuration data.

---

[1] OVADO[2]® is a RATP tool distributed and partly designed by Systerel (see https://www.ovado.fr).

© Springer Nature Switzerland AG 2022
S. Collart-Dutilleul et al. (Eds.): RSSRail 2022, LNCS 13294, pp. 143–148, 2022.
https://doi.org/10.1007/978-3-031-05814-1_10

2   OVADO Basic Use

The OVADO tool is an evaluation engine that takes as inputs configuration data and a formal model (in B language) of rules on the data and that verifies whether or not each rule holds. Figure 1 illustrates the tool's basic workflow. The tool consists of two independent tool chains, allowing it to be used in a SIL4 process. The first chain is developped in Java/Eclipse as an engine evaluating B language predicates and expressions untill getting to data values. The second chain first produces a B abstract machine gathering data values and rules modeled as B properties and then calls the B model-checker ProB to evaluate the rules.

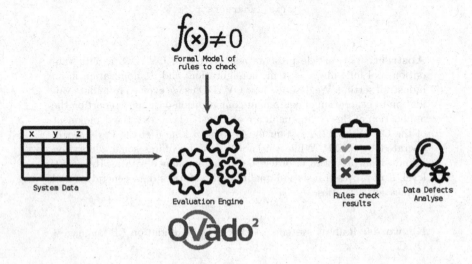

Fig. 1. Basic use of OVADO to check whether data comply with their rules.

OVADO can interface natively with data from XML or Excel files. To interface with other data formats, it is possible to develop specific extension modules. In this case 2 independent modules must be developed, one for each OVADO tool chain.

The formal model of the rules is composed of 3 parts: the interface with input data, intermediate definitions and the rules themselves. The intermediate definitions permit to develop intermediate abstractions, in order to avoid working directly with the raw configuration data and they also allow reusable library functions to be defined.

Then, OVADO can evaluate for each rule if the data respect the rule or not. To do so, it evaluates the rule as well as each intermediate definition transitively used till it gets to configuration data values. When a rule is not obeyed, OVADO produces a list of counterexamples to the rule and helps the user to analyze the causes of the rule violation.

3   OVADO Use to Check Railway Systems

To configure railway systems, the data is usually split into two parts: high level configuration data of the system provided in a user friendly format (e.g. XML or Excel) and low level configuration data loaded into the different devices of the system provided in a specific format (e.g. binary data). Low level data is deduced deterministically from system high level data. Until now, it was produced by software tools developed specifically for data generation with no safety requirement as the safety issues were entirely covered by the verification activity.

Data verification with OVADO consists in verifying the data rules issued by the various stakeholders in charge of the system configuration and verifying the consistency between the implementation data and the system data from which it is derived. To achieve this consistency check, the OVADO model includes the definition of the theoretical computation of the equipment configuration data from the system data, as well as the equality properties of the latter with the equipment configuration data produced by the data generation tools. Figure 2 illustrates this use of OVADO.

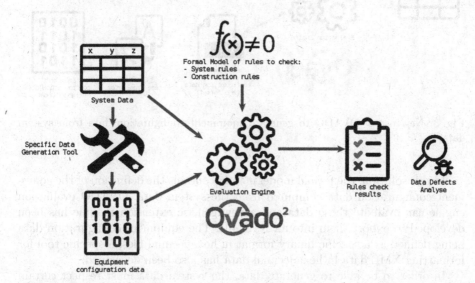

Fig. 2. A more complete use of OVADO in which the rules on the system data and the correct construction of the equipment configuration data in relation to the system data are checked.

4   A New Use of OVADO to Generate Data

Originally, the OVADO tool was only used to evaluate rules on configuration data, which means computing a Boolean result (TRUE or FALSE) for each evaluated rule. However, the tool can evaluate any intermediate expression modeled from the input data and not only Boolean expressions. Over the years, several OVADO extension modules have been developed to exploit some of these intermediate expressions, such as the module for displaying counterexamples of rules and the module for displaying interactively any expression to perform analyses on data or to debug the model. A data export module has been developed for this project, so that OVADO can now generate configuration data, as shown in Fig. 3.

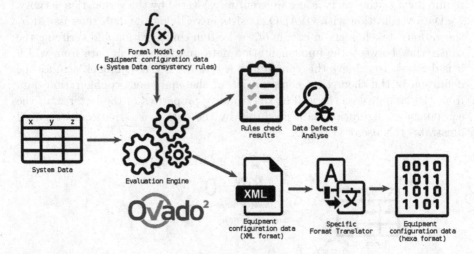

Fig. 3. New use of OVADO to generate equipment configuration data from system data.

In this solution, the formal model mainly contains the definition of the equipment configuration data computed from the system data. OVADO evaluation engine can evaluate those data and a new generic extension module has been developed to export them into an XML file. The equipment configuration data being defined as a specific binary format in hexadecimal files, a specific tool for formatting XML data in hexadecimal data has also been developed.

In order to be able to generate data, the system data must respect certain consistency constraints. Moreover, since the generated data must fill tables, the constraints of the format of these tables must also be obeyed. For instance, there should be no overflow of the number of elements and no overflow of the values of the elements. All these constraints constitute consistency rules that must be enforced. It was natural to verify these rules by integrating them into the formal OVADO data generation model. Before generating configuration data, it is necessary to check those rules in order to guarantee that this data generation is feasible and conforms to what is expected.

The safety strategy does not rely on producing safe configuration data. It relies on verifying safely that configuration data produced are correct. This strategy covers possible errors that may occur at any step of data production:

evaluation of data inside OVADO, generic export into XML files, translation into specific binary format or even while copying and delivering data configuration files. That is why only the first chain of OVADO is used to generate configuration data. However, both OVADO toolchains are still used for the verification activity.

This new use of OVADO changes its tool class according to the EN50128 standard. Indeed, it goes from being a T2-class tool (tool used for verification only) to a T3-class tool (tool contributing to the generation of code or data of the safety critical software).

This innovative approach has several advantages. It raises the quality level of the data generation solution, as it is now based on a formal model close to the data specification and on a generic evaluation engine (OVADO). It also reduces the costs by factoring out common activities between generation and verification.

5   Adaptation of the SIL4 Process

This approach requires to manage the common mode between data generation and verification in the OVADO model. Indeed, 80% of the OVADO model is dedicated to the computation of intermediate data used to produce the theoretical equipment configuration data. The remaining 20% represent the pure modeling of the rules.

Mitigation of a common mode error within the model is performed thanks to a detailed verification activity of the OVADO formal model. In this activity, each model element is verified independently and traced in auditable records by filling about fifteen criteria established following the feedback of both Systerel and RATP OVADO modeling experts. This verification activity has to be done once for a given OVADO model. When the input documents describing the data and rules evolve, the OVADO model creation activity and its detailed verification activity must be reworked, addressing only the differences. For each element of the OVADO model (rule, intermediate definition or interface with a constant), examples of verification criteria are: the presence of a natural language specification of the element and its completeness and consistency with the formal model, compliance with naming rules, data type verification, Well-Definedness verification, the presence of comments for case-based modeling or for tricky modeling points, traceability and compliance with the documents specifying the rules and the data format. There are also several criteria dedicated to the railway domain, such as consistency between the different references on the track, the consistency of the position of switch points on several tracks or unit consistency for the physical quantities. The Well-Definedness verification is done by providing an informal proof. For instance for a given $f(x)$ expression this proof may rely on f being a function and x being part of the domain of f.

From an industrial point of view, the cost of this detailed verification activity of the OVADO formal model is estimated at 10 to 15% of the development cost of the model.

6   Conclusion

To conclude, this article presented how the OVADO tool, that was primary used to the verification of configuration data of railway systems from a formal modeling of the rules on the data, was successfully used, in addition to its primary use for verification, to generate configuration data of railway equipment. This evolution brought the tool from the EN50128 T2 tool class to the T3 tool class. It brings advantages in terms of translation quality and factorization of data generation and verification activities. Finally, this new use of OVADO still complies with a SIL4 process.

References

1. Abo, R., Voisin, L.: Formal implementation of data validation for railway safety-related systems with OVADO. In: Counsell, S., Núñez, M. (eds.) SEFM 2013. LNCS, vol. 8368, pp. 221–236. Springer, Cham (2014). https://doi.org/10.1007/978-3-319-05032-4_17
2. CEN: Railway applications-communication, signalling and processing systems-software for railway control and protection systems (2011)

The 4SECURail Formal Methods Demonstrator

Franco Mazzanti[✉] and Dimitri Belli

Istituto di Scienza e Tecnologie dell'Informazione "A. Faedo",
Via G. Moruzzi 1, 56124 Pisa, Italy
{franco.mazzanti,dimitri.belli}@isti.cnr.it

Abstract. The need for high-quality standard interfaces is widely recognized as a mandatory step to reduce procurement costs and create safely operating complex railway infrastructures. That is why European initiatives like EULYNX have been set up precisely with the purpose of supporting standard interfaces development. The exploitation of formal methods during the phase of standardization plays an essential role in raising the quality of the generated specifications. 4SECURail is a recent project that aims to precisely show, with a structured evaluation (known as the formal methods demonstrator), how formal methods might help to improve the quality of a specific signalling interface selected as case study. This paper describes the experience gained with the experiment.

Keywords: Formal verification · Formal methods · System requirements · Standard interfaces · Railway signalling system

1 Introduction

The railway infrastructure is constituted by a large, heterogeneous, and distributed system with components that are on board, trackside, centralized, crossing regional and national borders, managed by different authorities, and developed by different providers. Not surprisingly, the current trend is to standardize the requirements of the various system components together with their interfaces (see, e.g., the EULYNX and the ERTMS initiatives[1]). Standardization, indeed, is expected to increase the market competition with the additional benefits of reducing both vendor lock-in effect and long-term life-cycle costs. However, the defined standard interfaces for the various system components must be *precise* and *correct* to produce the desired effects. They must not suffer from ambiguities in their interpretation and must not give rise to compatibility problems. In this respect, the Shift2Rail Joint Undertaking[2] aims to foster research and innovation in the railway sector by promoting the application of rigorous formal verification techniques to the standard interface development process.

---

[1] https://eulynx.eu, https://www.ertms.net/.
[2] https://shift2rail.org/.

© Springer Nature Switzerland AG 2022
S. Collart-Dutilleul et al. (Eds.): RSSRail 2022, LNCS 13294, pp. 149–165, 2022.
https://doi.org/10.1007/978-3-031-05814-1_11

Performing a formal analysis of a signalling standard is a very different - in the process adopted, the models generated, the tools used, the results expected - and more difficult task than performing a verification of a specific product design. In the case of the signalling standard, we are likely to have a more generic specification with many parameters and options, and its description is expected to be at a higher level, not forcing any unnecessary implementation detail. This is quite different from the case of a specific product design, where parameters and options can be somewhat constrained and where certain implementation choices can be deemed acceptable. So, while in the case of a specific product we might have the goal of validating the specification, e.g., with respect to its safety and functional requirements, in the case of a generic, abstract signalling standard, our goals cannot go further than a partial formal analysis of its properties, built on the definition of some specific scenarios. In doing that, we might need to abstract some aspects not needed for the verification of the intended properties and possibly make specific implementation choices. This does not mean at all that the partial formal analysis is not useful. In very simple terms, while the use of formal methods within the development process has the goal of ensuring that the final product satisfies the stated requirements, the use of formal methods within the system requirements specification phase has the goal of improving the confidence that the specification itself - usually expressed in natural language - is precisely what needed.

In line with the Shift2Rail philosophy, the 4SECURail project[3] aims to observe the possible approaches, benefits, limits, and costs of introducing formal methods in the system requirements definition process. This is done with the set up of a *structured evaluation* (a.k.a. the demonstrator), consisting in applying state-of-the-art tools and methodologies with the purpose to collect meaningful information and data on *one* of the possible paths that could be followed to associate a system requirements definition (or a standard interface) with a formal base. Notice, however, that it is not a purpose of the project the definition or the proposal of an overall methodology for the analysis of the requirements in the railway sector; the specific choices and the approaches exemplified with the demonstrator are simply those that have been considered the most fitting with respect to our specific case study, to our background, and to the project timelines. The project activity plan involves three steps:

1. Selection of a railway signalling case study and its initial specification expressed in natural language [1].
2. Derivation of semi-formal and formal models from the initial requirements specification and conduction of the formal analysis using all the generated evidence and artifacts to improve the initial specification [2–5].
3. Performing a quantitative analysis of the costs and benefits derived by the introduction of formal methods in the requirements definition process, leveraging the data collected during the demonstrator process [6].

In this paper, we introduce the first two steps of the above process, focusing on the presentation of the methodological approach followed in our demonstrator

---

[3] https://4SECURail.eu (November 2019–November 2021).

activity, without entering into the details of the formal analysis that has been conducted. The approach adopted for the quantitative cost/benefits analysis (partly still in progress) is not the subject of this paper. The rest of the paper is structured as follows: In Sect. 2, we give details about the case study that has been the object of the experimentation; in Sect. 3, we present the approach adopted by the demonstrator. In Sect. 4, we briefly describe some related studies, and in Sect. 5, we summarize the results of the experience, and we give insights for future research advancements in the field.

2   The 4SECURail Case Study

The transit of a train from an area supervised by a Radio Block Centre (RBC) to an adjacent area supervised by another RBC occurs during the so-called RBC-RBC handover phase and requires the exchange of information between RBCs according to a specific protocol. This exchange of information is supported by the communication layer specified within the UNISIG SUBSET-039 [7] and UNISIG SUBSET-98 [8]. Figure 1 summarizes the overall structure of the UNISIG standards supporting the handover of a train.

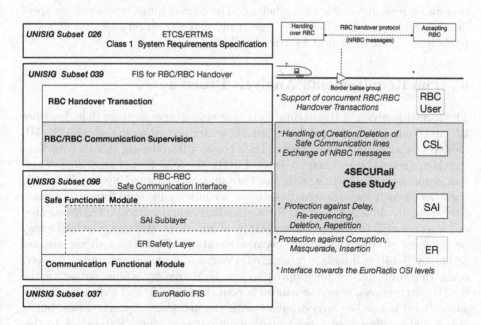

Fig. 1. Overall structure of the 4SECURail case study

The 4SECURail case study focuses on two main sub-components of the communication layers, supporting the RBC-RBC handover communications. The considered components are the Communication Supervision Layer (CSL) of the SUBSET-039 and the Safe Application Intermediate Sub-Layer (SAI) of the

SUBSET-098. These two components are the main actors that support the creation/deletion of safe communication lines and protect the transmission of messages exchanged on such lines. In particular, the CSL is responsible for requesting the activation - and in case of failure, the re-establishment - of the communication line for continuously controlling its liveliness and for forwarding the RBC handover transaction messages on the active line. The SAI is responsible for ensuring the absence of excessive delays, repetitions, losses, or reordering of messages during their transmissions. This is achieved by adding sequence numbers and time-related information to the RBC messages. The two sides of the communication line are configured one as initiator and the other as called.

With respect to the SUBSET-98, the 4SECURail case study does not include, for obvious time and budget constraints, the EuroRadio Safety Layer (ER), which is responsible for preventing corruption, masquerading and insertion issues during the communications, nor the lower Communication Functional Module (CFM) interface. With respect to the SUBSET-039, the 4SECURail case study does not include the description of the activation of multiple, concurrent RBC-RBC handover transactions when trains move from a zone supervised by an RBC to another one. From the point of view of the CSL, the RBC messages are forwarded to/from the other RBC side without the knowledge of the specific content or session to which they belong. The official initial requirements specification document describing the case study and the rationale for its choice is publicly available as project Deliverable D2.3 [1].

3   The Requirements Analysis Process

The formal analysis of the natural language system specification that describes the case study passes through an intermediate step consisting in designing SysML models of the various components. The choice of introducing this intermediate step is motivated by two main reasons. Firstly, the semi-formal modelling of system components is in line with the current trend adopted by the EULYNX initiative, which has selected SysML as accompanying semi-formal notation. And secondly, it is felt natural for a signalling standard to be complemented as far as possible by widely known graphical notations. However, the latter may be a source of troubles, mainly because SysML/UML, despite all the current attempts [9–14], still lacks a recognized, clear, and rigorous semantics. To overcome this problem, we have opted to use an extremely simple subset of the SysML instructions, whose semantics is considered stable and well-defined. The subset used is not the largest subset with the necessary characteristics, but it is just the smallest subset needed to model our case study. Extensions to this subset are definitely possible, but more investigations are needed, and this issue is out of our project goals.

In the modelling and analysis of the case study, a few choices have been made. In particular, the requirements of the SAI component allow two alternative options in modelling the safe connection initialization phase: One option is based on the "Triple Time Stamping (TTS)" approach, while the other is based on the

"Execution Cycle (EC) Defence Technique" approach. Our modelling takes into account the EC option which, at a first glance, seemed less dependent by real-time aspects.

The overall approach followed during the modelling and analysis process is incremental and iterative. About 53 versions of the system have been generated, each one widening the set of requirements of the case study modelled, and each one passing through the steps of semi-formal and formal modelling and analysis. During this iterative process, four kinds of artefacts have been generated and kept aligned:

1. A more abstract, semi-formal UML state machine design of the components under analysis.
2. A more detailed executable version of the same UML state machines.
3. A set of formal models derived from the executable UML state machine.
4. A natural language rewriting of the requirements based on the designed and analysed models.

Figure 2 depicts the relationship between these artefacts, whose detailed description is given in the following subsections. The activity of generating and elaborating most of the shown artefacts (currently) requires a human problem understanding and solving activity. The only part that can be mechanically automated (partly achieved within the project) is the generation of the formal models starting from the UML executable models.

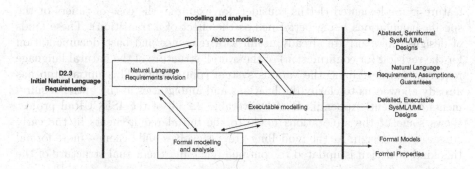

Fig. 2. The 4SECURail demonstrator generated artefacts

3.1   Semi-formal Designs

The first step in trying to associate an operational model to our input requirements specification consists in drawing an abstract design of the state machine describing the various components, putting the accent of the control flow relation between the most relevant system states, the events that trigger the corresponding state transitions, and the communication events occurring among such

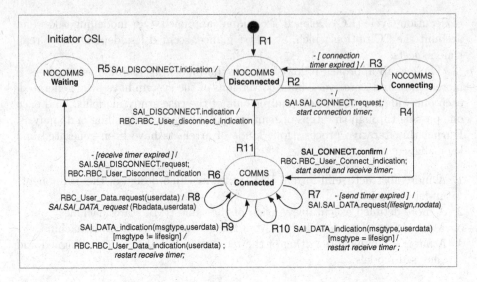

Fig. 3. The Initiator CSL (ICSL) abstract design

components. Figure 3 shows an example of such abstract/semi-formal design. The corresponding designs of the two sides of the modelled CSL and SAI components can be found in Appendix B of Deliverable 2.5 [4].

We can observe that no details are given at this step on how some abstract feature is implemented (let us consider, for example, the case of timers or the specific calculations being performed as the effect of a transition). These kinds of designs, however, are already useful as a reference and base documentation for the revision (or confirmation) of the overall structure of the natural language requirements describing the various system components. This initial step has already allowed us to clarify duplications and ambiguities in the initial requirements document. Appendix B of Deliverable 2.2 [3] of the 4SECURail project shows some of the annotations made to the initial requirements in the early stages of the design. As the modelling process evolves and becomes more formal this kind of design is updated to continue reflecting the actual structure of the system.

3.2   Executable UML Designs

The next step towards a formal model is the completion of the abstract design by providing an implementation of all the informally specified aspects. This means to precisely define all the needed local variables of the various components and clearly describe how they are manipulated within the effects of the various transitions. This also means providing a way to model a reasonable temporal flow since the overall system behaviour depends on several time-dependent aspects. Moreover, in order to generate a closed executable system, it is necessary to build parts of the environment capable of receiving data from our modelled components and stimulate them with appropriate events. In our specific case, we need three kinds of environment components: two components modelling the possible behaviour of the RBC users, and a component modelling the ER that allows the two SAI components to communicate. We also added a Timer component that allows all the components to proceed still in an asynchronous way, but relatively at the same speed. Figure 4 shows the resulting structure of the whole system. All the added environment and timer components can be designed in UML to facilitate the system encoding into the selected formal notations.

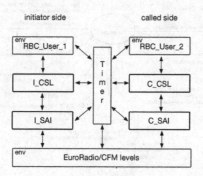

Fig. 4. The complete executable system structure

Figure 5 shows an example of executable state UML design corresponding to the abstract version of the component shown in Fig. 3.

3.3 Formal Modelling

The desirable approach for passing from a SysML/UML executable design (possibly generated with commercial tools like PTC, Yakindu, Rhapsody, Cameo Modeling Tool (once Magic Draw), SPARX-EA, Papyrus) to a set of formal models is to use available translation tools. During the initial phases of the project, we experimented with the SPARX-EA tool for the design of the executable SysML models. Still, no translation tool was found to be available, and an effort to build it was beyond the project effort and outside the project goals. Moreover, linking such translation tools to a specific commercial SysML design tool was considered not desirable. Our solution has been to make a first manual translation of the executable SysML design into the design notation accepted by the UMC tool of the in-house developed KandISTI [15] framework. The UMC notation for specifying a collection of interacting state machines is, in fact, a simple textual, user-friendly encoding of the state machines that allows an almost direct translation of the case study with minimal effort. A fragment of the UMC notation for the state machine depicted in Fig. 5 is shown in Fig. 6.

UMC allows to explore the possible system evolutions and verify branching time properties on it. This framework has been chosen as first target because

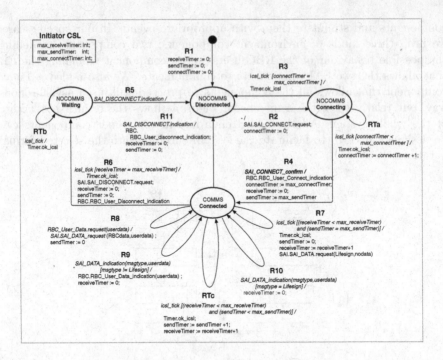

Fig. 5. The Initiator CSL executable model

it fits well the need for fast design prototyping. The resulting graph describing the evolutions of the system can be analysed or saved in the form of Labelled Transition System (LTS), where the user has the choice to specify which kind of information should be associated with the LTS edges. This information may include the UMC transition label, the outgoing events generated by the effects of a transition, or any other custom flag associated with the firing of the transition. However, UMC is essentially an academic prototype used mainly for research and teaching purposes. Therefore, we wanted to take into account also furthermore industry-ready formal verification frameworks.

The second framework that has been chosen to support the formal analysis of the system is ProB [16]. Indeed, according to several surveys (see, e.g., [17–19]) B/EventB appears to be one of the most adopted formal methods in railways. Moreover, ProB has a very user-friendly interface requiring a small effort to be learnt and powerful verification methods. Last but not least, it is freely available as an open-source product.

A third framework that has been taken into account is the CADP toolbox with its LNT language [20, 21]. One interesting aspect of this third approach is that the mathematical representation used for the models is based on process algebras, and can exploit the rich theory around LTS for supporting the verification process (e.g., minimizations, bisimulations, and compositional verification [22–24]). Another interesting aspect of the CADP framework is that the

```
Class I_CSL is                          Behaviour
Signals                                 R1_ICSL:
   -- from RBC                          initial -> Disconnected
   IRBC_User_Data_request(arg1: int);
                                        R2_ICSL_connecting:
   -- from I_SAI                           Disconnected -> Connecting
   ISAI_CONNECT_confirm;                   {- /
   ISAI_DISCONNECT_indication;             SAI.ISAI_CONNECT_request;
   ISAI_Error_report;                      connectTimer := 0;}
   ISAI_DATA_indication(arg1: Token,
                    arg2: int);         RTa_ICSL_okicsl_incr:
                                           Connecting -> Connecting
   -- from Timer                           {icsl_tick [connectTimer <
   icsl_tick;                                          max_connectTimer ] /
                                           Timer.ok_icsl;
Vars                                       connectTimer := connectTimer +1}
   ------ PORTS
   RBC_User: I_RBC;                     R3_ICSL_okicsl_connect:
   SAI: I_SAI;                             Connecting-> Disconnected
                                           { icsl_tick [connectTimer = /
   ------ CONFIGURATION PARAMS                       max_connectTimer ] /
   max_receiveTimer: int;                  Timer.ok_icsl}
   max_sendTimer:  int;
   max_connectTimer: int;              R4_ICSL_userconnind:
                                           Connecting -> COMMS
   ------ LOCAL VARS                        { ISAI_CONNECT_confirm /
   receiveTimer:       int := 0;            RBC_User.IRBC_User_Connect_indication;
   sendTimer: int := 0;                     connectTimer := max_connectTimer;
   connectTimer:      int := 0;             receiveTimer := 0;
                                            sendTimer := max_sendTimer}
                                        ...
                                        end I_CSL;
```

Fig. 6. The ICSL encoding in UMC (fragment)

model structure stands on events, and in particular on communication actions. The logic used to reason on these models is a very powerful, action-based, branching-time logic. This creates another point of view from the one supported

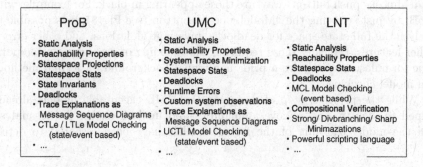

Fig. 7. Table of verification features

by ProB, which is more state-oriented. Similarly to ProB, CADP is freely usable with an academic licence.

Once available the UMC encoding of our model, we can exploit two other in-house translators to directly translate the UMC model into the ProB and LNT notations. We omit here the details of the translations, for which we refer to Appendix A of 4SECURail Deliverable D2.5 [4] and to [27].

The size of a complete (closed) executable model clearly depends on the complexity of the environment components used to stimulate our communication layer. In one of the simplest scenarios, the UMC executable model consists of about 2500 lines, resulting in a ProB model of about 3500 lines and in a LNT model of about 4000 lines. The modelling and analysis of the case study within the project have required an effort of about seven person-months.

These methods and tools are not meant to be, in general, "the best ones" or the "most fitting" the railway sector. Our selected frameworks are just those "most fitting" the project's expected efforts and goals. Alternative meaningful choices, similar in style, might have been mCRL2, nuXmv, Spin, TLA+, HLL.

The choice to model and analyse the system with more than one framework is considered very important for two reasons. Firstly, it allows to take advantage of the multiple verification methods provided by the different frameworks, e.g., analysis of state invariants with ProB, system and components property-driven minimizations with CADP, reachability explanations provided in the form of sequence diagrams with UMC (Fig. 7 shows a table of some of the features provided by our three frameworks). And secondly, the choice of using different formal notations allows us to verify the correctness of the mechanical translation from UML executable design (in UMC) into the other formal notations. All the three formal versions of the system can indeed be *proven* to reflect precisely the same system[4].

In Sects. 5.4 and 5.5, Appendix E and F of Deliverable D2.5 [4] are shown the various way in which all these frameworks have been used to analyse the system behaviour. Our experimentation shows that the selected formal frameworks can be used either in a "lightweight" or "advanced" way. In Fig. 7, the verification features that can be easily exploited without any advanced prior knowledge, and in an almost "push button" way, are those appearing in black. For example, with ProB, by just selecting the "Model Check" button (see Fig. 8), it is possible to analyse the full state-space for deadlocks, invariant violations, and other errors. Other features, typically those requiring the encoding of properties in temporal logic formulas, may require a prior non-trivial background on formal methods and model checking.

While the previous step of designing the UML executable models already helped to identify and remove ambiguities and unclarities, the static analysis and the model checking of the formal models have been essential to detect

---

[4] This has been done by comparing the formal semantics (in the form of an LTS) of the three versions of the system and mechanically proving that they are strongly equivalent.

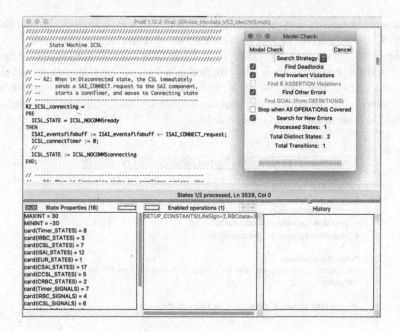

Fig. 8. Model Check GUI of ProB

missing requirements leading to loss events, missing assumptions leading to dead-locks, and implementation mistakes leading to properties violation expected to be guaranteed.

3.4   Revised Natural Language Requirements

Pragmatically, we are afraid that a system requirements specification of a standard interface is doomed to have an official natural language description as well. One of the goals of the 4SECURail demonstrator process is to show a way to improve such an initial natural language specification by backing it with formal models. This improvement has two goals:

1. Guarantee that the specification is based on a rigorous, clear structure, removing ambiguities and duplications.
2. Improve the confidence that the specification is correct, i.e., capable of inter-operating with other systems, with neither missing nor inconsistent requirements.

The generation of executable, formal models is the mean to achieve these goals, not the goal itself. Therefore, in our demonstrator process, we also tried to show a possible way of writing the requirements specification in a manner strictly tied to the executable, formal models but still in natural language.

The implementation choices that have been made in the construction of the executable, formal models should not appear in the natural language requirements specification, which is supposed to be at a higher level than an executable implementation. The abstract semi-formal design of a system, like the one shown in Fig. 3, appears to be at the correct level of abstraction for this task.

Figure 9 shows a possible example of a rigorous natural language description of the system resulting from the aligned generations of the various artefacts produced during the process. It is worth noticing the strict relation between the requirements describing the system behaviour, the semi-formal design, the executable design, and the formal models.

Requirements Specification for the *Initiator CSL* Component

Configuration Parameters
System parameters,
- *max connection delay;*
- *max delay between send operations;*
- *max delay between receive operationsr.*

External Interactions
The *Initiator CSL* can receive from the *Initiator RBC* component the following messages:
- ...

and can send to the *RBC* component the following messages:
...

States
The *CSL* can be in the following four main states:
- ...

External Guarantees
- The initiator CSL may send a *SAI_DISCONNECT.request* message only when in *Connected* (*COMMS*) state;
...

External Assumptions
- The *SAI* always replies with a *SAI_DISCONNECT.indication* message to *SAI_DISCONNECT.request* messages issued by the *CSL*.

Behavioral Requirements

R1: At startup, the *CSL* is in *Disconnected* state.

When in Disconnected State

R2: When in *Disconnected* state, the *CSL* immediately sends a *SAI_CONNECT.request* to the *SAI* component, starts a *connTimer*, and moves to the *Connecting* state.

When in Connecting State

R3: When in *Connecting* state the *connTimer* expires, the *CSL* moves to the *Disconnected* state.

R4: When in *Connecting* state a *SAI_CONNECT.confirm* is received from the *SAI* component, the *CSL* sends an *RBC_User_Connect.indication* to the *RBC* component, starts both the *sendTimer* and the *recTimer*, and moves to *Connected* state.

Fig. 9. Natural Language requirements for ICSL

At this level, an important role is played by the "guarantees" that each component should ensure to the other components making use of it, and the "assumptions" on the external environment which are supposed to hold. An example for all: When a connection request is sent from the initiator SAI to the ER, we should assume that it will always have a reply from ER either through a connection-confirmation or a disconnect-indication. The formal analysis of the system, indeed, allows to check if such an assumption is not satisfied by the ER level, and deadlocks may appear in the behaviour of the SAI component.

4   Related Works

The analysis of still "unstable" requirements has been widely investigated by Heitmeyer [25,26] with the Software Cost Reduction (SCR) tabular notation and method. While Avnur [28], differently, has based its analysis on Finite State Machines. In [29,30], Giannakopoulou, Mavridou et al. have exploited the FRET requirements elicitation tool for analysing requirements and generating Simulink models. In [31], Lutz and Ampo have used the Paradigm Plus tool to model the requirements and verify them with PVS, while Ferrari et al. [32] have used Simulink for modelling and verification of the system requirements. Another quite related effort is that one in [33], where Basile et al. have modelled and analysed part of the UNISIG SUBSET 98 using Uppaal.

Many more works have been done when starting from UML/SysML designs instead than from informal requirements. In [34], e.g., Caltais et al. have discussed the transformation of SysML models into NuSMV. While in [35], Snook and Butler have discussed the translation into the B notation of designs in the UML-B profile. Several other studies (e.g., [36]) instead describe the translation of UML/SysML models in mCRL2. Still, the approach which is the most similar to ours is the one by Bouwman et al. [37], which has the same goal of enriching EULYNX interfaces with formal models, that in this case, are encoded in mCRL2.

5   Conclusions

It is true that sometimes standard tends to prescribe vague goals and prohibitions, that they tend to be continuously revised to fix their weaknesses, and that implementations have often no strong legal incentive to fully comply with them. Our effort should be considered as a contribution towards the definition of clear, rigorous, stable, strongly enforced signalling standard, as required in the railway domain and as promoted by the Eulynx[5] and RCA[6] initiatives.

The executable and formal models generated during the analysis of the standard have the main purpose to provide the standard designer with some feedback from the analysis of some instantiations of the standardised interface. Surely this

---

[5] https://www.eulynx.eu/index.php.

[6] https://public.3.basecamp.com/p/jGh4E3ZdE8T1RtoxvbWLCYss.

is not sufficient to guarantee the generic correctness of the standard for all the allowed variation points, but it still much better than relying exclusively on a plain natural language description of the standardised interface for which no executable model has ever been devised and analysed.

From the point of view of the provider the generated executable UML models might be useful to shed some light on some aspects that might still be considered ambiguous in the natural language description of the standard, and to suggest the structure of a feasible implementation possibly reducing the design and debugging effort of the proprietary implementation.

The goal of the 4SECURail demonstrator has been the illustration - with a real experiment - of a possible way in which formal methods, in particular, can be exploited to improve the quality of system requirement specifications. The use of formal models is indeed considered important for the analysis of the interactions inside complex systems of systems, like those typical of the railway sector.

We have shown how creating an easy-to-understand and communicate executable model is an intermediate step that already allows to detect several possible weaknesses in the initial natural language requirements. However, this step is also a passage where errors can easily be made, and a formal analysis of executable models becomes important to detect and remove them. This can be done with a "lightweight" use of formal methods, since it does not require particular advanced background and experience. More advanced properties of the system, e.g., those related to the expected interoperability properties the system should guarantee, may require a more advanced knowledge of the formal frameworks and, therefore, higher costs in terms of effort and learning curve.

Adopting a formal methods diversity approach to analyse an executable model adds the advantage of having an alternative way to verify the correctness of the generated formal models and allows to exploit a broader range of verification features. The experience gained with our experimentation allowed us to confirm the essential importance of relying on an automatic/mechanical translation of executable models into the formal notations used for formal analysis. In their absence, we would not have been able to generate 53 releases of formal design in three different notations. The experimentation conducted within the 4SECURail project has put in evidence many aspects that deserve deeper studies. Among these:

- The precise role of SysML/UML as system design notation.
- The way to support the transition from executable designs generated in industry-ready Model-Based System Engineering frameworks to formal models.
- The way to support lightweight use of formal methods to make them more easily adaptable to the existing requirements definition processes.
- The way in which the formal models and the verified properties can be explained back in a rigorous natural language style.

Another piece of work that is still missing and that we hope to be able to complete in the near future is a thorough evaluation of the experimented approach and of its positioning with respect to the state of art. The project deliverables, the initial and revised case-study requirements, the UML designs, the formal models, the (open source) translation tools are all publicly available in the 4SECURail site and in open access repositories [38, 39].

Acknowledgements. This work has been partially funded by the 4SECURail project. The 4SECURail project received funding from the Shift2Rail Joint Undertaking under the European Union's Horizon 2020 research and innovation programme under grant agreement No 881775 in the context of the open call S2R-OC-IP2-01-2019, part of the "Annual Work Plan and Budget 2019", of the programme H2020-S2RJU-2019. The content of this paper reflects only the authors' view and the Shift2Rail Joint Undertaking is not responsible for any use that may be made of the included information. We are grateful to the colleagues of the Work Stream 1 of project 4SECURail, and in particular to Alessandro Fantechi, Stefania Gnesi, Davide Basile, Alessio Ferrari and Maurice ter Beek, for the comments and suggestions during the project.

References

1. Piattino, A.: 4SECURail deliverable D2.3 "Case study requirements and specification". In: The 4SECURail Work Stream 1 Deliverables, November 2020 (2020). https://doi.org/10.5281/zenodo.5807738
2. Mazzanti, F., Basile, D.: 4SECURail deliverable D2.1 "Specification of formal development demonstrator". In: The 4SECURail Work Stream 1 Deliverables, November 2020 (2020). https://doi.org/10.5281/zenodo.5807738
3. Mazzanti, F.; Basile, D.: 4SECURail deliverable D2.2 "Formal development Demonstrator prototype, first release". In: The 4SECURail Work Stream 1 Deliverables, November 2020 (2020). https://doi.org/10.5281/zenodo.5807738
4. Mazzanti, F., Belli, D.: 4SECURail deliverable D2.5 "Formal development demonstrator prototype, final release". In: The 4SECURail Work Stream 1 Deliverables, July 2021 (2021). https://doi.org/10.5281/zenodo.5807738
5. Basile, D., et al.: Designing a demonstrator of formal methods for railways infrastructure managers. In: Margaria, T., Steffen, B. (eds.) ISoLA 2020. LNCS, vol. 12478, pp. 467–485. Springer, Cham (2020). https://doi.org/10.1007/978-3-030-61467-6_30
6. Vaghi, C.: 4SECURail Deliverable D2.6 "Specification of Cost-Benefit Analysis and learning curves, Final release". In: The 4SECURail Work Stream 1 Deliverables. https://doi.org/10.5281/zenodo.5807738
7. UNISIG: SUBSET-039, FIS for the RBC/RBC Handover, 17 December 2015 (Issue 3.2.0)
8. UNISIG: SUBSET-098, RBC/RBC Safe Communication Interface, 21 May 2007
9. OMG: Unified Modelling Language version 2.5.1, December 2015
10. OMG: SysML 1.6 Specification, November 2019
11. OMG: Precise Semantics of UML State Machine version 1.0, May 2019
12. OMG: Action Language for Foundational UML (Alf), version 1.1, July 2017
13. OMG: Semantics of a Foundational Subset for Executable UML Models (fUML), Version 1.5, May 2020
14. OMG: Precise Semantics of UML Composite Structure (PSCS), Version 1.2

15. ter Beek, M.H., Fantechi, A., Gnesi, S., Mazzanti, F.: States and events in Kan-dISTI. In: Margaria, T., Graf, S., Larsen, K.G. (eds.) Models, Mindsets, Meta: The What, the How, and the Why Not? LNCS, vol. 11200, pp. 110–128. Springer, Cham (2019). https://doi.org/10.1007/978-3-030-22348-9_8

16. Leuschel, M., Butler, M.: ProB: an automated analysis toolset for the B method. Softw. Tools Technol. Transf. (STTT) **10**(2), 185–203 (2008)

17. ter Beek, M.H., et al.: Adopting formal methods in an industrial setting: the rail-ways case. In: ter Beek, M.H., McIver, A., Oliveira, J.N. (eds.) FM 2019. LNCS, vol. 11800, pp. 762–772. Springer, Cham (2019). https://doi.org/10.1007/978-3-030-30942-8_46

18. Ferrari, A., et al.: Comparing formal tools for system design: a judgment study. In: IEEE International Conference on Software Engineering (ICSE), June 2020 (2020)

19. Ferrari, A., et al.: Systematic evaluation and usability analysis of formal methods tools for railway signaling system design. IEEE Trans. Softw. Eng. (2021). https://doi.org/10.1109/TSE.2021.3124677

20. Champelovier, D., et al.: Reference Manual of the LNT to LOTOS Translator. https://cadp.inria.fr/publications/Champelovier-Clerc-Garavel-et-al-10.html

21. Garavel, H., Lang, F., Mateescu, R., Serwe, W.: CADP 2011: a toolbox for the construction and analysis of distributed processes. Int. J. Softw. Tools Technol. Transf. (STTT) **15**(2), 89–107 (2013)

22. Garavel, H., Lang, F., Mateescu, R.: Compositional verification of asynchronous concurrent systems using CADP. Acta Informatica **52**(4–5), 337–392 (2015)

23. Lang, F., Mateescu, R., Mazzanti, F.: Sharp congruences adequate with tempo-ral logics combining weak and strong modalities. In: Biere, A., Parker, D. (eds.) TACAS 2020. LNCS, vol. 12079, pp. 57–76. Springer, Cham (2020). https://doi.org/10.1007/978-3-030-45237-7_4

24. Lang, F., Mateescu, R., Mazzanti, F.: Compositional verification of concurrent systems by combining bisimulations. Formal Methods Syst. Des. **58**(1–2), 83–125 (2021). https://doi.org/10.1007/s10703-021-00360-w

25. Bharadwaj, R., Heitmeyer, C.L.: Model checking complete requirements specifica-tions using abstraction. Autom. Softw. Eng. **6**(1), 37–68 (1999)

26. Heitmeyer, C.L.: Formal methods for specifying, validating, and verifying require-ments. J. Univ. Comput. Sci. **13**(5), 607–618 (2007)

27. Mazzanti, F., Belli, D.: Formal modelling and initial analysis of the 4SECURail case study. In: Proceedings of 5th Workshop on Models for Formal Analysis of Real Systems, MARS 2022, EPTCS (2022, to appear)

28. Avnur, A.: A finite state machine model for requirements engineering, IREB Requirements Engineering Magazine, March 2015 (2015). https://re-magazine.ireb.org/articles/a-finite-state-machine-model

29. Mavridou, A., et al.: Bridging the gap between requirements and simulink model analysis. In: REFSQ-2020, Pisa, Italy, 24 March 2020 (2020)

30. Giannakopoulou, D., et al.: Formal requirements elicitation with FRET. In: Joint Proceedings of REFSQ-2020 Workshops, Pisa, Italy, 24 March 2020 (2020)

31. Lutz, R.R., Ampo, Y.: Experience report: using formal methods for requirements analysis of critical spacecraft software (1994)

32. Ferrari, A., et al.: The Metrô Rio case study. Sci. Comput. Program. **78**(7), 828–842 (2013)

33. Basile, D., Fantechi, A., Rosadi, I.: Formal analysis of the UNISIG safety appli-cation intermediate sub-layer. In: Lluch Lafuente, A., Mavridou, A. (eds.) FMICS 2021. LNCS, vol. 12863, pp. 174–190. Springer, Cham (2021). https://doi.org/10.1007/978-3-030-85248-1_11

34. Caltais, G., Leitner-Fischer, F., Leue, S., Weiser, J.: SysML to NuSMV model transformation via object-orientation. In: Berger, C., Mousavi, M.R., Wisniewski, R. (eds.) CyPhy 2016. LNCS, vol. 10107, pp. 31–45. Springer, Cham (2017). https://doi.org/10.1007/978-3-319-51738-4_3

35. Snook, C., Butler, M.: UML-B and Event-B: an integration of languages and tools. In: The IASTED International Conference on Software Engineering - SE2008, Innsbruck, Austria, 12–14 February 2008 (2008)

36. Hvid Hansen, H., Ketema, J., Luttik, B., Mousavi, M.R., van de Pol, J., dos Santos, O.M.: Automated verification of executable UML models. In: Aichernig, B.K., de Boer, F.S., Bonsangue, M.M. (eds.) FMCO 2010. LNCS, vol. 6957, pp. 225–250. Springer, Heidelberg (2011). https://doi.org/10.1007/978-3-642-25271-6_12

37. Bouwman, M., et al.: What is the point: formal analysis and test generation for a railway standard. In: Proceedings of the 29th European Safety and Reliability Conference (ESREL) (2020)

38. The 4SECURAil project. https://4securail.eu, https://doi.org/10.5281/zenodo.5807738

39. Mazzanti, F., Belli, D.: Supplementary material of 4SECURail Workstream 1. https://doi.org/10.5281/zenodo.4280773

ATO

Formal Design and Validation of an Automatic Train Operation Control System

Arturo Amendola[1], Lorenzo Barruffo[1], Marco Bozzano[2(✉)],
Alessandro Cimatti[2], Salvatore De Simone[1], Eugenio Fedeli[1],
Artem Gabbasov[2], Domenico Ernesto Garrubba[1], Massimiliano Girardi[2],
Diana Serra[1], Roberto Tiella[2], and Gianni Zampedri[2]

[1] Rete Ferroviaria Italiana, Osmannoro, Italy
[2] Fondazione Bruno Kessler, Trento, Italy
bozzano@fbk.eu

Abstract. In this paper, we report on the design of a complex control system, namely the Automatic Train Operation (ATO), which aims at enhancing the Grade of Automation in train operations (passenger transportation, infrastructure monitoring) in high-speed lines. The development of ATO is being conducted as an industrial project, with contributions from different research teams. The design of the system is complex in terms of architecture, functionality, safety and reliability requirements to be fulfilled, and geographical distribution of the development teams. Formal methods and model-based design are used to master the complexity of the design and of the system integration. Our approach is based on formal tools for system specification and validation, which support automatic code generation, early design validation, testing and simulation, and runtime verification. Moreover, we structured the development process in different phases and configurations, corresponding to increasing functionality of the system and different deployment configurations. The project is at an advanced stage of execution. In this paper, we demonstrate the effectiveness of the proposed approach and methodology, we discuss our experience and the lessons learned.

1 Introduction

The steady progress of the Information and Communication Technology and the limited efficiency of manual drive, which is mainly based on training and human experience, lead to the need for an automated management and control for railway traffic, which can best perform and react to different operating conditions or sudden changes. According to the International Association of Public Transport, there are five Grade of Automation (GoA) [8] that go from 0, which means absence of automation, up to 4, which indicates a fully automated train control and management without any staff on board.

In this context, Automatic Train Operation (ATO) systems aim to transferring the responsibility of train management from the driver to an automated

S. Collart-Dutilleul et al. (Eds.): RSSRail 2022, LNCS 13294, pp. 169–178, 2022.
https://doi.org/10.1007/978-3-031-05814-1_12

control system, optimizing the driving performances due to the characteristics and conditions of the track, the energy consumption and the passenger comfort and quickly reacting to unsafe situations. An additional protection level is guaranteed by the constant supervision of a vital computer (EVC) which interfaces with the infrastructure monitoring system following the ERTMS/ETCS standard for high-speed railway lines [5]. ETCS, with its direct connection to the braking system, protects the vehicle from some critical situations such as violating speed limits or running through places where it is not allowed.

In this paper, we report on the development of an ATO control system, which is carried out as an industrial project, with contributions from different research teams throughout the Italian territory (RFI, FBK and the Universities of Naples, Salerno and Bari, for a total of 4–6 persons per team). The design of the system is complex in terms of architecture, functionality, safety and reliability requirements to be fulfilled. In order to master the complexity of the design and of the system integration, we based our approach on the use of formal methods and model based-design for system specification and validation, which support automatic code generation, early design validation, testing, simulation and runtime verification.

ATO is currently at the stage of a prototype, but it will eventually evolve into a product. The objective is to have a GoA4 ATO operating on a prototype light-vehicle, equipped with devices for the infrastructure monitoring, running on an ERTMS/ETCS Italian high-speed line. This eventually could be the first step on the way to meet the challenge of adapting the design and control techniques from this prototype domain to applications on the high-speed mainline railway. The ATO project is at an advanced stage of execution. In this paper, we demonstrate the effectiveness of our design approach and methodology and discuss our experience and lessons learned.

The rest of the paper is structured as follows. In Sect. 2 we describe the ATO system, its architecture and requirements. In Sect. 3 we discuss the design challenges. In Sect. 4 we present our formal approach to the development and verification of ATO. In Sect. 5 we discuss the lessons learned. Finally, in Sect. 6 we draw some conclusions and outline directions for future work.

Related Work. For metropolitan railway lines, several approaches have been proposed to optimize train operation and energy consumption with autonomous driving [9], by combining high-level and low-level control of the ATO [10] or dealing also with train load and delays of the line [6]. However, the challenge of autonomous driving is still open for high-speed lines. Detailed modeling of high-speed trains is one of the most demanding research issues together with the development of powerful simulation platforms. Formal methods have been extensively applied in various industrial domains, including transportation [11], see e.g. [7] for a recent survey on the application to railway systems.

2   The ATO Control System

ATO consists of two cooperating systems: ATO Track Side (TS) and ATO On Board (OB). ATO-TS collects and forwards data on trains, tracks and timetables concerning the train journey, while ATO-OB receives such data and uses them to control and drive the train. ATO can be operated by a remote driver, who is responsible for activating autonomous driving. The architecture of ATO is described in Fig. 1. In the rest of this section, we focus on ATO-OB. The Interface Manager allows ATO to interface with the different modules such as ATO-TS, ETCS, SMO (Speed Monitoring and Odometry), SCS (Supervision and Control System) and TIU (Train Interface Unit). The Controller implements the main finite state machine for the different ATO functional operating modes. Track Database Manager uses odometry data to localize the train on the line and validates the journey received from the trackside before the start of the mission. Autonomous Driving Functions receives the track and journey profile data from the Track Database Manager and uses them to generate an optimal speed profile, and the brake and traction commands to forward to TIU. The Energy Manager uses the battery and fuel data and the traction system status to monitor the energy level and evaluate the consumption needed to achieve the current mission.

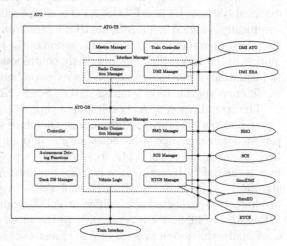

Fig. 1. ATO architecture

As an example, we consider the nominal scenario with a train stopped at a charging point. When the train is selected by an ATO-TS remote driver, ATO-OB verifies that its database version matches with the trackside one and performs some internal system tests. The remote driver plans the journey profile to be sent on board, and waits for an acknowledgment. When ETCS mode evolves to full supervision and other engagement conditions are fulfilled (e.g., ETCS and ATO are not applying full service or emergency brake, ATO-OB is localized on a specific Segment Profile sent by trackside, and train direction is forward), the remote driver can engage ATO-OB enabling autonomous driving. In such drive mode, the train reaches the final destination of the journey, respecting the related timetable of the assigned timing points and stopping points. An example of non-nominal scenario consists in using an autonomous vehicle equipped with ATO to rescue another vehicle that is blocking a high-speed line, due to a breakdown.

The design of ATO is subject to complex requirements. In order to meet specific project goals, we had to review and customize the functional and interface requirements defined by standard UNISIG subset, and add or discard some of them. For example, we provided train localizing function data on board, moving it from trackside; we discarded all the requirements related to doors management since the prototype light-vehicle has none; we added camera requirements to mitigate the absence of driver on board and we customized the interface protocol in order to manage the data for the new functions we added.

3   Challenges

The design of ATO is very challenging, due to the complexity of the system and of the associated requirements. The ATO system is distributed. It consists of on-board controller (ATO-OB) and a trackside counterpart (ATO-TS) which, in turn, are composed of several modules realizing different functions, and connecting to external systems, such as ETCS. ATO is composed of heterogeneous components, specifically it includes components that interact directly with the underlying HW, e.g., those commanding braking or traction of the train. Such components rely on models of the HW which are inherently continuous (e.g., specified using differential equations). For this reason, ATO relies on heterogeneous design tools, based on different specification languages (e.g., Scade, Simulink, C).

The specification of ATO relies on a complex and evolving set of (functional, safety and performance) requirements, therefore the design process needs to be robust against changes and adaptations, and support system evolution. Moreover, the architecture of ATO, its control logic and modules must be designed to match the Safety Integrity Levels (SIL) requirements, according to the EN50128 standard. A Preliminary Hazard Analysis is in progress to assign SIL to the product. It is expected that different ATO modules will be assigned different SIL, with the highest levels assigned to the most critical components.

Finally, the design process of ATO must take into account the distribution of the development teams. This makes system integration a particularly challenging task, which calls for suitable verification and validation and testing strategies.

4   Formal Design of ATO

The software specification and design of ATO is based on formal methods. The V-Model, as specified in the CENELEC EN-50128 [2] standard guides the software development process from the definition of the system requirements to testing, integration and validation phases. Model-based design takes advantage of co-design strategies and interdisciplinary effort, favoring cooperation between teams with skills in different disciplinary sectors.

Given the high assurance requirements of ATO, we based the design on tools such as ANSYS SCADE Suite[1] and Architect[2], which offer qualifiable/certified code generation capabilities and interoperability with other development tools

---

[1] https://www.ansys.com/products/embedded-software/ansys-scade-suite.

[2] https://www.ansys.com/products/embedded-software/ansys-scade-architect.

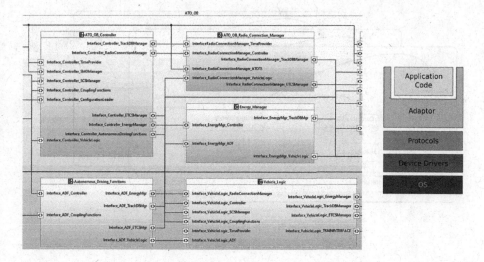

Fig. 2. An excerpt of an IBD for ATO-OB (left) and ATO process layers (right)

and platforms. The use of SCADE meets the production standards for SIL 3/4 SW, since it is compliant with the required metrics and constraints. Our approach integrates the capabilities offered by SCADE with other functionality for verification and validation implemented in our proprietary tool chain based on the nuXmv model checker [1]. In this section, we discuss how these solutions address the challenges outlined in Sect. 3.

4.1 Requirements and Architecture

The development of ATO is guided by an evolving set of requirements, and by a set of operational scenarios specifying some real case missions the system must fulfill. We grouped requirements by functionality and we identified the corresponding modules responsible for taking into account the set of assigned features. We further split requirements into those allocated to ATO-OB and those allocated to ATO-TS. Requirements have been analyzed to extract a hierarchical representation of ATO and the corresponding logical architecture. The architecture has been modeled using SCADE Architect, resulting in several Block Decision Diagrams (BDD) and Internal Block Diagrams (IBD). As an example, in Fig. 2 (left) we present (part of) an IBD focusing on a subset of ATO-OB. Since the design is distributed, it is of utmost importance to design a robust and stable architecture, in which interfaces between different modules are well defined and shared with all the involved teams. In this respect, scenarios have been formalized into sequence diagrams, which strictly refer to the architectural decomposition, and have then been used to guide the implementation of the components and to derive test suites to perform unit and integration testing.

The layered architecture of an ATO process is depicted in Fig. 2 (right): (a) *Application Code Layer* is a pure C function which computes abstract[3] outputs

---

[3] We use the term *abstract* for protocol-independent data.

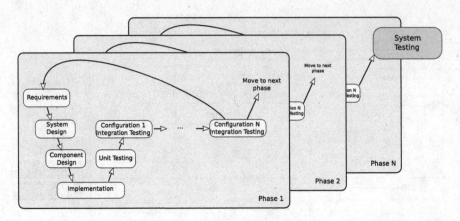

Fig. 3. Phased V-Model

from abstract inputs and current internal state. The layer is run at each execution cycle, (b) *Adaptor Layer* is in charge to periodically invoke the Application Code and to route abstract data from/to the layer below, (c) *Protocols Layer* handles incoming/outgoing data frames performing encoding/decoding operations mapping protocol data from/to abstract data, (d) *Device Drivers Layer* is in charge to cope with connected devices hiding communication details to the upper layers, finally (e) the underlying *OS Layer* provides required services such as scheduling and access to disks, network and other peripherals.

4.2   Development Process

Development Life-Cycle. The system is developed following a process that can be described as a *phased* V-Model (Fig. 3). To face the challenges implied by the novelty of the project, such as instability of requirements and variability of components interfaces, the process extends the classical V-Model with aspects borrowed from the Agile philosophy.

In details, the classical V-model is extended along two dimensions: *phases* and *configurations*. Phases concern functionalities and target a subset of system features. In a phase, the V-model is iterated refining requirement analysis, system architecture, implementation, unit and integration test until stability is reached. Once the last phase is terminated, the system will undergo a final system testing activity. Three phases were identified: remote operations, autonomous driving, and the full ATO system. Orthogonally, a *configuration* specifies which layers of the system are involved in the integration testing activities and, consequently, which running environment tests are run on. We identify three main configurations: (a) *Configuration 1* involves the Application Code Layer only. The code is tested in the simulation/testing environment of SCADE Suite (see next section for details), (b) *Configuration 2* extends Configuration 1 with the Adaptor and Protocols layers. The code is run on host, introducing asynchronous execution of subsystems and the interaction with services, e.g. logging service. Communication with devices is simulated, (c) *Configuration 3* adds the Device Layer and the Target OS Layer. Each subsystem is run on the proper target using real devices. Configuration 3 actually is subdivided in a set of subconfigurations (3a, 3b, etc.) that more and more integrate larger parts of the final physical system.

System Architecture, Component Design and Implementation. The development process follows the model-based approach, where a machine-readable formal representation of a system is built as the main project's artifact. Such a representation (model) is the input for all the downstream development activities, most notably allowing for formal verification of the properties of the system, i.e. model checking [4], certified source code and documentation generation. In details, the system architecture is specified in SCADE Architect using the SysML language. A SysML architectural model typically comprises hierarchical decomposition of the system, connections, interfaces and data types. SCADE Architect provides validation tools for early identification of flaws (see Sect. 4.3). Using the model generator provided by SCADE Architect, for each subcomponent we generate a skeletal behavioral model written in SCADE Suite language. The majority of subsystems/components are implemented using the SCADE Suite language. One subsystem is implemented using MathWorks Symulink and one data-intensive component is manually written in C. In total, the SW for ATO-OB contains about 75K lines of code. SCADE Suite comprises a code generator for translating models into C code which is certified under EN 50128:2011 at T3/SIL 3/4. The ratio of the C code we automatically generated for ATO-OB using Scade is about 75% of the whole code (including manually written code, and code generated by other means). Certification implies that unit/component testing activities can be performed on models instead of on generated code, reducing certification times and costs (the reduction is estimated in the order of 50%).

Moreover, to develop the Protocol Layer, we used ASN.1 as the interface description language, due to its flexibility, widespread use, and extensible format. In particular, we used ASN.1 to generate an intermediate formal specification to support component interaction. This approach can accommodate different communication protocols, including ad-hoc protocols described in textual or tabular form. Given that the protocols are constantly evolving and that the manual implementation of ASN specifications is time-consuming and error-prone, we generate them from tabular description for one protocol and from SCADE components based on textual description for others.

System Integration. When managing distributed teams and heterogeneous components, system integration becomes a highly important task. ATO contains some modules implemented using the SCADE language natively, while others are designed in different formats, e.g. Simulink and C. Source code generated from such models is linked to the rest of the code by means of a SCADE Suite language feature called 'external operators', i.e., operators whose interface is mapped to the interface of the corresponding external module via some glue code. We require a test suite associated to each module which must invoke all its nominal behaviors. Each test is then replicated in the SCADE framework so that we can mimic the same actions and prove that we obtain the same results even with the integrated system. Operational scenarios are then used to derive some integration test cases that are intended to simulate interactions between components and to prove that ATO behaves as expected. In order to avoid non regression failures, we followed a continuous-integration approach by designing a custom framework based on the python package 'pytest'. Moreover, we rely on the 'git' versioning tool to share the SW development effort among different teams and to freeze system implementation at specific milestones.

4.3   Verification and Validation

We used multiple and complementary ways to formally verify and validate the design and implementation of ATO. First, we used SCADE to perform early model validation. SCADE offers some checkers that can be used to validate the hierarchical composition of the architecture, in particular the compatibility of the component interfaces, and to check that sequence diagrams refer to valid data. This allows us to guarantee that the formalization of the scenarios is compliant with the architecture, before moving to the implementation. Then, we used SCADE Suite to design, simulate and

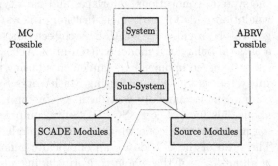

Fig. 4. Our approach to property-based formal verification

test the system by means of scenario validation, i.e. by specifying values on input ports and checking that the outputs are as expected. We performed this task starting from component level up to system level. In case of unit testing we also made use of the model coverage feature, which allows to highlight which (if any) paths of the model are not stimulated by tests; in this case, we enriched the test suite in order to reach the highest possible coverage. When scenarios need to be modified or we want to verify other sets of requirements (for instance when moving to a subsequent development phase), the same process is replicated, starting from the architecture up to system integration testing.

The ATO outcomes can be visualized and verified after executing a scenario by means of logging. A separate component (called ATOLOG) records all the relevant diagnostic information. It consists of: a server that receives and saves log packets from the log clients (written in C and Python) of other ATO components; a log client that provides an API for sending log packets; and various tools for decoding, analyzing, and visualizing raw binary data collected by the server. The collected diagnostic information is represented by the messages exchanged among components, and it can be processed with various tools to verify that the scenario execution results correspond to the expected behavior.

Finally, once system integration is consolidated and all the individual sub-modules have been validated, we used model checking (MC) techniques to perform property-based (runtime) verification. Namely, we used a custom tool-chain based on the nuXmv model checker [1] and NuRV, an extension of NuXmv for runtime verification [3], and we implemented a (in-house) translation from SCADE to nuXmv. Our approach is described in Fig. 4. The system to be verified is split into one part which is formally modeled in SCADE, hence amenable to formal verification, and one which is not. In the first case, we used model checking to automatically verify system-level properties. In the second case, we used techniques based on Assumption Based Runtime Verification (ABRV) to automatically generate monitors that can be used as test oracles, see [3]. Interestingly, this process is completely automatic and requires just a small effort to connect the generated monitors to the rest of the system, before conducting the tests. In this way, many verifiers can be generated from the properties, while the effort required for refactoring, when the module interface evolves, is negligible.

5   Lessons Learned

The design of ATO has raised many challenges, due to its inherent complexity, and the distribution of the development effort. The main problem we had to address was how to effectively split the work among different teams. Continuous integration, supported by custom strategies for testing and by versioning tools, was the natural choice to address the complexity of system integration, along with ad-hoc strategies to deal with system evolution, e.g. to deal with updates to the interfaces of the subsystems allocated to external development teams. In this respect, we were forced to agree with partners not only about the definition of the high-level interfaces, but also about the precise semantics of individual fields.

The phased V-model allowed us to progressively design and implement the functionality of the system in two different respects. First, it enabled us to streamline the support for different operational scenarios, concentrating on one scenario at a time. Second, it enabled us to test the implementation of the integrated system on different deployment configurations (using a simulator; on one or more hosts; on the final OS with the target HW in the loop), making it possible to progressively release the deployed system on different targets, as soon as the latter become available in the course of the project.

Finally, we have carried out verification and validation using a mix of strategies and tools, integrating the support given by tools such as Ansys Scade Suite and Architect, simulators, and our proprietary tool chain for formal verification, based on model checking. Particularly effective was our choice to use both *design-time* model verification, and custom techniques for *runtime* monitoring, in combination with testing. The latter enabled us to cover – via testing – the verification of system-level properties that were out of reach for model checking, due to the complexity of the models and the state explosion problem.

Based on our experience, the formal approach proved to be effective and gave numerous benefits. Indeed, most of the flaws we encountered during system integration were located in components that had been outsourced, and were designed and tested using traditional methodologies, without using formal methods.

6   Conclusions and Future Work

In this paper we discussed the design of a complex control system, the Automatic Train Operation, and we presented a formal methods approach, which guides the ATO development throughout all the development phases.

Currently, ATO is at the stage of a prototype. We estimate to execute first chassis dynamometer tests by March 2022 and then field tests by June 2022 on the Bologna San Donato railway test circuit, the first fully equipped laboratory in the field throughout Europe. ATO is designed on a single-unit unmanned prototype light-vehicle which does not require the presence of on board driver, cabin staff or passengers, with all the implications that such specific design brings. So far, possible future developments concern the design of an ATO which is able to control and drive a multiple-unit high-speed train, with passengers on board.

References

1. Cavada, R., et al.: The NUXMV symbolic model checker. In: Biere, A., Bloem, R. (eds.) CAV 2014. LNCS, vol. 8559, pp. 334–342. Springer, Cham (2014). https://doi.org/10.1007/978-3-319-08867-9_22
2. CENELEC: EN 50128, Railway applications - Communications, signaling and processing systems - Software for railway control and protection systems (2011)
3. Cimatti, A., Tian, C., Tonetta, S.: NuRV: a NUXMV extension for runtime verification. In: Finkbeiner, B., Mariani, L. (eds.) RV 2019. LNCS, vol. 11757, pp. 382–392. Springer, Cham (2019). https://doi.org/10.1007/978-3-030-32079-9_23
4. Clarke, E.M., Grumberg, O., Peled, D.A.: Model Checking. MIT Press, Cambridge (2000)
5. European Union Agency for railways: ERTMS - Making the railway system work better for society (2016)
6. Fernández-Rodríguez, A., Fernández-Cardador, A., Cucala, A., Domínguez, M., Gonsalves, T.: Design of robust and energy-efficient ATO speed profiles of metropolitan lines considering train load variations and delays. IEEE Trans. Intell. Transp. Syst. 16(4), 2061–2071 (2015)
7. Ferrari, A., ter Beek, M.H.: Formal methods in railways: a systematic mapping study (2021)
8. International Association of Public Transport: A global bid for automation: UITP Observatory of Automated Metros confirms sustained growth rates for the coming years, Belgium
9. Licheng, T., Tao, T., Jing, X., Shuai, S., Tong., L.: Optimization of train speed curve based on ATO tracking control strategy. In: Chinese Automation Congress (2017)
10. Su, S., Tang, T., Chen, L., Liu, B.: Energy-efficient train control in urban rail transit systems. J. Rail Rapid Transit 229(4), 446–454 (2015)
11. Woodcock, J., Larsen, P.G., Bicarregui, J., Fitzgerald, J.S.: Formal methods: practice and experience. ACM Comput. Surv. 41, 19:1–19:36 (2009)

Investigating Human Error Within GoA-2 Metro Lines

Josh Hunter[✉] and John McDermid

Assuring Autonomy International Programme, University of York, York, UK
{josh.hunter,john.mcdermid}@york.ac.uk

Abstract. The rail industry is progressing towards higher levels of automation and autonomy. Other industries, e.g. aviation, have discovered 'ironies of automation' where the reduction in workload actually contributes to unsafe events. The rail industry will not be immune from such issues as reductions in the complexity of workload often leads to work becoming mundane and routine. Further, without the need to be constantly reacting to their surroundings, drivers are ill-equipped to break the monotony to address anomalies which can lead to accidents. Such problems can arise in the transition from GoA-1 to GoA-2 and should lead to a rethink of system design, not to place blame on drivers. However, this redesign needs to consider both human workload and the system itself. The paper is a preliminary analysis of the challenges of increasing automation and identifies potential solutions such as reworking the transition by increasing the workload placed upon the driver within GoA-2 systems, increasing stress but decreasing monotony by making work non-routine and thus retaining driver attention. This is a positive trade-off and may be the cheapest and most effective solution, that isn't simply the transition to GoA-3.

Keywords: Automation · Human-error · Monotony

1 Introduction

Within Europe, rail is the safest mode of land transportation. Safety for rail has been improving for decades, with the annual rate of accidents resulting in a fatality falling by 5% every year. Further, a "major accident" which is defined as an accident where five or more fatalities occur have become very rare, with only two such accidents happening since 2018 (European Union Agency for Railways 2020). Not accounting for the 2019 pandemic which will have drastically affected travel for the past 2 years, rail has stayed relatively stable as a mode of transportation, with the general public using rail a similar amount each year for the previous five years (Gower 2021). This implies that all railway innovation within the past decade has either been for safety's sake, or has adequately considered safety, as the number of rail trips overall remains roughly constant as seen in Fig. 1, and the number of major accidents has fallen as seen in Fig. 2. Within the UK, the number of fatalities totals less than fifty per annum, excluding suicides (Rail Safety and Standards Board 2020).

S. Collart-Dutilleul et al. (Eds.): RSSRail 2022, LNCS 13294, pp. 179–191, 2022.
https://doi.org/10.1007/978-3-031-05814-1_13

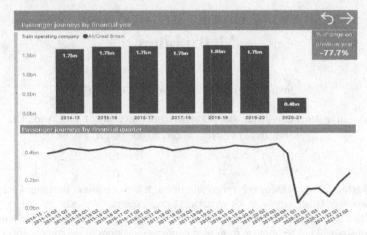

Fig. 1. Number of railway journeys within the UK per annum (Gower 2021)

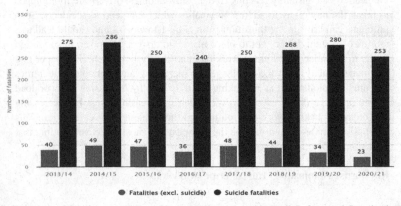

Fig. 2. Number of fatalities on rail within the UK per annum (Rail Safety and Standards Board 2021)

In the UK the most popular mode of transportation is the car. While the rate of accidents has been gradually decreasing over the past decade, total annual fatalities within the United Kingdom are still in four figures (UK Department for Transport 2020). There has been long-standing research on the safety of road vehicles, however road vehicles are inherently less safe than other modes of transportation, they are involved in more scenarios where accidents can happen, they take non pre-planned routes, get involved with non-scheduled traffic, and encounter more anomalies in general. In comparison, things are more planned within rail, so it is easier to account for and manage potentially hazardous situations. Rolling stock operates on a set path, meaning that it is easier to account for its surroundings. This is helpful because, whilst there are currently active programs to introduce autonomy within both rail and road, rail's more constrained environment should lead to its developments being smoother. With a clear path for the future of automation being constructed, there are good guidelines for where we should be looking regarding innovation.

1.1 Context of the Problem

At present, the majority of autonomous systems are within their infancy. The rail industry is no different, with automation being split into four stages, or four Grades of Automation (GoA), as shown within Fig. 3, GoA-0 is simply an unautomated train where movements are fully under the control of the driver. GoA-1 is essentially limiters that take control away from the driver, stopping them from speeding, this is known as Automatic Train Protection (ATP) and has been criticized for the ability to ignore the commands of the driver (Dave Keevill 2017) could cause reluctance to adopt the systems by the drivers who are used to having full control. Despite this, GoA-1 is the most common form of automation seen today (Brandenburger and Naumann 2021).

Railway	Road	Aircraft	Resp.	
Grades of automation	SAE levels	Levels of automation	👤	🚆
GoA-0 Sight train operator	L0 No automation	Level 1 Raw data, no automation at all	All time	Warn Protect
GoA-1 Manual train operation Automated train protection	L1 Driver assistance Park assist/cruise control	Level 2 Assistance Flight director Auto-throttle	Drivers	Guide Assist
GoA-2 Semi-automated train operation (STO). Autom. train op. (ATO)	L2 Partial automation Traffic jam assist	Level 3 Tactical use Autopilot	Monitors all time	Manage movements within limits
GoA-3 Driverless train operation (DTO) Automated control (ATC) Some control by attendant (operating doors, emergencies)	L3 Conditional automation L4 High automation Highway traffic jam system	Level 4 Strategic Flight management system Uninterrupted autopilot project (Boing) Drones (unmanned)	Ready to take back control May not take back control	Drives itself, may give back control Drives itself with graceful degradation
GoA-4 Unattended train op (UTO) Automated doors Platform screen doors	L5 Full automation (all situations)		Not required	All time

Fig. 3. Grades of automation (Dave Keevill 2017)

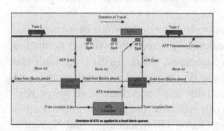

Fig. 4. ATS diagram (The Railway Technical 2021)

GoA-2 is defined as a locomotive with ATP and Automatic Train Operation (ATO), meaning the actual driving and braking of the train is automated with drivers taking over in case of disruption such as a tree falling on the rails or operating specific safety-related tasks such as door closure. It is worth noting that within GoA-2 and GoA-1 a driver is still required, and their average day doesn't change very much. GoA-2 has been set as a target for railway companies that are interested in automation (European Union Agency for Railways 2020). GoA-3 is the start of what could truly be considered self-sufficient automation, and GoA-4 is considered fully autonomous, and a goal of railway innovations as defined by the European Union (Shift2Rail EU 2019). In both GoA-3 and 4 ATO and ATP are utilized to ensure safety in basic driving operations. GoA-3 retains an attendant on-board to operate doors, assist passengers and operate the train in event of disruption but the bulk of the work is done either by automation or by remote operation from an off-site driver cabin. GoA-3 allows for Automatic Train Stopping (ATS/Fig. 4); if a train ahead is involved in an accident, ATS will "kick in" and stop the train from experiencing the same fate.

Scrutiny Within Automation

It is important to note that rail is such a safe mode of transportation with annual fatalities in the single or double digits in many countries, that we must treat each fatality with higher scrutiny than within road travel. When creating automation within cars and other road-based systems, there is leeway in the fact that accidents happen, the road is not an intrinsically safe place; accidents can be reduced but they are impossible to avoid altogether. In contrast, in railways, autonomous systems are expected to act as well as a human would, or even better, within a given scenario. Although that is hard to define on a philosophical level, on a quantitative level that would simply mean an autonomous railway system cannot be declared ready until it can run without incident and if an incident was to occur, accountability must be traceable within the system to find out why the incident happened.

Within rail travel we must discuss the possibility of even reducing minor incidents, while safety is the number one priority, it is also important to ensure that the public are getting the best possible experience while using an automated system. Thus, as well as having as few, or fewer, accidents as a human driver, an automated railway would be expected to achieve at least current levels of punctuality. Thus, automation within the railway industry requires scrutiny to ensure that the public are getting the best possible service.

Automation and Perceived Human Error

It is easy to look at the shortcomings of a system and blame it upon human error. However, when the human error is correlated with the introduction of a new system component, it is important to step back and consider whether or not there is an issue with the way that the new component is injected into the overall system and the assistance given to the individuals involved to help them to adapt.

Numerous reports have found that the exposure to extended periods of monotonous work within railways can cause drivers to experience "microsleep" which is defined as an individual experiencing a high Karolinska Sleepiness Score (KSS) (Åkerstedt and Gillberg 1989). In contrast, drivers who have the typical varied work schedule found within GoA-0 experience microsleep "substantially less" and often have lower KSS scores (Naumann 2016). The monotonous work typically linked with microsleep is attributed to the work commonly found within GoA-2 (Brandenburger and Naumann 2021). A potential critique of these trials is that they sometimes pushed the drivers to the limit for a short period of time in regard to monotony, not investigating the long term effects of minor daily monotony, the tests took place over two time variables, (PRE vs POST) the specifics of these variables were not published, however, they supported the overall point that there is an irony of automation, where during GoA-0, the gradient at which takeover time increases over the day is small, as seen in Fig. 5, but during GoA-2 the gradient gets much larger as seen in Fig. 6, but then decreases as Automation increases.

Being that the topic of monotony within the workplace is an incredibly wide area, it would be immature to suggest that GoA-2 is the only issue and the removal/reworking of GoA-2 systems would completely resolve any problems that may be linked, but there is sufficient evidence to suggest that it is a symptom of a wider problem.

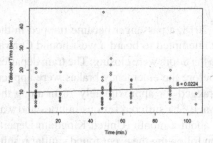 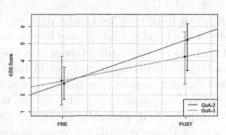

Fig. 5. Takeover time within GoA-0 systems (Brandenburger and Naumann 2021)

Fig. 6. KSS Score comparing GoA-2 and GoA-3 systems (Brandenburger and Naumann 2021)

2 Analysis

2.1 Real-World Examples of Problems

The world has slowly been adopting automated locomotives, which means that there are real-world examples of the potential issues within the different GoA. Several issues that have been declared as "human error" in that there are no specific issues with the software, with all computational components working as intended, meaning the drivers are fully to blame. However, while there are cases where this may be a fair attribution, there are several examples where extraneous circumstances have been identified:

Incidents Within the London Underground
Jubilee Incident (7 February 2018)
The majority of London Underground stations were converted to allow ATO between 2006 and 2008. When running in ATO, movement of the train is controlled automatically. At stations, the train operator is responsible for opening and closing the passenger doors, checking in-cab CCTV monitors for potential issues at the platform train interface (e.g. passengers or objects trapped in closed train doors) and initiating the start of the train. Between stations, the train operator is expected to monitor the ATO system, remain vigilant and look out for any obstruction on the track ahead of the train (United Kingdom Department for Transport 2018a, b). This can be considered as textbook GoA2.

Shortly after 09:00 h on Saturday 1 September 2018, a London Underground train travelled on the Jubilee line between Finchley Road and West Hampstead stations in north-west London with doors open at ten passenger doorways. The train travelled for 56 s and reached a maximum speed of 62 km/h between the two stations. There were approximately 30 passengers on the train, but no one fell out of it during the journey to West Hampstead, and there were no reported injuries or damage. After the incident, an investigation was undertaken and found a probable cause of this accident was the driver entering a microsleep, with them stating *"that he had 'zoned out' and made 'rushed decisions' when dealing with the door problems at Finchley Road. These are indicators that the sudden transition from a low workload to high workload situation, fatigue and/or low blood sugar levels were probably adversely affecting his capacity to deal with the stress caused by the unusual situation"* (Rail Accident Investigation Branch 2018).

Notting Hill Gate Incident (31 January 2018)

At about 16:00 h on Wednesday 31 January 2018, a passenger became trapped in the doors of a London Underground train as she attempted to board a west-bound Central Line service at Notting Hill Gate station while the doors were closing. The train departed and reached a maximum speed of 35 km/h before the emergency brakes were applied and the train stopped. The passenger was dragged for approximately 75 m along the platform, and about 15 m further into the tunnel. She suffered serious injuries and was taken to hospital, where she was treated for about a month (United Kingdom Department for Transport 2018a, b). An investigation following the event found similar results as Brandenburger stating *"Trains running with an active ATO system present a train operator with relatively low workload (compared to manual operation), and repetitive actions at stations. Research conducted by the Transport Research Laboratory for RSSB showed that, under such circumstances, it is possible for people to enter an automatic mode of responding, associated with faster reaction times but reduced attention and more errors. Witness evidence suggests that the ATO train operator's task can require effort to maintain attention, and that it can result in a reliance on the ATO system."* (United Kingdom Department for Transport 2018a, b).

Although the outcomes were different, within both the Notting Hill and the Jubilee Line incidents, the circumstances leading up to the two incidents were identical; the driver had low blood sugar and found it difficult to focus in the first place, tied up with the repeated monotonous work leads to microsleeps causing the driver to miss an important detail and unfortunately, cause an accident.

Further Incidents Taking Place on the London Underground

Numerous similar events have happened on the London Underground throughout the years since GoA-2 has been introduced, the reasoning behind them have all been similar, three of the events are listed, however more events do exist:

- Passenger trapped in a closed train door, Tooting Broadway, Northern line, London Underground, 1 November 2007 (RAIB report 17/2008).
- 1 Passenger dragged a short distance by a train at Holborn station, 3 February 2014 (RAIB report 22/2014).
- Victoria line of London Underground departed from Warren Street station with all the passenger doors open (RAIB 2011).

Bucharest Metro Line 2019 Incident

The main city centre of Romania's capital, Bucharest has had full GoA-2 rail infrastructure since 1995 (Hinojal 2017), however, the transition to a 2015 upgrade of the software seems to have caused some issues highlighting some problems with GoA-2. The upgrade saw the rail control system updated from relay-based technology in which commands were coded on rails to a computer-based system which increased operational efficiency and capacity while maintaining safety. An objectively positive change, should it all have worked correctly; however, through a combination of an inexperienced driver, poor weather and the software not receiving the proper updates on the situation, the upgrade ultimately led to a train derailing and crashing into a wall.

As an investigation was launched into the issue, it was brought to light that the onboard software was known to not work within extended icy conditions, with a representative of Metrorex, the company that supplied the train involved in the incident stating:

> "The train couldn't park because of the weather. It had to be parked outside, you couldn't park because of the ice. It may have been an incorrect maneuverer by the driver (…) I don't know (how experienced the locomotive driver is - ed.), But all the locomotive mechanics are experienced. I don't know (how long it will take them to get the train back in motion - ed.)."

(Șodolescu 2019) (Translated from Romanian)

Real-World Consequence

With the knowledge of past examples, it is reasonable to assume that this is an issue that we could blame on the "human factor" with drivers simply being unaccustomed to the software and its limitations. However, this would be premature as following further investigation it has been deemed a software issue by the Romanian Railway Investigation Agency (Leidig 2020) due to the ATP present within GoA-2 systems seizing control of the speed factor within the train due to a glitch caused by the poor weather conditions, an issue which is categorized as a structural one rather than an issue stemming from the driver. The lessons to be learned from this incident is both that drivers need more rigorous training before becoming acquainted with new software and that software must be ready for the scenarios in which it will be used and any extremes such as weather that it may encounter. Although GoA-2 serves to minimize the amount of work required by a driver, a manual override must be possible, and ATP must not have the final say (Leidig 2020).

Other similar events have taken place within GoA-2 metro systems throughout Europe's metro systems, however for the purposes of this paper it would be repeating points. The topic of modelling responsibility is not an easy one, it's impossible to say drivers are faultless, however there is sufficient evidence to suggest that the topic is not black and white.

2.2   Current Real-World Solutions

Since the failures of GoA-2 that have been presented, several specific solutions have been applied, often to ensure that the same problem doesn't happen twice. This is a desirable since it increases safety, is relatively cost effective and prevents recurrence of accidents with the same signature. However, it could be argued that this is not enough and that the fact these solutions were not implemented ahead of time shows a lack of critical understanding of the possible pitfalls within different grades of automation. It is still important to analyse the specific solutions and think of how they can help us to understand a more widespread and systematic one.

Passenger Report Buttons
In the event that any on-board protocol fails, drivers fail to note any anomalies such as in the Jubilee Line and Notting Hill Gate Incidents in 2018, passengers may take it upon themselves to cause a train to stop.

Year by year the number of alarm activations rises, despite the number of passenger journeys staying relatively stable. Indeed, 2019 actually had a 6% decline in railway usage compared to 2018 throughout all of Great Britain as shown in Fig. 7 (Gower 2021), meaning the 9% increase in emergency usage is implying either that passengers are getting more comfortable reporting issues or issues are becoming more commonplace. However, as discussed previously, the number of major incidents has been on a steady decline, but this has no real bearing on the usage of an emergency stop. There are reports of customers typically using the emergency stop button for smaller issues. There have been reports of passengers with bodily physical difficulties, such as the required use of a wheelchair using the emergency stop on a train to call for staff in order to assist them getting off the train, with one passenger telling the BBC "If I can't get off at my stop that's an emergency for me" and the Railways customer service representative declaring this a legitimate use of the emergency button, stating the company trusts passengers judgement in using the button (Rob-England 2020).

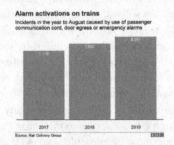

Fig. 7. (National Rail Delivery Group 2019)

As expected, 2020/21 saw a reduction in the total number of button presses compared to previous years, due to less people using the railway as shown in Fig. 8. However, the button presses per million passengers is up drastically. There could be several reasons behind this, but it is safe to assume that these results are anomalous and do not mean much for the purposes of reducing incident rates within GoA-2. It is not unreasonable to assume that, given a non-pandemic time, the alarm activation rate would have stayed steady (National Rail Delivery Group 2021). The purpose of the button is to help alleviate issues caused within GoA2 systems. At lower grades of automation there would always

	Period	Data / Results
Passenger Train Delay Incidents	2020/2021	6908
Passenger Train Delay Incidents	2021/2022	6952
Associated Passenger Train Delay minutes	2020/2021	129578
Associated Passenger Train Delay minutes	2021/2022	87563

Fig. 8. 2020/21 button usage (National Rail Delivery Group 2021)

be a staff member to help an individual with a wheelchair onto the station, for example, than within a higher grade of automation.

Aircraft Often Opting to Not Use Autoland Feature

Autoland as a feature has existed since 1937, being created by aircraft pioneers Captain Carl Crane, George Holloman and Raymond Stout (Larson 2012). However, the practise of using the feature is still not standard to this day for several reasons.

Software Not Fully Adaptable to All Forms of Weather

Much like the Bucharest 2019 metro incident, there have been cases in the past of aviation accidents caused partially by poor weather in which overcast clouds caused an auto-landing plane to crash onto grasslands near the landing zone (German Federal Bureau of Aircraft Accident Investigation 2011).

Causing Pilot Enjoyment to Dwindle

As shown within the open doorway incident within the London Underground, if a job becomes routine and unenjoyable there is a risk that the worker will enter a micro-sleep state while working. This is no different within air transport, with landing being one of the more difficult parts of the job, it is also the most engaging. Although the process can be automated, it seems counterintuitive to do so as, much like within rail, removing the more difficult parts of a pilot's job while still needing them in case of emergency can cause brainfog (Brandenburger and Naumann 2021).

Occasionally the Software Fails

Although piloting can theoretically be automated there are scenarios where the automation fails. Within these scenarios it is important that pilots can undertake the full extent of their jobs, else disaster may strike as it did within Asiana Airlines Flight 214, a flight in which crew had become dependent on autopilot to land and had gradually overtime forgotten their training and how to land at all, leading to several casualties (US National Transportation Safety Board 2013).

Complacency Within Aviation

Another irony within the working world is one of experience making workers less attentive, 'the better you get at work the less effort you put in to any given day' also known as complacency, a state of 'self-satisfaction with one's own performance coupled with an unawareness of danger, trouble' (Moray and Inagaki 2000). What all of this means is that overall as skill increases, less focus is needed to operate at average capacity. There has been some research into the overlap of complacency and over reliance on automation (Automation Bias) within aviation in which a link between the two was suggested stating that once experts (pilots) found an automated system to be reliable, they became complacent and allowed for their automation bias to take over (Parasuraman and Manzey 2010).

3   Synthesis

Using the knowledge of previous incidents, we now know the typical causes of most anomalies within GoA-2, so we are able to suggest methodologies to reduce the number of errors present and, hopefully, a methodology to better facilitate safe innovation within the rail industry. The key underlying factor with all examples of error in GoA-2 is the repetitiveness of a driver's task list combined with any negatives on the day (low blood sugar, lack of sleep etc.) which can lead to a driver easily getting distracted and switching to "auto-pilot" mode in which they enact their actions without sufficient thought. There are numerous ways to avoid this problem.

3.1   Solutions Within the Expansion of GoA-2

If the goal is to eventually get all rail to GoA-4, it is important to consider each step that will need to be taken in order to get there. If it is decided that GoA-2 is a necessary step towards total automation, it is important to consider its role. There is discussion to be had on expanding the definition of GoA-2 to reflect this transitionary period between the control being mostly in the drivers' hands in the case of GoA-1 and the system gaining more autonomy within GoA-3. This transitionary period could be used to identify potential issues within further automation, this process of identifying issues and applying solutions is sometimes called a "band-aid solution" the process of treating the symptoms of a problem instead of treating the cause. However, this is not necessarily bad if we think of GoA-2 as a transitionary period, it is important to learn from experience and ensure that accidents with a similar signature can be avoided within further automation.

The London Underground Jubilee incident, although unfortunate, serves as a perfect template for an expansion of automation. Currently GoA-2 systems use ATP in order to ensure trains operate at a safe speed and do not exceed the limits (Dave Keevill 2017). There is room for discussion whether ATP should include safety precautions related to doors, just as there is no reason why a locomotive should be allowed to speed, there is no reason the train should move with open doors. Within GoA-2 the job of opening and closing doors is a responsibility of the driver. GoA-2 technology is not reactive, meaning it cannot act autonomously regarding the irregular amount of time it will take for individuals to board from a platform, it cannot be suggested that GoA-2 should handle the opening and closing of doors, a driver will always be required to operate the doors within a GoA-2 system. However, in the cases where a driver makes a mistake and sets the train in motion with the doors still open, ATP should act as a backup and close the doors (or prevent movement) to ensure that incidents similar to that taken place on the London Underground Jubilee line cannot happen again.

3.2 Upgrading to GoA-3

GoA-3 typically operates with a Rail Operating Centre (ROC), an off-site location in which a single driver is responsible for the operation of numerous vehicles. This leads to both a higher intensity of work per individual and a lower overall number of staff needed than GoA-2, as each worker can be more specialized and each worker is more engaged in their job. A less repetitive environment leads to less worker fatigue, which leads to better work and less accidents, even if it causes a higher amount of stress for workers (Brandenburger and Naumann 2021).

While it would be simple to state that the most effective solution is simply to increase automation, that does not necessarily take into consideration the cost and scientific research required into so doing. Currently the usage of GoA 3 and 4 are very limited (UITP Observatory of Automated Metros 2018) so there is still much room for innovation, which leads to the question of whether or not we are even ready for increased automation; if we are to assume that the end goal is complete automation of railways then it would be reasonable to suggest that we should implement GoA-3 as soon as possible, something which is being discussed around the world already (Miller and Collet 2020). Costs of GoA-3 are higher initially than within other rail solutions (Zhou 2016) but the staff reductions could result in a much lower management and training cost, meaning lower costs in the long run, especially with the ever-increasing cost for labour. This, however, raises several questions about labour ethics and the discussion to be had with unions, topics which are out of scope for this discussion.

3.3 Decrease of Automation

If upgrading to GoA-3 is not an option, the reasonable suggestion is to rethink automation and how it is handled. Within GoA-2 the driver is acting as an assistant to the overall system, when naturally it seems safer if the roles were to be reversed. A GoA-2 system cannot detect anomalies, yet it is the one in control of acceleration and braking. There is an important question to be asked, are we giving control to a system that is not yet ready, if the driver needs to be within the cabin anyway, why not simply have them provide train operation? It is possible to put the driver back in control and give them the more stimulating job of acceleration and braking and simply have the GoA-2 system as a backup in case of emergency, in order to avoid events such as the Jubilee Incident, as well as taking advantage of the speed regulation and other features of ATP. Communication with other rolling stock is also a feature of GoA-2 which provides ATS given an incident that the driver could not have known about. Drivers within GoA-2 systems have less responsibility than drivers in GoA-1/unautomated systems, they do not have to maintain acceleration or pull into stations, it seems only natural to assume that economically this will mean that the drivers are cheaper. However, this is not the case, costs for a driver who operates the London Underground, using a GoA-2 system are no lower than drivers in an unautomated rail (Glassdoor 2021), the drivers still need to be trained for all scenarios in case the ATO fails.

If there are issues with GoA-2 from both an engineering and an economic standpoint there is discussion to be had about the definition of GoA-2. Currently a goal of railway innovation is the normalization of GoA-4 within passenger rails (Shift2Rail EU 2019) so it is important to ask if the current iteration of GoA-2 is an inevitable part of that journey or, if until automation gets to the point where it can run autonomously, it should take a back-seat and run in a limited capacity.

4   Conclusion

This paper presents a preliminary discussion on the topic of making work easier, with respect to introduction of automation on the railways. It poses the question of that being a good thing in the first place and more specifically it discusses the failure rate of work that is boring against work that is more challenging hence more engaging. Common beliefs would suggest that easier work will yield better results with less errors, however evidence suggests that is not the case. Although more research is required into just how much monotonous tasks within GoA-2 can lead to brainfog/microsleeping and it would be immature to suggest that the entire scope has been covered, it is safe to say that there is a link and to simply call each example "Human Error" is incorrect. Current safety precautions such as placing some responsibility on the consumer through an emergency button are effective in harm reduction however are more fixing the symptoms rather than fixing the cause. The most effective overall solution would be to simply increase the amount of automation and attempt to get to GoA-3 as soon as possible. However, until that time arrives, it would be useful to re-examine GoA-2's role in the future of railway automation. There is an irony of innovation, it is possible that a scientific breakthrough can happen but cannot be applied yet because the surrounding systems are not yet ready for it. Within piloting, although automated landing exists it is not commonplace because if you have a pilot in the cockpit, there is little-to-no reason for them not be the ones to land. Is this not the same within GoA-2, the driver is in the cab, what purpose is there to not have them drive? GoA-2 is in a sort of 'uncanny valley', meaning the automation is developed enough that it has surpassed being a novelty and somewhat demands respect; the train can move autonomously but also it has not developed to the point where it can be considered autonomous. Just because GoA-2 systems can be implemented doesn't necessarily mean they should. Thus, there is a discussion to be had on the overall need for, and definition of, GoA-2 within rail.

References

European Union Agency for Railways: Railway Safety and Interoperability in the EU. The Publications Office of the European Union, Luxembourg (2020)

Gower, T.L.: Passenger Rail Usage 2021–22. Office of Rail and Road, London (2021)

Hinojal, J.: Bombardier marks a quarter century of rail control excellence in Bilbao (2017). Accessed Bombardier Romania: https://rail.bombardier.com/en/about-us/worldwide-presence/romania/en.html/bombardier/news/2017/bt_20171124_bombardier-marks-a-quarter-century-of-rail-control-e/en

Leidig, M.: Stuck in the air train to be moved a year after crash (2020). Accessed Ananova news: https://ananova.news/stuck-in-the-air-train-to-be-moved-a-year-after-crash/

National Rail Delivery Group: Train Delay Incident Chart. National Rail, London (2019)

National Rail Delivery Group: 2020/2021 Passenger Train Delay Incidents. Reference Number 1/951612. National Rail, London (2021)

Naumann, J.S.: Monotony, fatigue and microsleeps - train driver' daily routine: a simulator study. In: 2nd German Workshop on Rail Human Factors, Berlin (2016)

Brandenburger, N., Naumann, A.: Task-Induced Fatigue When Implementing High Grades of Railway Automation. German Aerospace Center (DLR), Institute of Transportation Systems, Berlin (2021)

RAIB: Train departed with doors open, Warren Street, Victoria Line, London Underground, 11 July 2011. RAIB, London (2011)

Rail Accident Investigation Branch: Rail Accident Report - Train travelling with doors open on the Jubilee Line. RAIB, London (2018)

Rail Safety and Standards Board: Railway accidents: casualties by type of accident. Gov.uk, London (2020)

Rob-England: Train emergency alarm delays rise as more passengers call for help. BBC News, London (2020)

Miller, S., Collet, C.: World-first: Automatic Train Operation for regional passenger trains to be tested in Germany. Alstom, Berlin (2020)

Shift2Rail EU: Innovation in the Spotlight: towards unattended mainline train operations (ATO GoA 4). Shift2Rail, Brussels (2019)

Şodolescu, D.: Investigation in the case of the derailed subway at Berceni Depot. (Petre Dobrescu, N.R., Interviewer) (2019)

Åkerstedt, T., Gillberg, M.: Subjective and objective sleepiness in the active individual. Swedish Defence Research Establishment, Stockholm (1989)

UITP Observatory of Automated Metros: World Metro Figures 2018. UITP, Brussels (2018)

UK Department for Transport: Reported road casualties Great Britain, Annual report: 2020. Department for Transport, London (2020)

United Kingdom Department for Transport: Passenger trapped and dragged at Notting Hill Gate station, 31 January 2018. Rail Accident Investigation Branch, Department for Transport, London (2018a)

United Kingdom Department for Transport: Train travelling with doors open on the Jubilee Line. Rail Accident Investigation Branch, Department for Transport, London (2018b)

Zhou, Y.W.: Survey on Driverless Train Operation for Urban Rail Transit Systems. Urban Rail Transit, Beijing (2016)

Dave Keevill, P.: Implications of Increasing Grade of Automation. Parsons, Baltimore (2017)

Moray, N., Inagaki, T.: Attention and complacency. Guildford: Theoret. Issues Ergon. Sci. 1, 354–365 (2000)

Parasuraman, R., Manzey, D.H.: Complacency and bias in human use of automation: an attentional integration. Hum. Factors Ergon. Soc. 52, 381–410 (2010)

http://www.railway-technical.com/signalling/automatic-train-control.html

https://arc.aiaa.org/doi/abs/10.2514/3.56129?journalCode=jgcd

https://www.bfu-web.de/EN/Publications/Investigation%20Report/2011/Report_11_EX010_B777_Munic.pdf?__blob=publicationFile

https://www.ntsb.gov/investigations/accidentreports/reports/aar1401.pdf

https://www.glassdoor.co.uk/Salaries/london-train-driver-salary-SRCH_IL.0,6_IM1035_KO7,19.htm

A Vision of Intelligent Train Control

Francesco Flammini[1,2]([⊠]) [iD], Lorenzo De Donato[3] [iD], Alessandro Fantechi[4] [iD],
and Valeria Vittorini[3] [iD]

[1] School of Innovation, Design and Engineering, Mälardalen University,
Eskilstuna, Sweden
francesco.flammini@mdu.se
[2] Department of Computer Science and Media Technology, Linnaeus University,
Växjö, Sweden
[3] Department of Electrical Engineering and Information Technology,
University of Naples Federico II, Naples, Italy
{lorenzo.dedonato,valeria.vittorini}@unina.it
[4] Department of Information Engineering, University of Florence, Florence, Italy
alessandro.fantechi@unifi.it

Abstract. The progressive adoption of artificial intelligence and advanced communication technologies within railway control and automation has brought up a huge potential in terms of optimisation, learning and adaptation, due to the so-called "self-x" capabilities; however, it has also raised several dependability concerns due to the lack of measurable trust that is needed for certification purposes. In this paper, we provide a vision of future train control that builds upon existing automatic train operation, protection, and supervision paradigms. We will define the basic concepts for autonomous driving in digital railways, and summarise its feasibility in terms of challenges and opportunities, including explainability, autonomic computing, and digital twins. Due to the clear architectural distinction, automatic train protection can act as a safety envelope for intelligent operation to optimise energy, comfort, and capacity, while intelligent protection based on signal recognition and obstacle detection can improve safety through advanced driving assistance.

Keywords: Smart railways · Artificial intelligence · Machine learning · Trustworthy AI · Autonomous driving · Safety envelope · Certification

1 Introduction

Railway is undergoing a deep technological and organisational transformation since the beginning of this century. Such evolution was not limited to high speed trains and has been supported by important advancements of information and communication technologies, especially regarding train control systems.

In this paper we look at the impact of progressive adoption of artificial intelligence (AI) and advanced communication technologies within train control systems, with their huge potential in terms of optimisation, learning and adaptation,

S. Collart-Dutilleul et al. (Eds.): RSSRail 2022, LNCS 13294, pp. 192–208, 2022.
https://doi.org/10.1007/978-3-031-05814-1_14

together with the related dependability concerns, including the lack of measurable trust that is needed for certification purposes. Although AI can be applied to several functions and subsystems within railways, including monitoring, surveillance and predictive maintenance [2], which can be related to automatic control and safety of operations, in this paper we specifically focus on intelligent control for autonomous driving.

The vision of future intelligent train control described in this paper builds upon existing paradigms for automatic train operation, protection, and supervision. In particular, within intelligent railways, automatic train protection can be considered as a *safety envelope* for autonomous driving, something that is missing in other sectors such as automotive [30]. That allows optimising energy, comfort, and capacity through intelligent train operation. Moving a step further, we explore the possibility of intelligent train protection based on signal recognition and obstacle/anomaly detection to improve safety through advanced driving assistance when other safety technologies are missing or malfunctioning. In order to investigate autonomous driving in the railway domain, we will first define the basic concepts and then summarise opportunities, challenges, new paradigms and technology enablers, including trustworthy/explainable AI, autonomic computing, and digital twins.

The work described in this paper has been developed within Work Package 2 (AI for Rail Safety and Automation) of the RAILS (Roadmaps for A.I. Integration in the Rail Sector) research project[1] [15], funded by the European Union through the Shift2Rail Joint Undertaking.

The rest of this paper is structured as follows: Sect. 2 provides a brief overview about modern train control systems; Sect. 3 introduces a vision of intelligent railways focusing on grades of intelligence for future train control systems; Sect. 4 discusses essential technology enablers for intelligent train control; finally, Sect. 5 draws conclusions and mentions some open challenges.

2 Background on Modern Train Control Systems

In this section we provide a brief overview of modern train control systems, including basic concepts and some emerging paradigms.

2.1 Basic Definitions About Connected and Autonomous Trains

In order to provide a vision of intelligent train control, it is important to introduce some basic concepts of intelligent transportation and smart-railways. "Connected Vehicles" rely on Vehicle-to-Vehicle (V2V) and Vehicle-to-Infrastructure (V2I) communications (commonly referred to as V2X communication) to exchange information and *automatically* achieve a specified goal; instead, "Autonomous Vehicles (AVs)" are capable of elaborating information captured by on-board sensors to dynamically adapt to the environment's changes

---

[1] https://rails-project.eu/.

Table 1. Automatic train management functions

Automatic Train Operation	ATO	Used to automatically drive the train and stop at stations when needed
Automatic Train Protection	ATP	Used to automatically protect the train by applying brakes when needed
Automatic Train Control	ATC	Both ATP and ATO are in place to ensure full control of the train
Automatic Train Supervision	ATS	Used to manage train schedule and coordinate routes along whole tracks

Table 2. Grade of Automation (GoA) levels

GoA 0	Train operations are manually supervised by the driver, no automation
GoA 1	Train operations are manually supervised by the driver supported by ATP.
GoA 2	Semi-automatic train operation. ATO and ATP systems automatically manage train operations and protection while supervised by the driver.
GoA 3	Driverless train operation with on-board staff handling possible emergencies.
GoA 4	Unattended train operation, neither the driver nor the staff are required

and safely proceed along a requested journey. These categories are not mutually exclusive [10]: *connected* and *autonomous* solutions may be merged towards the realisation of future smart/intelligent vehicles. It is possible to distinguish between "automation" and "autonomy", with a focus on the role of AI. In reference [2], the following definition of AI has been given: *"AI is the discipline gathering all the aspects that allow an entity to determine how to perform a task and/or take a decision based on the experience matured by observing samples and/or by interacting with an environment, possibly competing against or cooperating with other entities"*. Such a definition allows for a clear distinction between what is attributable to intelligent behaviour and what not. For example, ATO and ATP (see Table 1) allow trains to *automatically* or *semi-automatically* perform a given task based on pre-specified rules; however, according to the definition given above, current driverless trains, which are often considered autonomous rather than automatic, cannot be considered "intelligent" since they miss any learning and adaptation capabilities. Actually, according to some reputable definitions, *Autonomy* refers to the capability of the system to dynamically adapt to unexpected scenarios by taking independent decisions [27] based on methods, procedures, or algorithms that may involve AI-based approaches. Indeed, "Intelligent Vehicles" can be seen as a special category of AVs that are capable of taking autonomous decisions, learning from experience, and adapting to changes in the environment.

ATO, ATP, and ATS are widely adopted, and connected trains are not a fully new concept [10]. ERTMS/ETCS (i.e., European Rail Traffic Management System - European Train Control System) and CBTC (i.e., Communication Based Train Control) systems rely on ATC and V2I communications to increase safety, performance, and reliability. Automation of train operation can be rated according to five different Grades of Automation (GoA, see Table 2), as defined by the International Association of Public Transport (UITP).

2.2 The ERTMS/ETCS Railway Standard Specification

ERTMS is an international standard aiming at unifying the European railway lines by replacing all the different control systems currently deployed, to allow trains to cross borders without the need to equip them with different systems or to change locomotive or driver [8]. ERTMS relies on the European Train Control System which is deemed to ensure that the maximum safe speed and minimum safe distance are respected [10]. Conventional train control systems are based on information captured by trackside equipment (such as track circuits or axle counter); ETCS is specified at four levels of operation (L0 to L3), depending on the role of the trackside equipment and on the way the information is transmitted to/from trains. Levels 2 and 3 can be considered as connected train systems.

At Level 2 (L2), track circuits or axle counters are used to detect the occupancy of sections of the track, determining the location of the trains. Then, this information is sent and processed by the Radio Block Centre (RBC) which sends to each train a Movement Authority (MA), computed by counting the free sections in front of the train; the MA specifies the maximum distance the train can travel and the allowed speed. Hence, the on-board European Vital Computer (EVC) uses the MA and on-board data (e.g. the braking capability of the train) to compute the maximum possible speed (i.e., the braking curve or the dynamic speed profile), triggering an emergency brake whenever this limit is exceeded. These communications are based on GSM-R (rail dedicated GSM) which allows a bidirectional communication among trains and RBC. While ETCS-L2 is based on *fixed-block* signalling, ETCS-L3 is based on *moving-block* signalling, where computation of the MA is performed using the position of the tail of the preceding train rather than the information from the interlocking system. This leads to a considerable reduction of the distance required to ensure safety between two consecutive trains, as depicted in Fig. 1, and improves upon Level 2 also by reducing wayside equipment for detecting track occupancy.

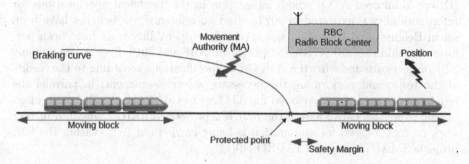

Fig. 1. Communication based moving block principle [10]

2.3   Segregated and Open Railway Environments

When it comes to connected or autonomous trains, it is necessary to make a clear distinction between "segregated" and "open" railway environments [27]. Segregated environments include the rail lines that are isolated from external influences (e.g. underground metro lines with platform screen doors). In these scenarios, moving block based on continuous communication and MA computation is currently implemented in several automatic metros, as a feature of CBTC systems [18]. Many metro lines are now equipped with GoA2 and 3 ATO systems, managing the train running from one station to another automatically adjusting the train speed with appropriate traction and braking commands allowing for train automated driving, and they are now moving towards GoA4 ones. Worth mentioning, in the ATO systems currently deployed as part of CBTC, autonomy with respect to the global train control is almost null, since the safety-critical decisions in a CBTC system are centralised in a Zone Controller. Differently, in open environments, i.e. all the railway market segments (mainline/high speed, urban/suburban, regional and freight) which are not completely isolated from external threats, the ATO implementation is still experimental due to the high interoperability requirements posed by such large, complex interconnected railway networks.

2.4   Automatic Train Operation over ETCS

In the last six years, the challenge of developing and validating a standard ATO up to GoA3/4 over ETCS (AoE) has been tackled by the Shif2Rail (S2R) Joint Undertaking (JU) under the H2020 research programme. Specifically, AoE is addressed by the S2R Innovation Programme 2 (IP2, "Advanced Traffic Management and Control Systems") with the objective to extend the existing applications from segregated (mostly subways) to open environments . The development of AoE is considered strategic [7] because great benefits can come from ATO and ATS in terms of increased system capacity, punctuality, resilience, flexibility, reduced operating costs and energy consumption. The research and the innovation solutions developed in IP2 through the projects funded by the S2R JU have brought important results, leading to the AoE GoA2 specification (Driver Monitored ATO) whose integration in the Technical Specifications for Interoperability is expected in 2022 [44]. Two reference test benches have been set in Belgium and Germany, and several interoperability tests have been performed within the S2R X2RAIL-1 project in 2018 and 2019. Recent and ongoing S2R projects are updating the AoE GoA2 specifications according to the results of the tests, and performing the necessary safety assessment; in parallel the requirements are being developed for ATO up to GoA4 (unattended train operations) over AoE GoA2 within the S2R IP2 project X2RAIL-4 [46], and further work on technologies for automation is being carried out (e.g., within the S2R projects SMART2 [38] and TAURO [40]).

2.5 Train Virtual Coupling

The availability of safe information about the position, speed, acceleration and deceleration of the preceding train, like that used in ETCS Level 3 and in CBTC, and the possibility of train to train communication, has inspired the Virtual Coupling concept, based on the idea of multiple trains which run one behind the other without physical contact, but at a distance comparable to mechanical coupling [4,41], with consequent high capacity and high flexibility. The concept inherits some of the principles of car platooning [1], that is being experimented in the automotive domain and it is currently under study by some S2R IP2 projects (e.g., see [28,45]). The strict real-time control of the dynamic parameters of the following train with respect to the parameters of the preceding one should allow the distance between trains to be minimized, therefore with consequent high capacity and high flexibility, for example in the forwarding of different segments of a train to different destinations through "run-time" composition and decomposition, without stopping the train.

2.6 Certification Challenges for Autonomous Trains

High levels of automation require new technologies and new generation of sensors such as obstacle detection sensors that are capable of providing artificial perception of the surrounding environment, vehicles and infrastructure, including shapes and distances. When dealing with safety related functions relying on new technologies, certification issues against current regulations are of paramount importance. Two major factors of uncertainties can be i) the opaque nature of underlying techniques and algorithms and ii) the reliability and accuracy of sophisticated sensors.

In the context of autonomous trains, it is possible to identify two types of safety [33]: *rule-based safety*, which is achieved by means of rules, formalisms, and protection measures, aiming at defining anticipated responses to foreseeable (i.e., known and predictable) situations, and *managed safety*, which aims at avoiding or mitigating unexpected (i.e., non predictable) hazardous events. In this paper, we mention safety envelopes [21,25,36] that are one declination of rule-based safety: the idea is that autonomous objects, i.e., self-driving trains, should move within an area, i.e., the safety envelope, that is free from any risk of collisions and other hazards, which is continuously computed and updated. Any movement outside the safety envelope should be detected in order to bring the system to a fail-safe state (e.g., application of emergency braking).

As already mentioned, the separation of concerns between ATP and ATO, which allows for rating at SIL4 only the former, can be framed in the concept of safety envelope. Indeed, only the two functions of safety envelope *computation* and *checking* need to be rated at SIL4, leaving the decision of how to optimally run the train to non safety-related and possibly complex software. Therefore:

– safety envelope computation should be based on sound and certified principles, that are simpler in railways than in automotive due to the train motion being constrained by the rails; these principles are enlarged to consider not only received Movement Authorities as in ETCS, but also any sensor input that conveys (only) information limiting the safety envelope, such as distance from leading train in Virtual Coupling;

- safety envelope computation should take into account all the uncertainties on measures from sensors (speed, position, distance, etc.) that impact safety of train actions (such as braking distance) on a probabilistic basis, so that the probability that the computation of producing a too permissive safety envelope is kept under the limits given by SIL4;
- safety envelope computation software should be formally proven to adhere to the above principles, by adoption of proper formal verification techniques;
- safety envelope checking is limited to verify at any time that driving commands to actuators do not bring the train outside the current safety envelope;
- safety envelope checking software should be formally proven by model-checking.

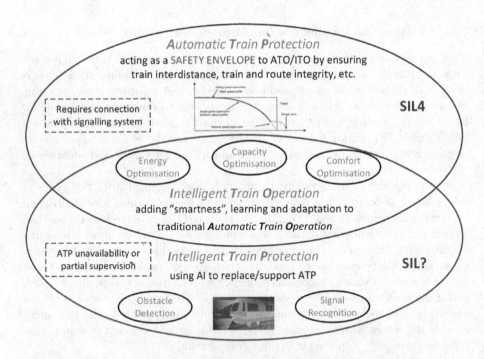

Fig. 2. Intelligent Train Control (ITC)

3   Intelligent Train Control

In this section we address AI applied to train control systems, starting from traditional ATC concepts and moving towards fully autonomous train driving in open environments.

3.1 Intelligent Train Operation and Protection

Figure 2 provides an overview of the Intelligent Train Control (ITC) concept, which integrates Intelligent Train Operation (ITO), ATP, and – possibly – Intelligent Train Protection (ITP). The main responsibility of the ATP is to ensure that the correct dynamic speed profile (also known as "braking curve") is applied to avoid collisions, derailments, and keep a safe distance between trains. ATP needs cooperation between the trackside system (e.g. interlocking – IXL –, plus RBC in case of ETCS L2) and the onboard system (e.g. EVC , for ETCS L2). If used in conjunction with ATP, ITO can safely extend the functionalities of traditional ATO to account for intelligent and adaptive behaviours, in order to optimise passenger comfort, energy consumption, and line capacity, e.g., through Virtual Coupling. In fact, just as the ATO, the ITO (i.e., the so-called "doer") is protected by the ATP (i.e., the so-called "checker"), following the safety envelope architectural pattern [21]. This allows certification against reference safety standards [39] using existing/traditional approaches. However, when ATP is not available, such as in old railways used in developing countries, or when ATP failures oblige to partial supervision, such as on-sight or staff-responsible operating modes, ITP could replace ATP by doing something similar to what automotive driving assistance systems do, i.e., automatically recognise signals and obstacles using artificial vision, possibly in combination with other sensors like radars and lidars. That would allow fully autonomous train driving.

As a last option, even if ATP is available and perfectly working, ITP can be a useful complement to detect events that are not managed by ATP, such as on-track obstacles different than rolling stock, trespassing, etc. The presence of those sensors can also aid special manoeuvres such as those needed to enable Virtual Coupling, by implementing what is know as "adaptive cruise control" for cars, i.e., keeping a constant and sufficiently short distance from the preceding vehicle. Differently from ATP, ITP uses artificial intelligence and machine learning in safety-critical applications, and therefore its SIL certification against international standards can be challenging. Therefore, an ITC implemented via ITO + ITP, although theoretically possible, does not seem to be practically viable yet as ad-hoc standards and regulations would be required to quantitatively assess the trustworthiness of AI systems, together with legal, ethical, robustness, and explainability implications [29].

However, ITP as a low-speed complement or fall-back system to ATP seems a promising option to improve safety in partial supervision, shunting, or during procedures such as the Track Ahead Free, where the driver is asked confirmation of no obstacles on the same track circuit the train is occupying during the ERTMS/ETCS "Start of Mission" scenario [8]. It is worth mentioning that the use of multiple redundant sensors, based on diverse technologies, together with explainable AI, might enable certification at higher SILs [12].

Another functionality referred to in Table 1 which is sometimes considered part of ATC is the ATS: similarly to the envisioned evolution from ATO to ITO, Intelligent Train Supervision (ITS) can take advantage of machine learning to efficiently learn and adapt, in order to optimise railway line utilisation and average throughput, and to promptly respond to disruptions by providing appropriate alternative train routing solutions. Similarly to ITO, ITS is not directly subject to safety-requirements, since safety checking of necessary conditions for train route formation is guaranteed by the IXL subsystem, which is rated at SIL4; therefore, the IXL can be considered a safety envelope for the ITS.

3.2 Grades of Intelligence in Train Control

As defined in Sect. 2, "automation" refers to the capability of a system to act automatically by following some pre-defined rules, therefore, GoA3 or GoA4 levels do not necessarily require AI. Reference [27] proposes another classification for "autonomous and semi-autonomous levels of automation"; however, an alignment of AI with levels of autonomy is missing in those classifications. Therefore, we introduce here a possible definition of Grades of Intelligence (GoI):

- **GoI 1**: This level includes all ATC implementations where AI is not used or it is used for limited functions such as optimisation within ATS. That means limited or no autonomy is normally possible in open environments.
- **GoI 2**: This level supports partial autonomy in open environments, by including only ITO as an adaptive ATO with energy, capacity and/or comfort optimisation capabilities, or only ITP for driving assistance and/or as a low-speed backup system in case of ATP unavailability or limited supervision.
- **GoI 3**: This level includes both ITO and ITP, allowing for full autonomy even in open environments, although with no advanced learning and adaptation capabilities. For instance, at GoI3, the artificial vision algorithms of ITP can be trained only once, e.g. to detect on-track obstacles, and never updated.
- **GoI 4**: This level includes both ITO and ITP, allowing for full autonomy in all environments, with advanced learning and adaptation capabilities, such as unsupervised and reinforcement learning. The system is typically fully connected, dynamically updated, and supported by higher levels of fog/cloud intelligence by using external AI models for big data analytics, such as those enabled by digital twins.

At all GoI levels, human driver/supervisor can be required or not, depending on whether the operating environment is open (e.g., commuter railways, high speed trains) or segregated (e.g., subways with platform screen doors, airport shuttles, etc.). At higher GoI levels in open environments, driverless/unsupervised trains can only be allowed if the ITP is certified to be trustworthy according to safety requirements of reference international standards. This might require extending the set of onboard sensors to allow for a full situation awareness that goes beyond ITP capabilities in signal recognition and obstacle detection. Remote driving/supervision might be allowed in some cases, if enough cameras and sensors are installed onboard, and related safety requirements are fulfilled. GoI4 is the most visionary level and represents the maximum development we can expect in the future of ITC. For instance, at GoI4 it would be possible to leverage digital twins to predict the risk of accidents such as derailments, based on data dynamically collected during system operation in several installations worldwide; therefore, GoI4 has the potential to significantly increase not only autonomy, but also safety well beyond the level achievable with current technologies.

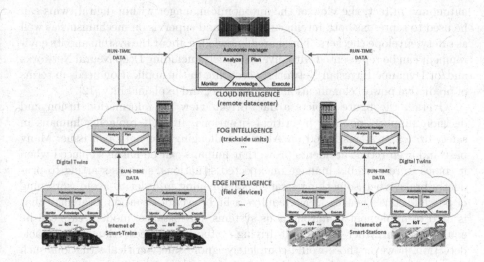

Fig. 3. Levels of intelligence in railway control and supervision.

4   Technology Enablers for Intelligent Train Control

In this section we provide a brief overview of relevant paradigms and technologies enabling ITC. Since a multitude of disciplines and research areas are connected to ITC, we will focus on those who are mainly connected with AI such as artificial vision and information fusion, rather than surveying all enabling communication and networking paradigms such as IoT and 5G (see, e.g., references [5] and [16]).

4.1   Autonomic Computing and Digital Twins in Railways

The vision of ITC provided so far does not address aspects related to where AI is located and how safety is managed in more general situations. Figure 3 shows an overview of the distribution of AI at different levels to implement railway control and supervision. Local autonomy is enabled by *edge intelligence*, with possible limitations in terms of computing power and data availability, due to constrained devices, and advantages in terms of response times and data security, due to shorter communication links. *Fog intelligence* represents trackside control where capacity optimisations such as Virtual Coupling can be orchestrated based on a larger view such as a whole track. Finally, *cloud intelligence* includes all aspects related to the elaboration of big amounts of data, possibly coming from multiple installations worldwide, with the aim of collecting information and knowledge to predict failures and make maintenance smarter.

We tried to generalise feedback control loops for autonomous railways by using the paradigms of autonomic computing (i.e., Monitor, Analyze, Plan, and Execute over a shared Knowledge, MAPE-K) and Digital Twins [11]. That means providing common frameworks for structured and systematic approaches to safe autonomy; in fact, the view of the autonomic manager within digital twins can be used to represent both intelligent control and supervision mechanisms as well as safety-envelope checkers. The shared knowledge about the system and its environment can be represented with diverse models, including Deep Neural Networks and/or Dynamic Bayesian Networks, according to the application needs in terms of predictive power, classification performance, and explainability [12].

Overall, the figure depicts a data-driven view for information fusion and decision support, possibly in critical situations. In fact, replacing humans in safety-critical systems based on AI is a challenging and hot open issue. Many past and even recent accidents prove that humans can be hardly replaced when it comes to responsibly manage unexpected situations, such as starting to prudently brake when something strange is happening in order to avoid worsening of possible consequences. That requires a high level of situation awareness that is hard to implement in autonomous systems: for instance, modern cars can be equipped with rather precise self-driving systems with pedestrian and obstacle detection, however those would completely ignore safety-critical situations such as anomalous vibrations or smoke coming from the engine if that event is not supposed to be monitored by the system, as it is in most cases.

When an appropriate number of sensors and information sources are available, safety-related data may be sufficient to autonomously manage most critical situations. When AI is employed to do that, its trustworthiness must be ensured in terms of robustness and explainability, as well as compliance to legal and ethical requirements [17]. Runtime model checking and online process mining can be used to perform anomaly detection and conformance checking of intelligent/adaptive systems against their specified "normative" behaviour. Depending on the level of knowledge about the system and the possible threats, the approach can be fine tuned including automatic process discovery; also, anomaly detection can be based on classification, clustering or statistical techniques, which means misbehaviour can be detected even when a threat signature is missing, e.g., when facing unknown scenarios [11].

4.2   Anomaly and Obstacle Detection, and Signal Recognition

Inspired from the framework for autonomous driving proposed in reference [3], as well as from the process discussed in reference [27], it is possible to instantiate the MAPE-K model for autonomic computing to the control loop that intelligent trains should adopt when taking autonomous decisions, as shown in Fig. 4. First, data related to the environment through different kinds of sensors (e.g., cameras, accelerometers), information from other trains or trackside infrastructures (V2X communication), and internal information coming from onboard sensors are collected. These data, together with the information already stored, constitute the knowledge of the single train and are then analysed to perceive the environment

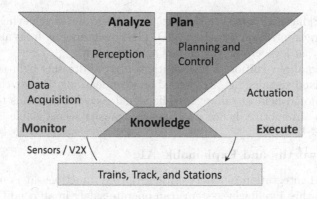

Fig. 4. MAPE-K loop for Intelligent Train Control

(e.g., obstacles, signals), the health status of the train (e.g., anomalies), and to identify the appropriate manoeuvres (e.g., acceleration, braking). Hence, the next activities are planned and set for execution based on these analyses. The last phase aims at physically actuating the decisions taken in the planning phase. Notably, the environment and the information from both onboard sensors and the other vehicles will continuously change, and AI has the potential to play a central role in this process (especially in the analysis phase), as intelligent systems are very efficient in detecting changes in data.

Anomaly detection is essential to increase safety, with Machine Learning (ML) offering several useful approaches. Sensors installed onboard for vehicle health monitoring and predictive maintenance can also be used to detect or even predict train anomalies in real-time. Anomaly detection mechanisms (e.g., [20,42]) are thus important enablers for ITC. In case an anomaly is detected/predicted, the system could warn the train driver or even start an automatic procedure to get the train to a fail-safe state, depending on the GoA and the level of confidence in anomaly classification.

Obstacle detection addresses the identification of an object when it is located within a specific region (or area) of the scene under examination. In order to take adequate and timely responses, obstacle detection requires real-time operation as well as high trustworthiness. Furthermore, if we focus on autonomous trains with onboard obstacle detection, we should consider the possible high speed of the rolling stock, environmental disturbances especially in open environments (vibrations, darkness, fog, rain, snow, etc.), and no possibilities to "skip" obstacles other than braking. On the other hand, the trajectory of railway vehicles is known and deterministic and the area in which obstacles must be detected is narrowed to rail tracks. Studies exist about detection of track obstacles (e.g., [22,47]) and other objects such as switch points (e.g., [48]) using onboard cameras and sensors. Those contribute to a better perception of the environment to enhance situation awareness. Additional measures are needed to ensure safe braking, including distance estimation, as obstacles must be recognised from long distances (hundreds of meters or even kilometres [34]). S2R projects including SMART [37] and

SMART2 [38] have addressed those aspects, with the aim of achieving long-range object and track intrusion detection (OD/TID) by leveraging front and trackside cameras (e.g., at level crossings), as well as drones [14].

As for signal recognition, a few solutions exist addressing light signals (e.g., [23,35]) or fixed signals (e.g., [6]), based on deep learning. Hence, this seems to be an unexplored field in railways, while signal recognition seems to be better developed in automotive, hence a technology transfer seems viable in principle.

4.3 Trustworthy and Explainable AI

To enable AI integration in safety-critical railway functions, it is necessary to demonstrate that intelligent systems can operate safely in all conditions. Safety certification of AI is still an open issue in all industry sectors. Some steps have recently been taken, such as the W-shaped development process [9] to properly assess the usage of neural networks in avionics, as proposed by the European Union Aviation Safety Agency (EASA) and Deadalean; however, further techniques are required to explain the input-output relationship in black-box AI approaches. AI applications are non-deterministic and they may be unstable, i.e., the output of the system may change drastically even with a slight variation of the input. This also exposes intelligent systems to new threats such as the so-called adversarial attacks (e.g., [31]). How to establish the cause-effect relationship between a given input and the produced output of many AI systems is currently challenging. Therefore, some of the key points established by the High Level Expert Group on AI of the European Commission [17], including transparency, robustness, and explainability, are not easy to address and represent an obstacle to high SIL certification of ITP.

In order to mitigate those issues, eXplainable AI (XAI) techniques (e.g., LIME [32], SHAP [24], and ELI5[2]) have been developed to generate interpretable models and explanations of ML decisions that can be comprehensible to humans to improve AI trustworthiness. XAI can be model-agnostic and applied a-posteriori on ML models, e.g. with LIME [32], or it can be part of system design (i.e., sort of "design for explainability"), e.g., if probabilistic models can be used such as Bayesian ones [26]. Amongst others, one Working Group of the IEEE Computational Intelligence Society Standards Committee (CIS/SC) is currently developing XAI standards [19].

5 Conclusions

In this paper, we have provided a vision of intelligent train control based on emerging paradigms and enabling AI technologies. We have shown that in order to move towards fully autonomous train driving, several steps needs to be taken, with AI being gradually introduced in train control and supervision systems. In the near future, AI can only be introduced in safety-critical train control applications if supervised by human operators and/or by existing high SIL systems such

---

[2] https://eli5.readthedocs.io/.

as the ATP. In driverless use, especially in open environments, intelligent train control must become capable of safely handling hazardous situations through self-X technologies (self-monitoring, self-diagnosing, self-healing), in order to enable early warning and situation assessment, considering both onboard and trackside risk factors. To that aim, we have shown that infrastructure and vehicle health monitoring for anomaly detection, together with obstacle detection and signal recognition, represent essential technologies to enable safe driverless ITC in all operating conditions. Future ITC evolution might include cooperative train driving developing from virtual coupling to swarm intelligence and game-based optimisation [43].

There are many open challenges that need to be tackled in order to enable a high SIL ITP, including those related to trustworthy and explainable AI. Together with formal approaches, simulation based techniques (e.g., abstract functional testing [13]) also need to be extended and adapted to cope with intelligent systems and ensure a sufficient coverage of AI functions.

Acknowledgements. This research has received funding from the Shift2Rail Joint Undertaking (JU) under grant agreement No 881782 RAILS. The JU receives support from the European Union's Horizon 2020 research and innovation program and the Shift2Rail JU members other than the Union.

References

1. Bergenhem, C., Pettersson, H., Coelingh, E., Englund, C., Shladover, S., Tsugawa, S.: Overview of platooning systems. In: 19th ITS World Congress, Vienna (2012)
2. Bešinović, N., et al.: Artificial intelligence in railway transport: taxonomy, regulations and applications. IEEE Trans. Intell. Transp. Syst. 1–14 (2021)
3. Braud, T., Ivanchev, J., Deboeser, C., Knoll, A., Eckhoff, D., Sangiovanni-Vincentelli, A.: AVDM: a hierarchical command-and-control system architecture for cooperative autonomous vehicles in highways scenario using microscopic simulations. Auton. Agents Multi-Agent Syst. **35**(1), 1–30 (2021). https://doi.org/10. 1007/s10458-021-09499-6
4. Di Meo, C., Di Vaio, M., Flammini, F., Nardone, R., Santini, S., Vittorini, V.: ERTMS/ETCS virtual coupling: proof of concept and numerical analysis. IEEE Trans. Intell. Transp. Syst. **21**(6), 2545–2556 (2020)
5. Dirnfeld, R., Flammini, F., Marrone, S., Nardone, R., Vittorini, V.: Low-power wide-area networks in intelligent transportation: review and opportunities for smart-railways. In: 2020 IEEE 23rd International Conference on Intelligent Transportation Systems (ITSC), pp. 1–7 (2020)
6. Etxeberria-Garcia, M., Ezaguirre, F., Plazaola, J., Munoz, U., Zamalloa, M.: Embedded object detection applying deep neural networks in railway domain. In: 2020 23rd Euromicro Conference on Digital System Design, pp. 565–569. IEEE (2020)
7. European Rail Research Advisory Council (ERRAC): Rail Strategic Research and Innovation Agenda - December 2020 (2020)
8. European Railway Agency: ERTMS - System Requirements Specification - UNISIG SUBSET-026 (2014). https://www.era.europa.eu/content/set-specifications-3-etcs-b3-r2-gsm-r-b1_en

9. European Union Aviation Safety Agency (EASA) and Daedalean: Concepts of Design Assurance for Neural Networks (CoDANN) II. Technical report (2021)

10. Fantechi, A.: Connected or autonomous trains? In: Collart-Dutilleul, S., Lecomte, T., Romanovsky, A. (eds.) Reliability, Safety, and Security of Railway Systems. Modelling, Analysis, Verification, and Certification, RSSRail 2019. LNCS, vol. 11495, pp. 3–19. Springer, Cham (2019). https://doi.org/10.1007/978-3-030-18744-6_1

11. Flammini, F.: Digital twins as run-time predictive models for the resilience of cyber-physical systems: a conceptual framework. Phil. Trans. R. Soc. A **379**(2207), 20200369 (2021)

12. Flammini, F., Marrone, S., Nardone, R., Caporuscio, M., D'Angelo, M.: Safety integrity through self-adaptation for multi-sensor event detection: methodology and case-study. Future Gener. Comput. Syst. **112**, 965–981 (2020)

13. Flammini, F., Mazzocca, N., Orazzo, A.: Automatic instantiation of abstract tests on specific configurations for large critical control systems. Softw. Test. Verif. Reliab. **19**(2), 91–110 (2009)

14. Flammini, F., Pragliola, C., Smarra, G.: Railway infrastructure monitoring by drones. In: 2016 International Conference on Electrical Systems for Aircraft, Railway, Ship Propulsion and Road Vehicles International Transportation Electrification Conference (ESARS-ITEC), pp. 1–6 (2016)

15. Flammini, F., Vittorini, V., Lin, Z.: Roadmaps for AI Integration in the Rail Sector - RAILS (2020). https://ercim-news.ercim.eu/en121/r-i/roadmaps-for-ai-integration-in-the-rail-sector-rails

16. Fraga-Lamas, P., Fernández-Caramés, T.M., Castedo, L.: Towards the internet of smart trains: a review on industrial IoT-connected railways. Sensors **17**(6), 1457 (2017)

17. High-Level Expert Group on AI: Ethics guidelines for trustworthy AI (2019)

18. IEEE: Vehicular technology society, 1474.1 - standard for communications- based train control (CBTC) - performance and functional requirements (2004)

19. IEEE CIS/SC: Standard for XAI - eXplainable Artificial Intelligence. https://development.standards.ieee.org/myproject-web/public/view.html#pardetail/8923. Accessed 15 Dec 2021

20. Kang, S., Sristi, S., Karachiwala, J., Hu, Y.C.: Detection of anomaly in train speed for intelligent railway systems. In: 2018 International Conference on Control, Automation and Diagnosis (ICCAD), pp. 1–6. IEEE (2018)

21. Koopman, P., Wagner, M.: Toward a framework for highly automated vehicle safety validation. Technical report, SAE Technical Paper (2018)

22. Li, J., Zhou, F., Ye, T.: Real-world railway traffic detection based on faster better network. IEEE Access **6**, 68730–68739 (2018)

23. Liu, W., Wang, Z., Zhou, B., Yang, S., Gong, Z.: Real-time signal light detection based on yolov5 for railway. In: IOP Conference Series: Earth and Environmental Science, vol. 769, p. 042069. IOP Publishing (2021)

24. Lundberg, S.M., Lee, S.I.: A unified approach to interpreting model predictions. In: Proceedings of the 31st International Conference on Neural Information Processing Systems, pp. 4768–4777 (2017)

25. Lyu, Y., Pan, Q., Zhao, C., Zhang, Y., Hu, J.: Vision-based UAV collision avoidance with 2D dynamic safety envelope. IEEE Aerosp. Electron. Syst. Mag. **31**(7), 16–26 (2016)

26. Mihaljević, B., Bielza, C., Larrañaga, P.: Bayesian networks for interpretable machine learning and optimization. Neurocomputing **456**, 648–665 (2021)

27. Milburn, D., Erskine, M.: Digital train control: functional safety for AI based systems. In: International Railway Safety Council Conference 2019, Perth, Australia (2019)
28. MOVINGRAIL: MOving block and VIrtual coupling New Generations of RAIL signalling. https://movingrail.eu/. Accessed 15 Dec 2021
29. RAILS: Deliverable D1.3: Application Areas (2021). https://doi.org/10.13140/RG.2.2.15604.07049, https://rails-project.eu/
30. Rajabli, N., Flammini, F., Nardone, R., Vittorini, V.: Software verification and validation of safe autonomous cars: a systematic literature review. IEEE Access 9, 4797–4819 (2021)
31. Ren, K., Zheng, T., Qin, Z., Liu, X.: Adversarial attacks and defenses in deep learning. Engineering 6(3), 346–360 (2020)
32. Ribeiro, M.T., Singh, S., Guestrin, C.: "Why should i trust you?" Explaining the predictions of any classifier. In: Proceedings of the 22nd ACM SIGKDD International Conference on Knowledge Discovery and Data Mining, pp. 1135–1144 (2016)
33. Richard, P., Boussif, A., Paglia, C.: Rule-based and managed safety: a challenge for railway autonomous driving systems. In: 31th European Safety and Reliability Conference (2021)
34. Ristić-Durrant, D., Franke, M., Michels, K.: A review of vision-based on-board obstacle detection and distance estimation in railways. Sensors 21(10), 3452 (2021)
35. Ritika, S., Mittal, S., Rao, D.: Railway track specific traffic signal selection using deep learning (2017)
36. Rudolph, A., Voget, S., Mottok, J.: A consistent safety case argumentation for artificial intelligence in safety related automotive systems. In: ERTS 2018 (2018)
37. SMART: Smart Automation of Rail Transport. http://www.smartrail-automation-project.net. Accessed 10 Dec 2021
38. SMART2: Advanced integrated obstacle and track intrusion detection system for smart automation of rail transport. https://smart2rail-project.net. Accessed 15 Dec 2021
39. European Committee for Electrotechnical Standardization, C.: EN 50128:2011 - Railway applications - Communications, signalling and processing systems - Software for railway control and protection systems (2011)
40. TAURO: Technologies for the AUtonomous Rail Operation. https://projects.shift2rail.org/s2r_ipx_n.aspx?p=tauro. Accessed 15 Dec 2021
41. UIC: Virtually coupled trains (2002). http://www.railway-energy.org/static/Virtually_coupled_trains_86.php. Accessed 15 Dec 2021
42. Wang, C., Liu, J.: An efficient anomaly detection for high-speed train braking system using broad learning system. IEEE Access 9, 63825–63832 (2021)
43. Wang, Q., Chai, M., Liu, H., Tang, T.: Optimized control of virtual coupling at junctions: a cooperative game-based approach. Actuators 10(9), 207 (2021)
44. X2Rail-1: Start-up activities for Advanced Signalling and Automation Systems. https://projects.shift2rail.org/s2r_ip2_n.aspx?p=X2RAIL-1. Accessed 15 Dec 2021
45. X2Rail-3: Deliverable D6.1 Virtual Train Coupling System Concept and Application Conditions (2020). https://projects.shift2rail.org/s2r_ip2_n.aspx?p=X2RAIL-3. Accessed 15 Dec 2021
46. X2Rail-4: Advanced signalling and automation system. Completion of activities for enhanced automation systems, train integrity, traffic management evolution and smart object controllers. https://projects.shift2rail.org/s2r_ip2_n.aspx?p=X2RAIL-4. Accessed 15 Dec 2021

47. Xu, Y., Gao, C., Yuan, L., Tang, S., Wei, G.: Real-time obstacle detection over rails using deep convolutional neural network. In: 2019 IEEE Intelligent Transportation Systems Conference (ITSC), pp. 1007–1012. IEEE (2019)

48. Ye, T., Zhang, Z., Zhang, X., Zhou, F.: Autonomous railway traffic object detection using feature-enhanced single-shot detector. IEEE Access **8**, 145182–145193 (2020)

Safe and Secured Telecom for Railway

Analysis of Safety-Critical Communication Protocols for On-Premise SIL4 Cloud in Railways

Benjamin Rother[1]([⊠]), Frank Golatowski[1], Zeeshan Ansar[2], Don Kuzhiyelil[2], Stefan Resch[3], Reinhard Hametner[3], and Prashant Pathak[4]

[1] Universität Rostock, 18051 Rostock, Germany
{benjamin.rother,frank.golatowski}@uni-rostock.de
[2] SYSGO GmbH, Am Pfaffenstein 8, 55270 Klein-Winterheim, Germany
{zeeshan.ansar,don.kuzhiyelil}@sysgo.com
[3] Thales Austria GmbH, Handelskai 92, 1200 Vienna, Austria
{stefan.resch,reinhard.hametner}@thalesgroup.com
[4] DB Netz AG, Stresemannstr. 123, 10963 Berlin, Germany
prashant.pathak@deutschebahn.com

Abstract. In this paper, we address the question of how SIL4 railway applications within on-premise cloud environments can communicate safely with internal and external systems.

The EN 50159 standard is the railway standard applicable for safety-related communication. For IT/OT Security IEC 62443 can be considered. Most standardized protocols developed according to EN 50159 are peer-to-peer protocols involving two communication partners. To leverage the cloud environment, contemporary applications of other domains use a different communication scheme, namely publish-subscribe, to connect internal and external components and enable scalability.

Based on this challenge, the goal of this paper is to investigate emerging communication protocols from different domains and their suitability for the railway system. We will first determine the requirements for the railway communication infrastructure and applications executed in a SIL4 cloud, i.e., an environment provided by on-premise data centers utilizing technologies such as virtualization and with other cloud-like features, such as scalability and flexible usage of resources. Furthermore, a brief comparison of the potential application-layer communication protocols from industrial domains with railway-specific safety-critical protocols will be presented. Finally, we will present a system architecture that demonstrates how safe communication can be realized by middleware protocols such as DDS or OPC UA and how they fulfill the previously established requirements for the railway system.

Keywords: SIL4 · Safety · Railway · SIL4 cloud · Protocols · Safe computing platform

© Springer Nature Switzerland AG 2022
S. Collart-Dutilleul et al. (Eds.): RSSRail 2022, LNCS 13294, pp. 211–220, 2022.
https://doi.org/10.1007/978-3-031-05814-1_15

1 Introduction

1.1 Motivation

As with computation, communication in railway systems is heterogeneous and incorporates safe and unsafe communication. An example for unsafe communication is a command requesting the setting of a route from the automatic train routing system, e.g., the CTMS[1] [15] to the interlocking system. This is not safety-critical, since the interlocking system guarantees the safe setting of routes.

However, a command from the operator to the interlocking system changing the state of a switch marked as occupied is safety-critical. This command overrules the route protection of the interlocking system; thus, the safe execution has to be guaranteed [4].

For the communication data that is safety relevant, the communication protocol used on top by the respective safety relevant applications must be compliant to EN 50159. Errors, such as transmission errors, repetitions, deletions, insertions, re-sequencing, corruption and delays of messages must be considered. So far most of the used standardized protocols developed according to EN 50159 are peer-to-peer protocols involving two communication partners. This is well fitted in the traditional railway architectures that are hierarchically organized and distributed along the railway network. However, the question arises as to which communication protocols will be suitable for the on-premise SIL4 cloud in the future. To answer this question, the first step is to determine the requirements for the communication infrastructure and to find protocols based on these requirements. Furthermore, we analyze potential application-layer communication protocols used in other domains such as industrial or automotive and find their suitability for railway-specific safety-critical use cases. Finally, we present a system architecture that demonstrates how safe communication can be realized by middleware protocols such as DDS and how they fulfill the previously established requirements for the railway system.

1.2 Purpose of Paper

The purpose of this paper is to investigate emerging SIL4 communication protocols from different domains and their suitability for a cloud-like computing platform for the railway system. The following points are examined:

1. Identification and understanding of communication requirements of SIL4 cloud
2. Overview of railway-specific safety-critical protocols
3. Brief survey of potential communication protocols and comparison with 2
4. Present a system architecture to show how DDS can be used to meet requirements

2 SIL4 Communication Requirements

2.1 Safe Computing Platform

Deutsche Bahn, as part of the Digitale Schiene Deutschland sector initiative, and other railways in Europe are aiming to introduce a large degree of digitalization in rail operation, which will for instance be characterized by highly or fully automated driving, an

---

[1] Capacity and Traffic Management System.

AI-based disposition of rail traffic in real-time, and fully automated incidence management. As a fundament for the future rail system RCA[2] and OCORA[3] have initiated the
work toward a functional Safe Computing Platform (SCP) architecture for the onboard
and trackside functions as depicted in Fig. 1. A key prerequisite for the envisioned digitalization of rail operations is a highly performant IT infrastructure that allows to decouple
the different life cycles of railway applications, middleware and hardware and explicitly leverage the latest developments in the IT sector, e.g., virtualization and flexible
communication in the context of safety [5].

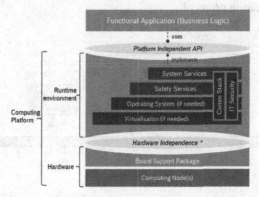

Fig. 1. Logical reference architecture of the Safe Computing Platform (SCP) [5]

Following the SCP approach, communication can be categorized in the following
five categories, as depicted in Fig. 2:

1. Communication within one SCP implementation
2. Communication between different SCP implementations in the same cloud environment
3. Communication between an SCP and other IT systems within an on-premise SIL4
   cloud boundary
4. Communication between a SIL4 cloud and other IT systems outside of the on-premise
   SIL4 cloud boundary
5. Communication between an SCP and external Systems (e.g., Point machines in the
   field)

The categorization is based on the zoning concept of safety-critical systems for which
there might be different ways to separate them. As illustrated in Fig. 1, functional applications are decoupled from the underlying SCP and isolated from each other. The communication between two functional applications on the same SCP instance is considered
in the domain of the SCP vendor, meaning that it can be established via platform independent (PI) API commands with the SCP as a middleware. The PI API approach allows

---

[2] Reference Control Command and Signalling Architecture.

[3] Open Control Command and Signalling On-board Reference Architecture.

safety-critical railway applications to run unchanged on different SCP implementations, hence maintaining application portability. The vendor can decide which communication protocol to use, as it is hidden behind the PI API. There is the possibility to distribute redundant applications, executed on the SCP, to different geographical locations, which will be needed in SIL4 cloud environments. Communication protocols must provide safety capabilities if safety-critical applications want to exchange data safely with each other. Nevertheless, important communication connections to other systems in the private and external network must be enabled. In today's railway systems, communication with external systems, such as object controllers or signalling systems, is enabled by the RaSTA[4] communication protocol.

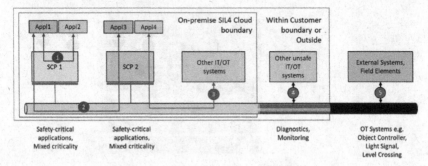

Fig. 2. Communication categories in the railway domain

2.2 Requirements

The EN 50159 standard defines requirements for communication between safety-related railway applications. The key properties for safe communication are authenticity, integrity, timeliness and sequence.

The standard discriminates network architectures in three categories:

Category 1 applies to closed transmission systems with a fixed number of participants, negligible risk of unauthorized access, and static physical characteristics of the transmission system during its life cycle. Categories 2 and 3 concern open transmission systems, which may have a changing set of participants and possibly unknown participants, which are not part of the railway application and may generate:

- arbitrary communication loads
- changing properties of the transmission media
- changing message routes through the system.

Only in category 3, the open transmission system may also be subject to unauthorized, malicious access. Based on this categorization, the standard identifies possible threats and lists measures and methods that protect the safety-related communication against

---

[4] Rail Safe Transport Application.

these threats. The appropriate measures have to be implemented in an independent layer above the transmission system according to EN 50128 and EN 50129 [1, 4].

According to the OCORA requirements for the SCP, the following non-exhaustive list of requirements arise for future communication infrastructures:

- R1: The communication protocol evolves independently from a specific computing platform realization.
- R2: The computing platform shall support point-to-point, point-to-multipoint and publish-subscribe communication model to support different application communication models. Publish-subscribe model helps to achieve location transparency for applications running on platform(s).
- R3: Safe communication should be applied end-to-end, so that the whole communication link between remote functional applications can be considered safe.
- R4: Safe communication protocols will be transparent to Functional Applications
- R5: The computing platform provides a communication protocol which is based on open and standardized specification to achieve interoperability.

3   Railway-Specific Safety-Critical Protocols

RaSTA is a network protocol that is tailored to the specific needs of railway signalling systems which fulfills requirements of EN 50159 e.g., message integrity, message authenticity, message timeliness, and message sequence for safety-critical communication. In this case, authenticity is to be understood as a safety property [3].

The protocol supports safe data transmission in networks classified as category 1 or 2 (according to EN 50159). If transmission over a category 3 network is necessary, additional means of encryption need to be foreseen. This could be within the upper layer (application layer) or the lower layer (e.g., IPsec).

From experiences of the railway supplier Thales it is clear that the use of the protocol in a cloud environment is severely restricted. In particular, the reduced flexibility of the peer-to-peer protocol and limited integration of security functions are highlighted in this context. Other safe and secure protocols therefore have to be investigated or designed for suitability in the cloud environment, especially for communication among newly developed applications specified by RCA.

4   Potential SIL4 Communication Protocols

In the following we present OPC UA[5] and DDS[6] as potential candidates for such a multi-point communication since they are widely used in industrial control systems.

---

[5] Open Platform Communication Unified Architecture.
[6] Data Distribution Service.

4.1 OPC UA

OPC UA supports communication scalability between distributed systems including reliable data transmission end-to-end. It supports extensible security features including authentication, authorization, encryption, checksums along with security key management. With its flexibility, interoperability and scalability, it can be addressed as reference standard to meet all the requirements and trends in industry 4.0. OPC UA is an open standard without dependence on or binding to proprietary technologies or individual vendors. Hence, all OPC UA communications are independent of the vendors who implement them, the programming languages used, and the platforms those products run on. It supports both publish-subscribe over UDP and client/server over TCP communication patterns. OPC UA over TSN provides deterministic communication via Ethernet [2]. OPC UA is already used in railways for non-safety-critical communication such as the collection of diagnostics data from various systems including safety-critical ones [13].

The specification of OPC UA Safety extends OPC UA to fulfill functional safety requirements as defined in the IEC 61508 and IEC 61784-3 standards. IEC 61508 is the basis of many derived standards in functional safety context therefore it should be considered as feasible to use OPC UA Safety as well in railway domain [14]. The safety measures such as the assignment of safety IDs to change communication partners at run-time, cyclic-redundancy check (CRC), codenames, monitoring numbers, watchdog, diagnostic data and SIL 4 monitors to identify and rectify communication errors, can be employed as a standard at the safety layer for safe communication over OPC UA [7]. This could limit the certification effort to the correctness of implementation of safety layer on a functionally safe computing platform.

OPC UA has been developed for machine-to-machine communication and is therefore well suited for communication with field elements and external systems in the context of railway systems, as depicted in Fig. 2. Due to its application-independence, OPC UA Safety does not pose requirements concerning the length or structure of the application data [6].

4.2 DDS

The open standard DDS middleware provides a data centric connectivity framework based on a publish-subscribe model for a real-time system. To provide the interoperability between DDS implementations from different vendors, specifications are formulated to define the wire protocol called RTPS (real-time publish-subscribe). DDS-RTPS enables seamless interoperability across vendor implementations, programming languages and platforms. DDS enables modular application development and reliable and real-time data exchange [9–11].

In order to use DDS middleware over standard IP networks for safety-critical applications, additional safety measures are required to meet the requirements of safety-critical applications. DDS employs a variety of Quality of Service (QoS) mechanisms to ensure reliability, system health, security and real-time behavior [9]. These QoS mechanisms can be used to detect and, in some cases, rectify communication errors such as data corruption, unintended repetition, incorrect sequence numbers, lost messages and delay. For security, DDS employs additional features such as access control, data flow path enforcement and data encryption [12]. These security measures can also handle integrity issues which may be caused by errors such as message insertion and masquerade.

DDS's comprehensive QoS and security mechanisms make it a potential candidate for safe communication in railways.

5 Safe Communication Architecture for Railway Systems

This section describes an example design and architecture for safe communication on a black channel applicable for safety-critical railway applications deployed on a distributed SIL4 cloud environment. The safety standard EN 50159 allows for black channel communication, where only the endpoints are considered safety-relevant and the transmission is protected via a safety protocol. This means that only the safety protocol has to be developed according to EN 50159 and EN 50128 and executed in a safe context. The safety layer which implements the safety protocol will sit between the application and the potentially unreliable transport layer. The safety layer will provide safety measures to detect communication errors such as sequence numbering, timeout, sender/receiver identification and data consistency checks.

A separation kernel isolates the safety-critical partition from the non-safety-critical partition, however, applications running inside these partitions are allowed to communicate via inter-partition queuing/sampling ports provided by the separation kernel. Due to the strong separation provided by a qualified separation kernel, we could limit the certification efforts to the components in the safety-critical partition and use an unqualified, off-the-shelf network stack inside a non-safety-critical partition.

Figure 3 shows a system architecture where a communication middleware such as DDS or OPC UA runs in a separate safe partition with a POSIX runtime along with the safety-critical railway application and safety component. The TCP/IP stack and Ethernet driver run inside an unsafe virtualized Linux partition which provides the black channel. The black channel stack running inside the unsafe Linux partition implements a software switch that either directly transfers the data by memory copy to the destination port when it is located on the same CPU, or calling a socket write using an Ethernet driver when it's on a different CPU.

A DDS/OPC UA middleware framework running inside the safe partition on a separation kernel provides a Modular Open Systems Approach (MOSA) to create a common data communication framework for railway applications that can communicate across any data transport while providing fault tolerance, resiliency and security. Based on the evaluation of a state-of-the-art industrial implementation of DDS such as RTI Connext [10], this approach allows the systems to distribute the right data from the right railway applications to the right operators. This is achieved in real-time across different data transports and can additionally be used to enable safety mechanism such as fault handling and safety measures against performance limitations using QoS mechanisms [9].

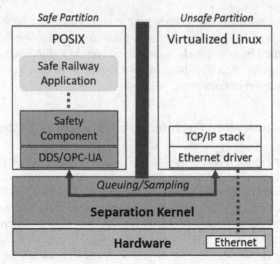

Fig. 3. Example of a safe communication system architecture based on DDS/OPC UA and a separation kernel

6 Evaluation

The proposed safe communication architecture fulfils all requirements R1 to R5, described in Sect. 2.2, with the integration of potential SIL4 communication protocols. To compare the safe protocols RaSTA, DDS and OPC UA Safety, key properties of the protocols are listed in Table 1. With the integration of DDS and OPC UA Safety, the architecture is able to support different communication patterns, such as publish-subscribe and peer-to-peer connections (R2). This allows for changing the safety communication partners at runtime by transparently exchanging data (R4). As a limitation it should be mentioned that safe multicast is resolved in OPC UA as a point-to-point connection on the layer below [7].

Both protocols are based on an open standard and have strong international support (R5). By covering the EN 50159 key properties, they are potential candidates for the railway sector. With suitable safety measures, which have to be integrated into the application appropriately, OPC UA and DDS are able to support communications up to SIL4 (R3). In particular, safe communication between field elements and the safe communication architecture can be achieved with OPC UA Safety using Safety Multicast. According to [8], OPC UA supports semantic interoperability and large-scale application scenarios and is therefore suitable for EN 50159 category 1 and 2 networks.

Table 1. Comparison of safe protocols

	RaSTA	DDS	OPC UA safety
Communication pattern PubSub architecture	P2P	PubSub, point-to-multipoint	PubSub, point-to-multipoint
EN 50159 key properties (authenticity, integrity, timeliness, sequence)	Supported	Supported	Supported
Open standard with strong international support	No (used in railway industry)	Yes	Yes
Safety features (excerpt)	• Black channel principle • Detection of communication errors	• Black channel principle • Changing communication partner during runtime • Detection of communication errors	• Black channel principle • Changing communication partner during runtime • Detection of communication errors • Safety Multicast
Security features	Limited (secure code)	Extensive (authentication, access control, cryptography, logging)	Adequate (secure channel)

7 Conclusion

In this paper, a brief comparison of the potential application layer communication protocols from industrial domains with railway-specific safety-critical protocols was presented. Both OPC UA and DDS protocols have the potential to be used in on-premise SIL4 cloud for safety-critical communication. Still, RaSTA is applicable for on-premise SIL4 cloud, but is limited to point-to-point communication. Finally, a safe communication architecture for railway was presented that shows how safe communication can be realized through middleware protocols such as DDS and OPC UA and how these fulfil the requirements previously defined for the railway system.

The investigation for a safety-critical communication protocol is an important subject in the context of SIL4 cloud environments and needs to be examined further to analyze protocols differences in terms of their performance under real conditions and how it affects the safe communication architecture.

References

1. CENELEC, "EN50159: Railway applications - Communication, signalling and processing systems - Safety-related communication in transmission systems". European Committee for Electrotechnical Standardization (2010)
2. Drahos, P., Kucera, E., Haffner, O., Klimo, I.: Trends in industrial communication and OPC UA. In: Cybernetics and Informatics (K&I), Lazy pod Makytou (2018)
3. Heinrich, M., Vieten, J., Arul, T., Katzenbeisser, S.: Security analysis of the RaSTA safety protocol, pp. 199–204 (2018)
4. Kantz, H., Resch, S., Scherrer, C.: Communication in train control. In: Industrial Communication Technology Handbook. CRC Press (2017)
5. An Approach for a Generic Safe Computing Platform for Railway Applications. https://github.com/OCORA-Public/. Accessed 28 Jan 2022
6. OPC Foundation: OPC UA for Field Level Communications - A Theory of Operation. (2020)
7. OPC Foundation: OPC UA Specification Part 15 - Safety (2019)
8. Pfrommer, J.: Semantic interoperability at big-data scale with the open62541 OPC UA implementation. In: Podnar Žarko, I., Broering, A., Soursos, S., Serrano, M. (eds.) Interoperability and Open-Source Solutions for the Internet of Things, vol. 10218, pp. 173–185. Springer, Cham (2017). https://doi.org/10.1007/978-3-319-56877-5_11
9. Madden, M.M., Glaab, P.C.: Distributed simulation using DDS and cloud computing. In: Proceedings of the 50th Annual Simulation Symposium (ANSS 2017), vol. 3, pp. 1–12. Society for Computer Simulation International, San Diego (2017)
10. Data Distribution Service (DDS) for Complex Systems|RTI. https://www.rti.com/products/dds-standard. Accessed 22 Feb 2022
11. OMG, "The Real-time Publish-Subscribe Protocol (RTPS) DDS Interoperability Wire Protocol Specification." September 2018. https://www.omg.org/spec/DDSI-RTPS/2.3/Beta1/PDF. Accessed 02 Feb 2022
12. Corsaro, A.: A Tale of Two Industrial IoT Standards: DDS and OPC-UA, RTInsights, 15 August 2016. https://www.rtinsights.com/dds-opc-ua-industrial-iot-standards/. Accessed 22 Feb 2022
13. OPC UA Used in Deutsche Bahn Signaling System – OPC Connect. https://opcconnect.opcfoundation.org/2015/06/opc-ua-used-in-deutsche-bahn-signaling-system/. Accessed 22 Feb 2022
14. SYSGO expands safety cert to IEC 61508 and EN 50128, highest level security PikeOS now available to industrial sector, Embedded.com, 10 January 2011. https://www.embedded.com/sysgo-expands-safety-cert-to-iec-61508-and-en-50128-highest-level-security-pikeos-now-available-to-industrial-sector/. Accessed 22 Feb 2022
15. Thales will digitize Deutsche Bahn Stuttgart signalling system to substantially improve capacity, punctuality and comfort, Thales Group. https://www.thalesgroup.com/en/group/journalist/press_release/thales-will-digitize-deutsche-bahn-stuttgart-signalling-system. Accessed 22 Feb 2022

TASC: Transparent, Agnostic, Secure Channel for CBTC Under Failure or Cyberattack

Utku Tefek[1]([⊠]), Ertem Esiner[1], Lin Wei[1], and Yih-Chun Hu[1,2]

[1] Advanced Digital Sciences Center, Singapore 1 Create Way, #14-02 Create Tower, 138602, Singapore
{u.tefek,e.esiner,lin.wei}@adsc-create.edu.sg
[2] University of Illinois at Urbana Champaign, Champaign, IL, USA
yihchun@illinois.edu

Abstract. Modern railway systems rely on communication-based train control (CBTC) for traffic management and automation. CBTC provides the controller with precise, timely updates on the position/speed of trains and communicates the corresponding control information to the trains. However, disruptions due to potential component failures and jamming attacks threaten the communication availability in CBTC. To improve availability, we propose a countermeasure based on redundant communications. The proposed Transparent, Agnostic, Secure Communication (TASC) system sniffs and tunnels the CBTC messages through an alternative network to their intended receivers. Prior works mitigate the impact of jamming and failures through hardware modifications to CBTC. In contrast, TASC is transparent to the underlying system, causing no interference unless signaling is disrupted, and designed to be agnostic to communication protocols above the physical-layer. Unlike commonly adopted active redundancy via the duplication of components, TASC steps in only upon signaling disruptions, employing standby redundancy.

Keywords: Availability · CBTC · Communication redundancy · Jamming attack

1 Introduction

Railway systems offer an efficient, safe, cost and environment-friendly way of transporting masses. Modern information and communication technologies known as communication-based train control (CBTC) in railways enable high resolution, automated, real-time train state and control information exchange

This work was supported in part by the National Research Foundation (NRF), Prime Ministers Office, Singapore, under its National Cybersecurity R&D Programme (Award No. NRF2014NCR-NCR001-031) and administered by the National Cybersecurity R&D Directorate, and in part by the National Research Foundation, Prime Minister's Office, Singapore under its Campus for Research Excellence and Technological Enterprise (CREATE) programme.

S. Collart-Dutilleul et al. (Eds.): RSSRail 2022, LNCS 13294, pp. 221–237, 2022.
https://doi.org/10.1007/978-3-031-05814-1_16

between the train and the wayside equipment, which increases the line capacity by safely reducing the train headway [7]. However, as railways become more reliant on automated systems, they inevitably become vulnerable to hardware and communication failures and cyberattacks.

Multiple serious incidents due to the disruptions in CBTC have occurred in recent years. Intermittent signal interference caused loss of communication and delays on the Circle Line of Singapore metro from 2 November to 9 November 2016. Postmortem analysis of data logs revealed that one of the trains with faulty signaling hardware emitted erroneous signals, preventing other trains in its vicinity from communicating with the wayside radio equipment [18]. The disruption in signaling led to the activation of emergency brakes as a safety mechanism, causing long and sustained delays. Another incident where the loss of communication contributed to the collision of two trains caused the injury of over 30 commuters in the East-West Line of Singapore metro on 15 November 2017 [22]. In March 2019, two subway trains in Hong Kong Tsuen Wan Line have collided during a trial ride for the newly installed signaling system, reportedly due to a software glitch [12].

Since the railway systems are critical infrastructure, CBTC has stringent requirements on the availability and integrity of signaling data exchanged between the wayside and the trains. Although the safety in railway systems has been taken very seriously, the security measures are mostly proprietary and confidential, thus relying on physical isolation and obscurity to limit the attack surface [19]. However, it is well known that the security of a system should not depend solely on the secrecy of a given system implementation [15]. Due to the deep involvement of humans in rail transport and the widespread availability of software-defined radios, the bar for the attackers to interfere and disrupt the signaling in the train-to-wayside wireless communication link is low.

Based on our discussions with our industry partner SMRT Corporation Ltd., and considering the distinct features of CBTC and further relying on the general security principles of cyberphysical systems, we adhere to the following design guidelines.

Transparency: The deployed CBTC systems are expected to operate for decades because any major modification may be very costly, requiring a re-design of security mechanisms that are already in place. In this regard, compatibility and interoperability with the legacy CBTC are indispensable. Unlike existing solutions, TASC is designed to be an independent system. It can detect failures with no feedback from the underlying system. Upon failure detection, TASC sniffs, tunnels and injects packets at desired locations as if the packets were sent directly by their source.

Agnostic Design: Since most CBTC systems utilize proprietary technologies rather than commercial off-the-shelf networking equipment, the details of communication protocols are kept confidential. Any proposed design should be applicable even with limited information on the existing CBTC system. TASC performs its functions without any knowledge of the communication protocols above the physical-layer of the underlying system.

Improved Availability: The past incidents have shown that communication failures may disrupt the CBTC operation and even contribute to accidents [12,18,22]. Furthermore, CBTC is shown to be vulnerable to jamming attacks, and the impact of jamming is further amplified if waveguides are deployed as the CBTC wireless medium [1]. TASC relies on communication redundancy to improve the availability of communications.

Uncompromised Integrity and Confidentiality: The interconnected digital elements of CBTC present potential attack surfaces [2]. As a critical cyberphysical system, CBTC must be guarded against information altering and loss through proper authentication and integrity checking mechanisms. We designed the TASC backbone communication to provide message authentication, freshness, and optionally confidentiality by employing lightweight cryptographic primitives.

2   Related Work

Relying on channel hopping commonly employed in cognitive radio networks [20], a countermeasure against jamming in CBTC has been proposed in [13]. The authors proposed the use of frequency hopping spread spectrum (FHSS) not only at the transmitter-receiver pair but also at the wayside repeaters, which are located at regular intervals on the waveguide to amplify CBTC signals in some continuous antenna based implementations of CBTC. Although FHSS repeaters are effective in mitigating the effect of jamming by amplifying the legitimate signal only, interference from the legitimate but malfunctioning transmitters may also be amplified.

Improving the resilience of CBTC against component failures has been studied. Cooperative relaying in CBTC [6,21] eliminates the need for train-AP association and hence reduces the risk of AP failure. However, the communication chain in a relaying scenario is prone to disruption in the event of a single-node failure. Inspired by the Coordinated Multi-point (CoMP) technique of LTE, a train-to-wayside communication system to allow trains to communicate with a cluster of APs simultaneously was proposed in [23]. Our proposed TASC system also benefits from redundant APs for train-to-wayside communication. However, unlike [23], the redundant APs in TASC remain in standby mode, taking over the functions of primary APs only upon failure. Our redundancy approach is also known as *standby redundancy*, which has been employed predominantly in high reliability, non-repairable systems such as in space exploration and satellites. The likelihood of failure in standby redundancy is much lower, since the redundant components are shielded from the operational stress (e.g., software glitches, hardware failures and cyberattacks in CBTC) until they are required to substitute for a failed component [3].

3   Overview of CBTC and Attack/Failure Model

CBTC requires uninterrupted radio communication between the wayside and the trains. The trains send their real-time location, speed, and direction to the wayside over the radio connection. Based on the information aggregated from all trains on the track, as well as considering other variables such as the trains' braking capability, the Zone Controller (ZC)[1] continuously calculates the maximum speed and the distance (collectively referred to as the *limit-of-movement authority* or LMA) for each train. LMA data is then shared with the trains over the same radio connection, for the onboard automatic train control (ATC) functions to adjust the speed and headway accordingly. This real-time information exchange (or *signaling*) between the train and the wayside ZC enabling a dynamic headway and speed adjustment is also known as the *moving-block* operation and allows driverless trains to operate with a higher density than the conventional *fixed-block* operation. The frequency of CBTC messages is about 0.1–0.6 s. If a train fails communicate up-to-date information (i.e., train state and LMA), timeout occurs and emergency brakes are applied [7].

3.1 Train-to-Wayside Radio Network

The trains communicate with the access points (APs) through a wireless network known as the train-to-wayside radio network. APs are responsible for relaying CBTC messages between the ZC and trains. Since the wayside depends on the trains to obtain the train data and the trains rely on the wayside to get LMA in a timely manner, the reliability of the train-to-wayside radio network is crucial for CBTC to function.

As railways are deployed in a variety of environments including subway tunnels and viaducts, various wireless network protocols and propagation mediums have been considered for CBTC signaling over the train-to-wayside radio network [8]. While the deployment of the leaky-waveguides or radiating cables are costlier than discrete antenna implementations, they provide a more reliable performance thanks to the significantly reduced path-loss attenuation and protection from interference. A continuous antenna configuration of CBTC is shown in Fig. 1.

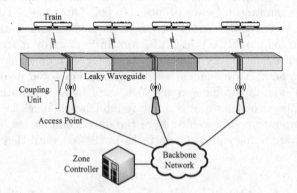

Fig. 1. CBTC system with continuous antennas.

---

[1] Zone Controller, also known as the Wayside Controller, is responsible for controlling a particular section comprising of multiple access points in the railway network.

In continuous antenna configurations, the APs are wired to disjoint segments of the propagation medium, e.g., the leaky-waveguide as in Fig. 1, through a coupling unit. The leaky waveguide is deployed along the railway track so that the train antenna travels a few decimeters above it as the train moves. In discrete antenna configurations, the wayside is divided into multiple virtual cells, each of which is served by AP over a wireless interface. The APs are responsible for converting the signals received over the wired backbone network into wireless signals and vice versa. In both configurations, the trains communicate with APs using wireless protocols such as Wi-Fi or the supplier's proprietary protocols. These wireless links are the weakest links in the CBTC signaling system since they are vulnerable to interference from signals in the same frequency band transmitted by coexisting devices.

3.2 Attack and Failure Model

Communication failures occur despite the built-in redundancy in CBTC systems at multiple levels, e.g., through the use of multiple radios, antennas, frequencies, and overlapping AP coverage [7,14]. The built-in active redundancy of train radio equipment and overlapping AP coverage cannot prevent the failures entirely because the design principles and the software running on each radio unit is typically the same, causing multiple redundant units to fail simultaneously. Furthermore, a failed radio unit may emit interfering signals, acting as a jammer, which in turn causes the loss of communication between other trains and APs as had happened in the rogue train incident of Singapore metro [18].

Strong interference caused by a jamming attack may also prevent the receiver from decoding the legitimate signal and renders any security measure above the physical-layer (e.g., cryptography and network security) irrelevant. As discussed in [4], the railway infrastructure is a potentially high-value victim of electromagnetic jamming attacks. The effect of jamming is further amplified in continuous antenna configurations. As shown in [1,13], while a jamming signal in free-medium communication has an impact over a limited range due to natural signal attenuation, jamming in continuous antenna configurations can extend to a much longer range due to the limited longitudinal attenuation provided by the leaky-waveguide. Ironically, a seemingly useful feature of reduced signal attenuation in continuous antenna configurations potentially magnifies the scale of a jamming attack.

In line with the past incidents and demonstrated the risk of signal jamming attacks, we include the following in our attack/failure model.

i. A train radio or an AP emits unwanted signals in addition to the legitimate signals, causing interference to other train-AP pairs.
ii. An adversary injects jamming signals to the train-to-wayside radio network. For instance, the adversary in close proximity to the track, or on-board the train can transmit jamming signals using a high-gain antenna.
iii. The AP breaks down, fails to relay the LMA to the train and/or train data to the ZC. The AP failure can be either in a single direction or unidirectional.

Our solution covers the communication failures, e.g., the message is lost or corrupted as per the attack and failure model, from the point the message leaves its source, to the point it reaches its destination. If the message is not sent by its source in the first place (e.g., the train radio equipment or ZC breaks down), an agnostic design to cover communication failures is unattainable. In such a case, redundant signaling mechanisms such as track circuits or inductive loop systems [16] are possible mitigation techniques.

3.3   Alternative Networks for CBTC Signaling

The CBTC signaling systems commissioned during the early 2000s or before mostly utilized proprietary technologies, because the extent to which wireless communication would proliferate in the form of Wi-Fi or LTE was not commonly perceived. Today, even though CBTC signaling converges towards said standards thanks to their availability, interoperability, high capacity, and low-cost equipment, replacing the proprietary CBTC systems altogether within their life span of operation is not desirable. Instead, using commercial-off-the-shelf equipment to provide back-up signaling, and doing so only when anomalies are detected on the main train-to-wayside radio network could be a viable solution.

Multiple networks already co-exist with the train-to-wayside radio network. Ubiquitous LTE coverage is increasingly more available in a majority of railways including underground metro systems for passengers' use. Besides, supplementary radio networks such as Terrestrial Trunked Radio (TETRA) are sometimes deployed to implement critical functions (e.g., emergency communication and alarms) in railways. For instance, in the Circle Line of Singapore Metro, an LTE access network is deployed to provide mobile access to commuters, and TETRA is used for passenger emergency communication, passenger announcement, and security camera requests along with the train-to-wayside radio network providing CBTC signaling over waveguides.

4   Transparent, Agnostic, Secure Channel (TASC) System

To improve the train-to-wayside radio network's resilience, we propose the use of alternative networks for re-routing the CBTC messages in a transparent, agnostic, and secure (to the desired level in terms of confidentiality, integrity, and availability) manner. Our proposed TASC system relies on proxy devices, referred to as TASC devices, attached to communicating CBTC components. TASC devices monitor traffic in standby mode and relay the CBTC messages through a substitute channel only when the primary CBTC channel fails. A redundant AP, referred to as the Slave-AP, is also controlled by the TASC system for standby AP redundancy.

Our approach resembles performing a relay attack [9], or more closely, a wormhole attack [11] which are targeted against ad-hoc networks. In a wormhole attack the attacker records packets from a location in the network, then (selectively) tunnels them to another location and replays them into the network, without manipulating or even reading the messages. Similarly, the proxy TASC devices, agnostic to the underlying CBTC protocols, overhear and tunnel the CBTC packets using secure communication protocols over alternative channels, rendering themselves transparent to the CBTC system. Unlike these attacks, however, TASC performs this tunneling honestly and reliably. Therefore, it provides a useful service in improving the communication availability.

Figure 2 depicts the TASC system attached to a CBTC train-to-wayside radio network. The following entities constitute the TASC system: a set of identical TASC devices for each train, another set of identical TASC devices for each AP, at least one other TASC device for each ZC, and a slave-AP to be exclusively used by the TASC system. This slave-AP is identical to those used in the CBTC network, and the rationale for its use will be explained in Sect. 4.2. As shown for a single train-to-wayside link in Fig. 2, the first TASC device is deployed near the train, second near the AP, and third connected to the backbone network, controlling the slave-AP. All TASC devices are interconnected through a backbone network such as LTE or TETRA.

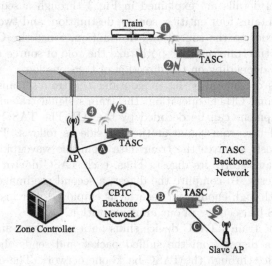

Fig. 2. TASC system and its connections with a CBTC network. Wireless and wired interfaces to the CBTC backbone are denoted by 1–5 and $A - C$ respectively.

Each TASC device is equipped with monitoring (sniffing) and injection capabilities compatible with the physical layer protocols of the CBTC system. The wireless interfaces which the TASC devices can sniff and inject to are denoted by numbers 1–5, whereas the wired connections are denoted by letters A-C in Fig. 2. The TASC system is indifferent to train-to-wayside communication protocols above the physical layer (e.g., interpretation of messages/headers, data encapsulation/framing, encryption scheme). However, we assume that the TASC devices are equipped with a mechanism to distinguish between the packets sniffed from 1 and 2, as well as those from 3 and 4. I.e., the train's TASC device can differentiate the signals transmitted from the train and those sniffed from the waveguide; the AP's TASC device can differentiate the signals transmitted from the AP and those sniffed from the waveguide. This function could be procured without the need or the ability to interpret CBTC messages, for instance by installing two antennas for TASC devices: one directly wired to the host device (1 or 4), another as an air interface (2 or 3). Through these interfaces, TASC passively monitors the CBTC, and activates signaling through the alternative network only when failures are detected.

4.1   Resilience Against Jamming/Interference

In order to maintain signaling in the case of a jamming attack or interference from faulty CBTC components, the TASC system detects such events, then reroutes the CBTC messages exchanged between the train and its associated AP until the failure is resolved. The idea is to sniff frames from interface 1 and to tunnel and inject them to interface 4 – and vice versa – upon failure detection. The system-level details are explained in Fig. 3 through a sequence diagram. The diagram contains four entities: source, destination, and two TASC devices deployed as proxies to the source and destination. Since the CBTC signaling is bidirectional, the train and AP both take the role of source and destination interchangeably, depending on the direction of transmission.

Without loss of generality, let us consider the train's transmission to the AP. During normal CBTC operation, the train's signal transmitted from the train radio equipment can be decoded by the AP. The TASC system verifies the reception of the train signal at the AP side as follows. The AP's TASC device continuously receives the train data from the waveguide (interface 3), then computes and stores its digest. Thus, each TASC device keeps an array of past data digests. To compute the digest, a second pre-image resistant hash function [17] with high enough bit security is employed. For instance, we chose SHA-256 for 128-bit security in our implementation.

Whenever the train's TASC device sniffs data from the train over interface 1, it computes a digest from the sniffed packet and sends the digest to the AP's TASC device through the TASC backbone network. The digest should be accompanied by an authentication mechanism to deter signal injection attacks. For example, after generating the digest of the train data, the TASC device generates a hash-based message authentication code (HMAC)[2] of this digest and sends the digest together with its HMAC to the AP's TASC device. Thus, the AP's TASC device verifies the authenticity and integrity (and freshness) of the digest. Such authentication and integrity checking mechanism is necessary if TASC backbone channels are not secure, e.g., the adversary can spoof and inject packets with random digests, fooling the TASC system into the Error state despite a functional CBTC. The *Verify* process is triggered via the receipt of this current digest from the train's TASC device. It checks whether this current

---

[2] For 128-bit security, we chose SHA-256 as the digest function of the employed HMAC. We concatenate a timestamp to the input of HMAC for freshness.

digest matches any of those previously received from interface 3. If a certain number of consecutive digests received from the train's TASC device cannot be found among the past digests stored at the AP's TASC device, Error state is switched on. The required number of consecutively received packets without a matching digest, to switch into the Error state should be determined based on the emergency braking timeout duration of the CBTC system.

The benefits of sending a digest rather than the train data itself are twofold. The first is the bandwidth savings accrued from sending a digest rather than the larger data. Second, the CBTC messages are not directly exposed to the backbone network during orderly CBTC operation (when the Error state is off).

While the Error state is on, instead of the digests, the TASC system re-routes CBTC data packets, through the TASC backbone network. In particular, the *Sniff* process running at the train's TASC device continuously sniffs packets from interface 1 and sends them to the AP's TASC device. Integrity checking and authentication mechanisms may be needed if the TASC backbone network is not secure.[3] Meanwhile, AP's TASC device stores the data packets, if any, received from interface 3. The *Inject* process is triggered at the AP's TASC device when a packet is received from the authenticated TASC device attached to the train. The *Inject* process checks whether the received packet matches any of those already sniffed from 3. If no match is found, the packet is injected to the AP as a valid wireless frame via interface 4. Otherwise, continuously receiving matching packets prompts TASC to exit the Error state. The injection rate of all TASC devices is hardware constrained by the rate of transmissions necessitated by the underlying CBTC network. The rationale behind this implementation feature is explained in Sect. 5.

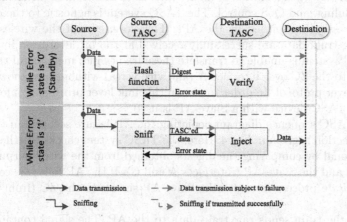

Fig. 3. Jamming/interference resilience.

---

[3] Likewise, HMAC can be sent along with the train data for authentication and integrity. Encryption may be considered if confidentiality is of concern. We used 128-bit AES for 128-bit security.

In TASC backbone communications, the sniffed messages are expected to pass through two TASC devices, i.e., proxies of source and destination. To add another layer of security, one may opt to employ a provenance checking mechanism [5] at the receiving side of the destination, checking whether the data injected by the destination TASC had been initiated by the source TASC.

The TASC system relies on the phenomenon of Physical Layer Capture, which suggests that the received signal with sufficiently higher power than others can be successfully decoded even if it collides with other signals on the same channel. Thus, even if a continuous jamming signal is present and collides with the CBTC signals, the TASC'ed (tunneled) signal containing this legitimate frame can still be successfully received by the AP over interface 4 as the TASC devices can be wired (via RF connectors), or deployed near the CBTC components, hence are not subject to coupling and propagation losses, unlike the adversary and faulty CBTC components.

4.2   Resilience Against AP Failure

The described TASC system with two TASC devices, each of which is attached to the train and AP, improves the resilience against interference and jamming attacks to the train-to-wayside radio network. As will be described throughout the rest of this section, resilience against AP failures to relay the LMA to the train and/or train data to the ZC can be improved by utilizing another TASC device, controlling a Slave-AP.

As the train movements are controlled solely by the ZC, the APs do not modify the train data or LMA. Nevertheless, the APs still perform data link layer processing, e.g., encapsulation of higher layer data into frames, physical addressing, scheduling, and QoS control. The TASC system is agnostic to the data link layer processing performed by the APs. Therefore, even if the wireless frames containing train data are successfully received at the bit level from interface 1, the TASC system is unable to translate these frames into meaningful train data and send to the ZC over interface A (and vice versa) without any knowledge on the link-layer protocol. In order to obtain this link layer processing information, the third TASC device with a Slave-AP is used.

The TASC sequence diagram depicting the AP failure scenario in the train-to-ZC direction is given in Fig. 4. Here, the TASC system checks whether the AP is operational by comparing the digests obtained from the wired output signals of the AP and the Slave-AP (interfaces A and C). If the AP failure is confirmed, the *Substitute* process re-routes the Slave-AP signals to the ZC (from interface C to B).

First, the train sends raw train data to the AP. The signal containing this raw train data is also decoded at the bit level by the train's TASC device and TASC'ed to the ZC's TASC device over the TASC backbone. As stated above, authentication and integrity checking may be required for communication over the TASC backbone. For instance, HMAC should be sent along with the train data. Encryption can be considered if confidentiality is also desired. The *Relay* process running on ZC's TASC relays the raw train data (after authentication/decryption) to the Slave-AP over interface 5. The AP is expected to convert the received raw train data into a wired backbone signal to be sent to the ZC. Upon this conversion and transmission (if successful), the *Hash function* process running on AP's TASC device sniffs the wired signal, generates its digest and sends the digest to the ZC's TASC device (with an accompanying authentication code). The ZC's TASC device stores the train data digest when received from the AP's TASC device. Therefore, ZC's TASC device possesses the digests of past train data. The *Substitute* process is triggered whenever a response is received from the Slave-AP over interface C. The *Substitute* process compares the digest of this response with those received from the AP's TASC device. If no match is found for a certain number of times, the *Substitute* process injects the train data as received from interface C to the ZC via interface B. Recovery from the Error state occurs if a certain number of digests received from the AP's TASC match the train data from the Slave-AP.

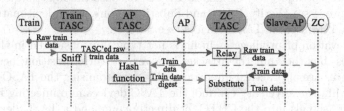

Fig. 4. Train-to-ZC for AP redundancy.

TASC operation for the AP failure scenario in the ZC-to-train direction is similar to the above, from the other way around. The sequence diagram is given in Fig. 5, however, its description is omitted due to space constraints.

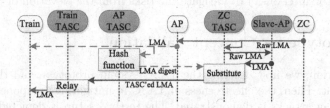

Fig. 5. ZC-to-train for AP redundancy.

5   Security Discussion of TASC

As with many redundancy mechanisms [10], the introduction of TASC increases the attack surface of the host cyberphysical system. Here, we briefly discuss potential attacks to TASC, their consequences, and countermeasures.

We have categorized attacks based on the STRIDE (Spoofing, Tampering, Repudiation, Information disclosure, Denial-of-service, Elevation of privilege) threat model. Since TASC uses symmetric keys, it does not provide non-repudiation. TASC is susceptible to information disclosure attacks as much as the host CBTC network. It can be addressed by encrypting the TASC backbone communication. This leaves us with the following broad class of methods an adversary may use to attack the TASC system in an attempt to disrupt the CBTC.

i. Spoofing, Tampering: e.g., injecting false data to the TASC backbone.
ii. Denial-of-service: e.g., jamming the TASC backbone.
iii. Elevation of privilege: e.g., compromising the secret keys of TASC or taking full control of one or more TASC devices.

In i., the false data packets are dropped by the TASC device in order, thanks to the integrity checking mechanism (i.e., HMAC) used by TASC. ii. may result in the loss of TASC functionality. Even when TASC functionality is lost, TASC system does not inject any signals to CBTC, because the injection is triggered in TASC processes (Verify, Inject and Substitute) only when legitimate packets are received from other TASC devices (see Sect. 4).

The elevation of privilege as in iii. is not typically considered in theoretical approaches, but they put the attacker in a very powerful position; hence, their consequences are of practical importance. By compromising the TASC keys and devices in iii., the adversary can fool the TASC devices into injecting false data or jamming signals into the CBTC, or directly command a TASC device to do so. If the underlying CBTC system has its own integrity checking and authentication mechanisms in place (i.e., EN 50159), false data will not be verified by the CBTC system. The adversary may also choose to flood the CBTC network through TASC with the said capabilities. Thanks to the hardware constraints on the frequency of injected packets (or bits) by TASC devices as mentioned in the previous section, the effect of jamming by data flooding through TASC is mitigated. TASC devices can also employ hardware-based security (e.g., TPM, ARM TrustZone, or Intel SGX) to mitigate the risks from the elevation of privilege.

6   Prototype for Concept Validation

In this section, we first describe the TASC system prototype and the testbed environment. Then, the effectiveness of TASC in mitigating component failures and jamming attacks is demonstrated. The testbed setup is depicted in Fig. 6. Here, the whole testbed diagram is given in the top figure, and each of the two areas covered by the red ovals is set up as shown in the photo below. We used seven computers, each running Kali Linux. The ZC is emulated by a virtual machine running on a PC. The train, AP, Slave-AP, and their corresponding three proxy TASC devices are each emulated by a sub-$40 Raspberry Pi 3B+ device (hereby referred to as Pi). For connectivity, we attached external Wi-Fi adapters to these six Pi's. We used Alfa 802.11ac ultra-range wireless adapters (model: AWUS036ACH for their support of coaxial RF connections, and monitor and injection modes) for the AP, train and their two proxy TASC devices; and used RangePlus wireless USB adapters (model: WUSB 100 ver. 2) for the Slave-AP and its proxy TASC. We connected the AP and the train to their respective proxy TASC devices through coaxial cables for protection against jamming and interference. This RF connection between the AP (or that of the train) to its TASC device is shown in the photo from the actual testbed in Fig. 6. An RF connection is not necessary between the Slave-AP and its proxy TASC, because these devices can be kept in an isolated environment.

The AP and ZC are interconnected through a backbone Ethernet network representing the CBTC backbone network. The TASC devices are also interconnected through another Ethernet network representing the TASC backbone. In our setup, we used multi-port Ethernet switches (bottom-right of Fig. 6). In line with the TASC model, the proxy TASC devices of the AP and slave-AP are also connected to the CBTC's Ethernet network. Additionally, an Ethernet connection provides communication between the slave-AP and its proxy TASC. All backbone communications over Ethernet are managed by TCP/IP, to provide reliable backbone communications while focusing on the wireless link failures.

We used a modified version of the aircrack-ng software suite (version 1.5.2) for wireless monitoring and packet injection. Aircrack-ng enables over-the-air capturing of Wi-Fi frames, the export of captured data for further processing by third-party tools, as well as injecting Wi-Fi frames with desired content. We also used OpenSSL cryptography library to implement cryptographic hash, HMAC, and AES encryption/decryption.

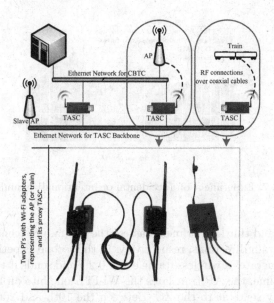

Fig. 6. Testbed diagram (top) and a photo (bottom) depicting the RF connection between the AP (bottom-left), its proxy TASC device (bottom-middle) and the TASC backbone consisting of ethernet cables and switch (bottom-right).

We tested the scenarios in our attack model, described in Sect. 3.2. The first experiment tests accidental and intentional jamming, and the second and third experiments test the AP failure scenarios. In the first experiment, the Pi's representing the AP and train listen to each other and continuously send wireless frames to each other in 0.2-s intervals, over 2.4 GHz Wi-Fi. Then, starting from second 10, we turn on a jamming device for 10 s, and record down the number of packets received at the AP (train), transmitted by the train (AP) and the AP's (train's) TASC device.

Figure 7 illustrates the results from the average of five trials of the experiment. As shown by the dark blue bars, the communication between the AP and train was maintained at 5 frames per second before the jamming started. When jamming started, however, no packets were exchanged between these CBTC components. Here, the light blue bars in between represent the lost packets. The TASC activation threshold is set to 20 packets or 4 s. Therefore TASC becomes active at around the 14th second (orange bars) and the number of legitimate frames received by the intended receiver climbs back to around 5/s (black dots). Occasional errors could be due to packet losses during sniffing or injection, or timing mismatches between different experiments. After the jamming ceases, the TASC system does not deactivate immediately. Thus, the number of packets received by the intended receiver briefly climbs up to 10 frames per second. These packets include both the original packets sent by the AP/train and their duplicates injected by TASC. This is due to the intentional de-activation delay of TASC, which is set to 10 successful transmissions or 2 s.

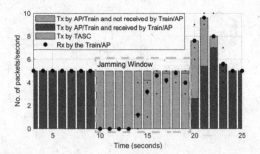

Fig. 7. Experiment on (accidental or intentional) jamming.

The second and third experiments assess the AP failure scenario in train-to-ZC and ZC-to-train directions, respectively. In the second experiment, the train continuously generates a wireless frame every 0.2 s and sends it to the AP. Upon receiving the frame, the AP translates the Wi-Fi frame into an Ethernet packet and immediately sends it to the ZC. Between the 10th and 20th s, we disable the AP.

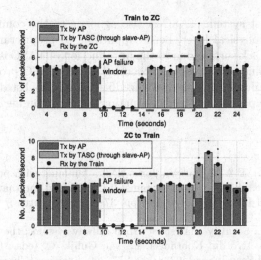

Fig. 8. Experiments on AP failure in train-to-ZC and ZC-to-train directions.

As can be seen from the top plot of Fig. 8, no translations (i.e., link layer processing), hence no transmissions were made by the AP during the failure window (blue bars). The TASC system, however, continued to obtain the correct translation from the slave-AP and started injecting the Ethernet packet containing train data to the ZC, after the intentional activation delay was observed (orange bars starting at the 14th s). As such, the number of packets received by the ZC (black dots), rose back to around 5 frames per second. After the AP was up at the 20th second, the total number of packets successfully received per second by ZC rose to 10 due to duplicate transmissions by TASC. Then, using the slave-AP translations as a reference, the TASC system stopped injection upon the confirmation of 10 correct translations. The third experiment (bottom plot of Fig. 8) is similar, except that the AP receives LMA data encapsulated as an Ethernet packet by the ZC, and translates it to Wi-Fi frames instead.

Note that, not all transmitted packets reached their destination, i.e., the number of received packets per second is slightly below 5 even outside the failure windows. This is due to the noise or interference from coexisting devices operating in the same frequency band. Packets from such devices are also sniffed by TASC, only to be dropped as their source is not authenticated.

7   Conclusion

This paper presents a standby redundancy approach to improve communication availability in CBTC and similar critical cyberinfrastructure. The proposed TASC solution sniffs packets from its hosts in the network; and upon failure detection, it tunnels and injects them to their intended destination. TASC is transparent to its underlying cyberphysical system, and requires no structural change on the host system. TASC is also agnostic to the communication protocols above the physical layer, hence applicable to proprietary systems. The increase in the attack surface due to the introduction of TASC is limited, thanks to the cryptographic primitives employed by TASC. TASC prototype detected communication failures with no direct feedback from its host devices, and reliably tunneled the packets to their destinations under jamming and AP failure.

References

1. Chang, S., Tran, B.A.N., Hu, Y., Jones, D.L.: Jamming with power boost: leaky waveguide vulnerability in train systems. In: IEEE 21st International Conference on Parallel and Distributed Systems, pp. 37–43 (2015). https://doi.org/10.1109/ICPADS.2015.13
2. Chen, B., et al.: Security analysis of urban railway systems: the need for a cyber-physical perspective. In: Koornneef, F., van Gulijk, C. (eds.) Computer Safety, Reliability, and Security, vol. 9338, pp. 277–290. Springer, Cham (2015). https://doi.org/10.1007/978-3-319-24249-1_24
3. Coit, D.W.: Cold-standby redundancy optimization for nonrepairable systems. IIE Trans. **33**(6), 471–478 (2001). https://doi.org/10.1023/A:1007689912305
4. Deniau, V.: Overview of the European project security of railways in Europe against Electromagnetic Attacks (SECRET). IEEE Electromagn. Compat. Mag. **3**(4), 80–85 (2014). https://doi.org/10.1109/MEMC.2014.7023203
5. Esiner, E., Mashima, D., Chen, B., Kalbarczyk, Z., Nicol, D.: F-Pro: a fast and flexible provenance-aware message authentication scheme for smart grid. In: IEEE SmartGridComm, pp. 1–7 (2019). https://doi.org/10.1109/SmartGridComm.2019.8909712
6. Farooq, J., Bro, L., Karstensen, R.T., Soler, J.: A multi-radio, multi-hop ad-hoc radio communication network for communications-based train control (CBTC). In: IEEE 86th Vehicular Technology Conference (VTC-Fall), pp. 1–7 (2017). https://doi.org/10.1109/VTCFall.2017.8288281
7. Farooq, J., Soler, J.: Radio communication for communications-based train control (CBTC): a tutorial and survey. IEEE Commun. Surv. Tutor. **19**(3), 1377–1402 (2017). https://doi.org/10.1109/COMST.2017.2661384
8. Fitzmaurice, M.: Wayside communications: CBTC data communications subsystems. IEEE Veh. Technol. Mag. **8**(3), 73–80 (2013). https://doi.org/10.1109/MVT.2013.2269191
9. Francis, L., Hancke, G., Mayes, K., Markantonakis, K.: Practical NFC peer-to-peer relay attack using mobile phones. In: Ors Yalcin, S.B. (ed.) Radio Frequency Identification: Security and Privacy Issues, RFIDSec 2010. LNCS, vol. 6370, pp. 35–49. Springer, Heidelberg (2010). https://doi.org/10.1007/978-3-642-16822-2_4
10. Ge, M., Kim, H.K., Kim, D.S.: Evaluating security and availability of multiple redundancy designs when applying security patches. In: 47th Annual IEEE/IFIP International Conference on Dependable Systems and Networks Workshops (DSN-W), pp. 53–60 (2017). https://doi.org/10.1109/DSN-W.2017.37
11. Hu, Y.C., Perrig, A., Johnson, D.B.: Packet leashes: a defense against wormhole attacks in wireless networks. In: IEEE INFOCOM, vol. 3, pp. 1976–1986, March 2003. https://doi.org/10.1109/INFCOM.2003.1209219
12. Huang, C.: Hong Kong MTR train crash blamed on Thales signalling system linked to Joo Koon collision, March 2018. https://bit.ly/2ukEueR. Accessed 21 Mar 2018

13. Lakshminarayana, S., et al.: Signal jamming attacks against communication-based train control: attack impact and countermeasure. In: Proceedings of the 11th ACM Conference on Security and Privacy in Wireless and Mobile Networks, pp. 160–171. WiSec, ACM, New York (2018). https://doi.org/10.1145/3212480.3212500

14. Liu, Y., Wu, Y., Kalbarczyk, Z.: Smart maintenance via dynamic fault tree analysis: a case study on Singapore MRT system. In: 47th Annual IEEE/IFIP International Conference on Dependable Systems and Networks (DSN), pp. 511–518, June 2017. https://doi.org/10.1109/DSN.2017.50

15. Mercuri, R.T., Neumann, P.G.: Security by obscurity. Commun. ACM **46**(11), 160 (2003)

16. Pascoe, R.D., Eichorn, T.N.: What is communication-based train control? IEEE Veh. Technol. Mag. **4**(4), 16–21 (2009). https://doi.org/10.1109/MVT.2009.934665

17. Rogaway, P., Shrimpton, T.: Cryptographic hash-function basics: definitions, implications, and separations for preimage resistance, second-preimage resistance, and collision resistance. In: Roy, B., Meier, W. (eds.) Fast Software Encryption, vol. 3017, pp. 371–388. Springer, Heidelberg (2004). https://doi.org/10.1007/978-3-540-25937-4_24

18. Sim, D.: How the circle line rogue train was caught with data (2016). https://blog.data.gov.sg/how-we-caught-the-circle-line-rogue-train-with-data-79405c86ab6a. Accessed 23 Feb 2022

19. Taylor, J.M., Sharif, H.R.: Security challenges and methods for protecting critical infrastructure cyber-physical systems. In: MoWNeT, pp. 1–6, May 2017. https://doi.org/10.1109/MoWNet.2017.8045959

20. Tefek, U., Lim, T.J.: Channel-hopping on multiple channels for full rendezvous diversity in cognitive radio networks. In: IEEE GLOBECOM, pp. 4714–4719, December 2014. https://doi.org/10.1109/GLOCOM.2014.7037552

21. Tefek, U., Esiner, E.: Coverage analysis of cooperative relaying for urban transportation systems in tunnels. In: IEEE International Conference on Communications (ICC), pp. 1–6. IEEE (2020). https://doi.org/10.1109/ICC40277.2020.9148695

22. The Land Transport Authority: Executive summary of investigation report into train collision at Joo Koon station westbound platform on 15 November 2017, December 2017. https://tinyurl.com/tp8j3bv. Accessed 10 Mar 2020

23. Zhu, L., Yu, F.R., Ning, B., Tang, T.: Design and performance enhancements in communication-based train control systems with coordinated multipoint transmission and reception. IEEE Trans. Intell. Transp. Syst. **15**(3), 1258–1272 (2014). https://doi.org/10.1109/TITS.2014.2298409

Author Index

Printed in the United States
by Baker & Taylor Publisher Services